To: Mommy Oldest Bab...

Nuke, You're ...
and my on...
can't describe of how...
loves you.

I pray that as you read this
boy it will strengthen you
in and out ward.

Love You
Always Nuke

Mommy
(♡)

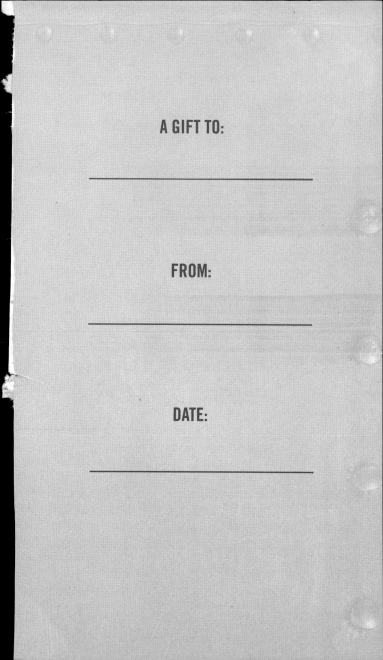

A GIFT TO:

_____

FROM:

_____

DATE:

_____

THE
BIBLE
IN 366 DAYS
FOR MEN
OF
FAITH

ANGUS BUCHAN™

CHRISTIAN ART
PUBLISHERS

The Bible in 366 Days for Men of Faith

Published by Christian Art Publishers
PO Box 1599, Vereeniging, 1930, RSA

© 2012
First edition 2012

Cover designed by Christian Art Publishers

Images used under license from Shutterstock.com

Scripture quotations are taken from the *Holy Bible*,
New Living Translation®, second edition. Copyright © 1996, 2004
by Tyndale House Publishers Inc., Carol Stream, Illinois 60188.
All rights reserved.

Set in 9 on 12 pt Arial by Christian Art Publishers

Printed in China

ISBN 978-1-4321-0307-1

15 16 17 18 19 20 21 22 23 24 – 17 16 15 14 13 12 11 10 9 8

"Love the LORD your God
with all your heart,
all your soul, all your strength,
and all your mind."

~ Luke 10:27

Foreword

How do you get to know somebody intimately?

The answer is very simple – by spending time with that person. Not every now and again, but every single day. That is how you get to know someone.

The greatest compliment for any Christian is when someone says, "Do you see that man? I see Jesus Christ in him."

I encourage you today to have regular quiet times with the Lord each day. Colossians 1:27 says, "Christ lives in you. This gives you assurance of sharing His glory."

This type of relationship can never be earned by doing good works or obtaining a university degree. It can only happen by spending time with Jesus Christ.

We are instructed to "love the Lord your God with all your heart, all your soul, all your strength, and all your mind" (Luke 10:27). I really believe that this is the secret ingredient to a contented and happy life: Spend time with your Savior, Jesus Christ.

~ Angus Buchan

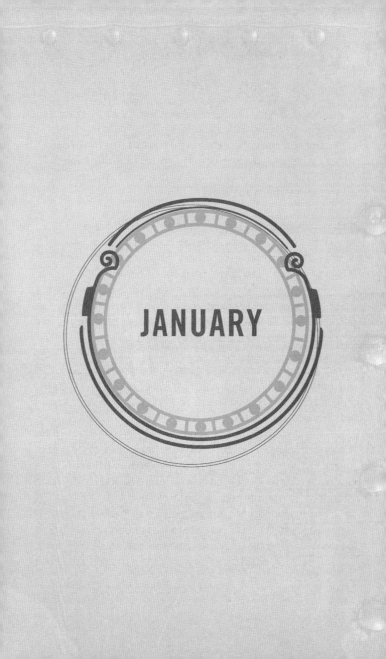

JANUARY

As the sun rises and sets at the start of this new year, let's praise God for His marvelous creation. Experience the colors, fragrances and sounds of creation and enjoy them anew every day.

[1]In the beginning God created the heavens and the earth.

[3]Then God said, "Let there be light," and there was light. [5]And evening passed and morning came, marking the first day. [6]Then God said, "Let there be a space between the waters, to separate the waters of the heavens from the waters of the earth." [8]And evening passed and morning came, marking the second day. [9]Then God said, "Let the waters beneath the sky flow together into one place, so dry ground may appear." [13]And evening passed and morning came, marking the third day. [14]Then God said, "Let lights appear in the sky to separate the day from the night. [19]And evening passed and morning came, marking the fourth day. [20]Then God said, "Let the waters swarm with fish and other life. Let the skies be filled with birds of every kind." [23]And evening passed and morning came, marking the fifth day. [24]Then God said, "Let the earth produce every sort of animal. [26]Then God said, "Let us make human beings. [29]Then God said, "Look! I have given you every seed-bearing plant throughout the earth and all the fruit trees for your food. [30]I have given every green plant as food for all the wild animals—everything that has life." And that is what happened. [31]Then God looked over all he had made, and he saw that it was very good!

And evening passed and morning came, marking the sixth day.

~ Genesis 1:1, 3, 5-6, 8-9, 13-14, 19-20, 23-24, 26, 29-31

REST

God never intended for us to work seven days a week. If our Creator took a day to rest from His work of creating, how much more are we, His creation, not in need of quiet rest?

¹So the creation of the heavens and the earth and everything in them was completed. ²On the seventh day God had finished his work of creation, so he rested from all his work. ³And God blessed the seventh day and declared it holy, because it was the day when he rested from all his work of creation.

⁴This is the account of the creation of the heavens and the earth.

When the LORD God made the earth and the heavens, ⁵neither wild plants nor grains were growing on the earth. For the LORD God had not yet sent rain to water the earth, and there were no people to cultivate the soil. ⁶Instead, springs came up from the ground and watered all the land. ⁷Then the LORD God formed the man from the dust of the ground. He breathed the breath of life into the man's nostrils, and the man became a living person.

⁸Then the LORD God planted a garden in Eden in the east, and there he placed the man he had made. ⁹The LORD God made all sorts of trees grow up from the ground—trees that were beautiful and that produced delicious fruit. In the middle of the garden he placed the tree of life and the tree of the knowledge of good and evil.

¹⁰A river flowed from the land of Eden, watering the garden and then dividing into four branches.

~ Genesis 2:1-10

GOD CREATED MAN

It's wonderful to know that God has created us in His own image. Unlike the animals, we have a soul and a spirit. Praise God that you are able to have a personal relationship with Him.

[7]Then the LORD God formed the man from the dust of the ground. He breathed the breath of life into the man's nostrils, and the man became a living person.

[15]The LORD God placed the man in the Garden of Eden to tend and watch over it. [16]But the LORD God warned him, "You may freely eat the fruit of every tree in the garden— [17]except the tree of the knowledge of good and evil. If you eat its fruit, you are sure to die."

[18]Then the LORD God said, "It is not good for the man to be alone. I will make a helper who is just right for him."

[21]So the LORD God caused the man to fall into a deep sleep. While the man slept, the LORD God took out one of the man's ribs and closed up the opening. [22]Then the LORD God made a woman from the rib, and he brought her to the man.

[23]"At last!" the man exclaimed.
"This one is bone from my bone,
    and flesh from my flesh!
She will be called 'woman,'
    because she was taken from 'man.'"

[24]This explains why a man leaves his father and mother and is joined to his wife, and the two are united into one.

[25]Now the man and his wife were both naked, but they felt no shame.

~ Genesis 2:7, 15-18, 21-25

THE SADDEST CHAPTER

This is possibly the saddest chapter in the Bible. Adam and Eve were content until they gave in to the serpent's temptation. From that time on, man has had to work the soil and struggle to grow crops in order to survive. Yet in His love, God showed us mercy in sending His Son to save us.

¹The serpent was the shrewdest of all the wild animals the LORD God had made. One day he asked the woman, "Did God really say you must not eat the fruit from any of the trees in the garden?"

⁸When the cool evening breezes were blowing, the man and his wife heard the LORD God walking about in the garden. So they hid from the LORD God among the trees. ⁹Then the LORD God called to the man, "Where are you?"

¹⁰He replied, "I heard you walking in the garden, so I hid. I was afraid because I was naked."

²³So the LORD God banished them from the Garden of Eden, and he sent Adam out to cultivate the ground from which he had been made. ²⁴After sending them out, the LORD God stationed mighty cherubim to the east of the Garden of Eden. And he placed a flaming sword that flashed back and forth to guard the way to the tree of life.

~ Genesis 3:1, 8-10, 23-24

FAITH

God told Noah to build an ark and he did so with-out questioning. That is incredible faith, considering that it had never rained on the earth before. He also had to endure mockery and humiliation from others. When your faith is being tested, stand firm like Noah.

¹⁰Noah was the father of three sons: Shem, Ham, and Japheth.

¹¹Now God saw that the earth had become corrupt and was filled with violence.

¹³So God said to Noah, "I have decided to destroy all living creatures, for they have filled the earth with violence. Yes, I will wipe them all out along with the earth!

¹⁴"Build a large boat from cypress wood and waterproof it with tar, inside and out. Then construct decks and stalls throughout its interior. ¹⁵Make the boat 450 feet long, 75 feet wide, and 45 feet high. ¹⁶Leave an 18-inch opening below the roof all the way around the boat. Put the door on the side, and build three decks inside the boat—lower, middle, and upper.

¹⁷"Look! I am about to cover the earth with a flood that will destroy every living thing that breathes. Everything on earth will die. ¹⁸But I will confirm my covenant with you. So enter the boat—you and your wife and your sons and their wives. ¹⁹Bring a pair of every kind of animal—a male and a female—into the boat with you to keep them alive during the flood. ²⁰Pairs of every kind of bird, and every kind of animal, and every kind of small animal that scurries along the ground, will come to you to be kept alive. ²¹And be sure to take on board enough food for your family and for all the animals."

²²So Noah did everything exactly as God had commanded him.

~ Genesis 6:10-11, 13-22

THE FLOOD

During the flood it rained for forty days and nights and the floodwaters covered the earth for 150 days. Noah and his family had to wait patiently for the floodwaters to subside. Patience is so important when God is doing a sovereign work.

¹²The rain continued to fall for forty days and forty nights. ¹³That very day Noah had gone into the boat with his wife and his sons—Shem, Ham, and Japheth—and their wives. ¹⁴With them in the boat were pairs of every kind of animal— domestic and wild, large and small—along with birds of every kind. ¹⁵Two by two they came into the boat, representing every living thing that breathes. ¹⁶A male and female of each kind entered, just as God had commanded Noah. Then the LORD closed the door behind them.

¹⁷For forty days the floodwaters grew deeper, covering the ground and lifting the boat high above the earth. ¹⁸As the waters rose higher and higher above the ground, the boat floated safely on the surface. ¹⁹Finally, the water covered even the highest mountains on the earth, ²⁰rising more than twenty-two feet above the highest peaks. ²¹All the living things on earth died— birds, domestic animals, wild animals, small animals that scurry along the ground, and all the people. ²²Everything that breathed and lived on dry land died. ²³God wiped out every living thing on the earth—people, livestock, small animals that scurry along the ground, and the birds of the sky. All were destroyed. The only people who survived were Noah and those with him in the boat. ²⁴And the floodwaters covered the earth for 150 days.

~ Genesis 7:12-24

GOD'S PROMISES

Noah was obedient and God blessed him and his sons. God made a covenant with Noah. He promised never to flood the earth again. He set a rainbow in the clouds as a sign of this covenant. The next time you see a rainbow, be filled with hope as you are reminded that God's promises are true.

[7]"Now be fruitful and multiply, and repopulate the earth."

[8]Then God told Noah and his sons, [9]"I hereby confirm my covenant with you and your descendants, [10]and with all the animals that were on the boat with you—the birds, the livestock, and all the wild animals—every living creature on earth. [11]Yes, I am confirming my covenant with you. Never again will floodwaters kill all living creatures; never again will a flood destroy the earth."

[12]Then God said, "I am giving you a sign of my covenant with you and with all living creatures, for all generations to come. [13]I have placed my rainbow in the clouds. It is the sign of my covenant with you and with all the earth. [14]When I send clouds over the earth, the rainbow will appear in the clouds, [15]and I will remember my covenant with you and with all living creatures. Never again will the floodwaters destroy all life. [16]When I see the rainbow in the clouds, I will remember the eternal covenant between God and every living creature on earth." [17]Then God said to Noah, "Yes, this rainbow is the sign of the covenant I am confirming with all the creatures on earth."

~ Genesis 9:7-17

OBEDIENCE

Only when you own a piece of ground yourself can you fully understand what Abram did. Abram was a successful and wealthy farmer and he left his home for an unknown destination because God told him to. Abram was obedient to God and is the only man in the Bible called God's friend. God blessed Abram for his obedience.

¹The LORD had said to Abram, "Leave your native country, your relatives, and your father's family, and go to the land that I will show you. ²I will make you into a great nation. I will bless you and make you famous, and you will be a blessing to others. ³I will bless those who bless you and curse those who treat you with contempt. All the families on earth will be blessed through you."

⁴So Abram departed as the LORD had instructed, and Lot went with him. Abram was seventy-five years old when he left Haran. ⁵He took his wife, Sarai, his nephew Lot, and all his wealth—his livestock and all the people he had taken into his household at Haran—and headed for the land of Canaan. When they arrived in Canaan, ⁶Abram traveled through the land as far as Shechem. There he set up camp beside the oak of Moreh. At that time, the area was inhabited by Canaanites.

⁷Then the LORD appeared to Abram and said, "I will give this land to your descendants." And Abram built an altar there and dedicated it to the LORD, who had appeared to him. ⁸After that, Abram traveled south and set up camp in the hill country, with Bethel to the west and Ai to the east. There he built another altar and dedicated it to the LORD, and he worshiped the LORD.

~ Genesis 12:1-8

IMPATIENCE

God promised Abram that his wife would bear a son. Yet, Sarai became impatient and asked her husband to sleep with her maidservant, Hagar. A son, Ishmael, was born to Hagar. Since then, Ishmael's descendants have been the thorn in the side of the Jewish people. God's timing is not our timing and we must wait patiently for Him to do what He promises to do.

¹Now Sarai, Abram's wife, had not been able to bear children for him. But she had an Egyptian servant named Hagar. ²So Sarai said to Abram, "The Lord has prevented me from having children. Go and sleep with my servant. Perhaps I can have children through her." And Abram agreed with Sarai's proposal. ³So Sarai, Abram's wife, took Hagar the Egyptian servant and gave her to Abram as a wife. ⁴So Abram had sexual relations with Hagar, and she became pregnant. But when Hagar knew she was pregnant, she began to treat her mistress, Sarai, with contempt. ⁵Then Sarai said to Abram, "This is all your fault! I put my servant into your arms, but now that she's pregnant she treats me with contempt."

⁶Then Sarai treated Hagar so harshly that she finally ran away.

⁷The angel of the Lord found Hagar beside a spring of water in the wilderness, along the road to Shur. ⁸The angel said to her, "Hagar, Sarai's servant, where have you come from, and where are you going?"

"I'm running away from my mistress, Sarai," she replied.

⁹The angel of the Lord said to her, "Return to your mistress, and submit to her authority." ¹⁰Then he added, "I will give you more descendants than you can count."

~ Genesis 16:1-10

DON'T EVER DOUBT

When God promised Abraham that his wife would have a baby, Sarah laughed, thinking that it was impossible. If the Lord makes a promise, He keeps it. It doesn't matter how impossible it may seem, we need to stand on God's word. God honored Abraham and gave them a son, who they named Isaac. Nothing is too difficult for God.

⁹"Where is Sarah, your wife?" the visitors asked.

"She's inside the tent," Abraham replied.

¹⁰Then one of them said, "I will return to you about this time next year, and your wife, Sarah, will have a son!"

Sarah was listening to this conversation from the tent. ¹¹Abraham and Sarah were both very old by this time, and Sarah was long past the age of having children.

¹²So she laughed silently to herself and said, "How could a worn-out woman like me enjoy such pleasure, especially when my master—my husband—is also so old?"

¹³Then the Lord said to Abraham, "Why did Sarah laugh? Why did she say, 'Can an old woman like me have a baby?' ¹⁴Is anything too hard for the Lord? I will return about this time next year, and Sarah will have a son."

¹⁵Sarah was afraid, so she denied it, saying, "I didn't laugh."

But the Lord said, "No, you did laugh."

21The Lord kept his word and did for Sarah exactly what he had promised. ²She became pregnant, and she gave birth to a son for Abraham in his old age. This happened at just the time God had said it would. ³And Abraham named their son Isaac.

~ Genesis 18:9-15; 21:1-3

Abraham was God's friend (Isa. 41:8). God tested Abraham and he did not fail Him. God was so touched by Abraham's obedience and unwavering faith that He promised, "I will certainly bless you. I will multiply your descendants beyond number" (Gen. 22:17).

²"Take your son, your only son and go to the land of Moriah. Go and sacrifice him as a burnt offering on one of the mountains."

⁶So Abraham placed the wood for the burnt offering on Isaac's shoulders, while he himself carried the fire and the knife. As the two of them walked on together, ⁷Isaac turned to Abraham and said, "Father?"

"Yes, my son?" Abraham replied.

"We have the fire and the wood," the boy said, "but where is the sheep for the burnt offering?"

⁸"God will provide a sheep for the burnt offering, my son," Abraham answered. And they both walked on together.

⁹When they arrived at the place where God had told him to go, Abraham built an altar and arranged the wood on it. Then he tied his son, Isaac, and laid him on the altar on top of the wood. ¹⁰And Abraham picked up the knife to kill his son as a sacrifice. ¹¹At that moment the angel of the Lᴏʀᴅ called to him from heaven, "Abraham! Abraham!"

"Yes," Abraham replied. "Here I am!"

¹²"Don't lay a hand on the boy!" the angel said. "Do not hurt him in any way, for now I know that you truly fear God. You have not withheld from me even your son, your only son."

¹³Then Abraham looked up and saw a ram caught by its horns in a thicket. So he took the ram and sacrificed it as a burnt offering in place of his son.

~ Genesis 22:2, 6-13

GOD PERSEVERES

Here we see how Jacob, a dishonest man, tricked his brother out of his birthright. Yet God didn't give up on Jacob and he became one of the great spiritual fathers in Israel. This story confirms that God loves sinners. If God can redeem Jacob after what he did to his brother, then there is hope for you and me.

⁵But Rebekah ⁶ said to her son Jacob, "Listen. I overheard your father say to Esau, ⁷'Bring me some wild game and prepare me a delicious meal. Then I will bless you in the LORD's presence before I die.' ⁸Now, my son, listen to me. Do exactly as I tell you. ⁹Go out to the flocks, and bring me two fine young goats. I'll use them to prepare your father's favorite dish. ¹⁰Then take the food to your father so he can eat it and bless you before he dies."

¹⁸So Jacob took the food to his father. "My father?" he said.

"Yes, my son," Isaac answered. "Who are you—Esau or Jacob?"

¹⁹Jacob replied, "It's Esau, your firstborn son. I've done as you told me. Here is the wild game. Now sit up and eat it so you can give me your blessing."

²⁰Isaac asked, "How did you find it so quickly, my son?"

"The LORD your God put it in my path!" Jacob replied.

²¹Then Isaac said to Jacob, "Come closer so I can touch you and make sure that you really are Esau." ²²So Jacob went closer to his father, and Isaac touched him. "The voice is Jacob's, but the hands are Esau's," Isaac said. ²³But he did not recognize Jacob, because Jacob's hands felt hairy just like Esau's. So Isaac prepared to bless Jacob. ²⁴"But are you really my son Esau?" he asked.

"Yes, I am," Jacob replied.

~ Genesis 27:5-10, 18-24

PERSEVERANCE

Jacob wrestled with God. He would not let God go until God blessed him. By the morning, God had dislocated Jacob's hip and for the rest of his life, Jacob walked with a limp. God also changed his name to Israel (meaning prince of God). From that time onwards, God walked very closely with Israel. No matter how tough times may be, keep going.

²²During the night Jacob got up and took his two wives, his two servant wives, and his eleven sons and crossed the Jabbok River with them. ²³After taking them to the other side, he sent over all his possessions.

²⁴This left Jacob all alone in the camp, and a man came and wrestled with him until the dawn began to break. ²⁵When the man saw that he would not win the match, he touched Jacob's hip and wrenched it out of its socket. ²⁶Then the man said, "Let me go, for the dawn is breaking!"

But Jacob said, "I will not let you go unless you bless me."

²⁷"What is your name?" the man asked.

He replied, "Jacob."

²⁸"Your name will no longer be Jacob," the man told him. "From now on you will be called Israel, because you have fought with God and with men and have won."

²⁹"Please tell me your name," Jacob said.

"Why do you want to know my name?" the man replied. Then he blessed Jacob there.

³⁰Jacob named the place Peniel (which means "face of God"). ³¹The sun was rising as Jacob left Peniel, and he was limping because of the injury to his hip.

~ Genesis 32:22-31

FAVORITISM

The story of Joseph and his coat of many colors teaches us to never show favoritism. Joseph was sold into slavery by his brothers because they were jealous of him. We need to be wise and sensitive as parents, employers and elders.

³So one day Jacob had a special gift made for Joseph—a beautiful robe. ⁴But his brothers hated Joseph because their father loved him more than the rest of them. They couldn't say a kind word to him.

²³So when Joseph arrived, his brothers ripped off the beautiful robe he was wearing. ²⁴Then they grabbed him and threw him into the cistern. Now the cistern was empty; there was no water in it. ²⁵Then, just as they were sitting down to eat, they looked up and saw a caravan of camels in the distance coming toward them. It was a group of Ishmaelite traders taking a load of gum, balm, and aromatic resin from Gilead down to Egypt.

²⁶Judah said to his brothers, "What will we gain by killing our brother? We'd have to cover up the crime. ²⁷Instead of hurting him, let's sell him to those Ishmaelite traders. After all, he is our brother—our own flesh and blood!" And his brothers agreed. ²⁸So when the Ishmaelites, who were Midianite traders, came by, Joseph's brothers pulled him out of the cistern and sold him to them for twenty pieces of silver. And the traders took him to Egypt.

³¹Then the brothers killed a young goat and dipped Joseph's robe in its blood. ³²They sent the beautiful robe to their father with this message: "Look at what we found. Doesn't this robe belong to your son?" ³³Their father recognized it immediately. "Yes," he said, "it is my son's robe."

~ Genesis 37:3-4, 23-28, 31-33

TAKE THE OPPORTUNITY

Everybody gets opportunities in life. In Joseph's case, he accepted the opportunity to interpret Pharaoh's dream and as a result Pharaoh showed him favor and he became the second most powerful man in Egypt. Grab the opportunities you get.

[17]So Pharaoh told Joseph his dream. "In my dream," he said, "I was standing on the bank of the Nile River, [18]and I saw seven fat, healthy cows come up out of the river and begin grazing in the marsh grass. [19]But then I saw seven sick-looking cows, scrawny and thin, come up after them. I've never seen such sorry-looking animals in all the land of Egypt. [20]These thin, scrawny cows ate the seven fat cows. [21]But afterward you wouldn't have known it, for they were still as thin and scrawny as before! Then I woke up.

[22]"Then I fell asleep again, and I had another dream. This time I saw seven heads of grain, full and beautiful, growing on a single stalk. [23]Then seven more heads of grain appeared, but these were blighted, shriveled, and withered by the east wind. [24]And the shriveled heads swallowed the seven healthy heads. [25]Joseph responded, "Both of Pharaoh's dreams mean the same thing. God is telling Pharaoh in advance what he is about to do. [26]The seven healthy cows and the seven healthy heads of grain both represent seven years of prosperity. [27]The seven thin, scrawny cows that came up later and the seven thin heads of grain, withered by the east wind, represent seven years of famine." [39]Then Pharaoh said to Joseph, "Since God has revealed the meaning of the dreams to you, clearly no one else is as intelligent or wise as you are. [40]You will be in charge of my court, and all my people will take orders from you."

~ Genesis 41:17-27, 39-40

RECONCILIATION

When a man of God is touched by the Holy Spirit, he is able to forgive. Joseph was able to forgive his brothers. Never be slow to forgive, because it is only by the grace of God that we are forgiven.

4"Please, come closer," he said to them. So they came closer. And he said again, "I am Joseph, your brother, whom you sold into slavery in Egypt. 5But don't be upset, and don't be angry with yourselves for selling me to this place. It was God who sent me here ahead of you to preserve your lives. 6This famine that has ravaged the land for two years will last five more years, and there will be neither plowing nor harvesting. 7God has sent me ahead of you to keep you and your families alive and to preserve many survivors. 8And he is the one who made me an adviser to Pharaoh—the manager of his entire palace and the governor of all Egypt.

9"Now hurry back to my father and tell him, 'This is what your son Joseph says: God has made me master over all the land of Egypt. So come down to me immediately! 10You can live in the region of Goshen, where you can be near me with all your children and grandchildren, your flocks and herds, and everything you own. 11I will take care of you there, for there are still five years of famine ahead of us.'"

12Then Joseph added, "Look! You can see for yourselves, and so can my brother Benjamin, that I really am Joseph! 13Go tell my father of my honored position here in Egypt. Describe for him everything you have seen, and then bring my father here quickly." 14Weeping with joy, he embraced Benjamin, and Benjamin did the same. 15Then Joseph kissed each of his brothers and wept over them, and after that they began talking freely with him.

~ Genesis 45:4-15

GOD-INCIDENCES

There are no coincidences, only God-incidences. Moses was not raised in Pharaoh's palace by accident. God has a plan and purpose for every person's life. He puts men in the right place at the right time and equips them to do His work.

²The woman became pregnant and gave birth to a son. She saw that he was a special baby and kept him hidden for three months. ³But when she could no longer hide him, she got a basket made of papyrus reeds and waterproofed it with tar and pitch. She put the baby in the basket and laid it among the reeds along the bank of the Nile River. ⁴The baby's sister then stood at a distance, watching to see what would happen to him.

⁵Soon Pharaoh's daughter came down to bathe in the river. When the princess saw the basket among the reeds, she sent her maid to get it for her. ⁶When the princess opened it, she saw the baby. The little boy was crying, and she felt sorry for him. "This must be one of the Hebrew children," she said.

⁷Then the baby's sister approached the princess. "Should I go and find one of the Hebrew women to nurse the baby for you?" she asked.

⁸"Yes, do!" the princess replied. So the girl went and called the baby's mother.

⁹"Take this baby and nurse him for me," the princess told the baby's mother. "I will pay you for your help." So the woman took her baby home and nursed him.

¹⁰Later, when the boy was older, his mother brought him back to Pharaoh's daughter, who adopted him as her own son. The princess named him Moses, for she explained, "I lifted him out of the water."

~ Exodus 2:2-10

AN ORDINARY MAN

Moses was an ordinary man just like you and me. After forty years in the wilderness God called Moses to perform a great task. At first Moses found the task daunting, but God persisted with him and he went.

¹One day Moses was tending the flock of his father-in-law, Jethro, the priest of Midian. He led the flock far into the wilderness and came to Sinai, the mountain of God. ²There the angel of the Lord appeared to him in a blazing fire from the middle of a bush. Moses stared in amazement. Though the bush was engulfed in flames, it didn't burn up. ³"This is amazing," Moses said to himself. "Why isn't that bush burning up? I must go see it."

⁴When the Lord saw Moses coming to take a closer look, God called to him from the middle of the bush, "Moses! Moses!"

"Here I am!" Moses replied.

⁵"Do not come any closer," the Lord warned. "Take off your sandals, for you are standing on holy ground. ⁶I am the God of your father—the God of Abraham, the God of Isaac, and the God of Jacob." When Moses heard this, he covered his face because he was afraid to look at God.

¹⁰Now go, for I am sending you to Pharaoh. You must lead my people Israel out of Egypt." ¹¹But Moses protested to God, "Who am I to appear before Pharaoh? Who am I to lead the people of Israel out of Egypt?"

¹²God answered, "I will be with you. And this is your sign that I am the one who has sent you: When you have brought the people out of Egypt, you will worship God at this very mountain."

~ Exodus 3:1-6, 10-12

DELIVERANCE

After the many plagues, Pharaoh was irritated and angry with Moses. That was the beginning of deliverance for the Israelites. The last plague was the death of the firstborn in each Egyptian household. Pharaoh broke down and chased the Israelites away.

²¹Then the Lord said to Moses, "Lift your hand toward heaven, and the land of Egypt will be covered with a darkness so thick you can feel it." ²²So Moses lifted his hand to the sky, and a deep darkness covered the entire land of Egypt for three days. ²³During all that time the people could not see each other, and no one moved. But there was light as usual where the people of Israel lived.

²⁴Finally, Pharaoh called for Moses. "Go and worship the Lord," he said. "But leave your flocks and herds here. You may even take your little ones with you."

²⁵"No," Moses said, "you must provide us with animals for sacrifices and burnt offerings to the Lord our God. ²⁶All our livestock must go with us, too; not a hoof can be left behind. We must choose our sacrifices for the Lord our God from among these animals. And we won't know how we are to worship the Lord until we get there."

²⁷But the Lord hardened Pharaoh's heart once more, and he would not let them go. ²⁸"Get out of here!" Pharaoh shouted at Moses. "I'm warning you. Never come back to see me again! The day you see my face, you will die!"

²⁹"Very well," Moses replied. "I will never see your face again."

11Then the Lord said to Moses, "I will strike Pharaoh and the land of Egypt with one more blow. After that, Pharaoh will let you leave this country."

~ Exodus 10:21-11:1

FIGHTING FOR YOU

I find this passage truly inspiring. Moses was pressed on all sides. He was stuck in a very difficult situation. The most powerful army was behind him and the Red Sea was in front of him. Yet he held fast to the Lord's promises. Remember that, "The Lord Himself will fight for you" (Exod. 14:14).

¹Then Moses and the people of Israel sang this song to the Lord:
"I will sing to the Lord,
    for he has triumphed gloriously;
he has hurled both horse and rider
    into the sea.
²The Lord is my strength and my song;
    he has given me victory.
This is my God, and I will praise him—
    my father's God, and I will exalt him!
³The Lord is a warrior;
    Yahweh is his name!
⁴Pharaoh's chariots and army
    he has hurled into the sea.
The finest of Pharaoh's officers
    are drowned in the Red Sea.
⁵The deep waters gushed over them;
    they sank to the bottom like a stone.
⁶"Your right hand, O Lord,
    is glorious in power.
Your right hand, O Lord,
    smashes the enemy."

~ Exodus 15:1-6

BREAD FROM HEAVEN

The Israelites complained that they had no food to eat and that they were better off in Egypt. So God sent manna and quail from heaven. God always takes care of His people.

⁴Then the LORD said to Moses, "Look, I'm going to rain down food from heaven for you. Each day the people can go out and pick up as much food as they need for that day. I will test them in this to see whether or not they will follow my instructions. ⁵On the sixth day they will gather food, and when they prepare it, there will be twice as much as usual."

⁶So Moses and Aaron said to all the people of Israel, "By evening you will realize it was the LORD who brought you out of the land of Egypt. ⁷In the morning you will see the glory of the LORD, because he has heard your complaints, which are against him, not against us. What have we done that you should complain about us?" ⁸Then Moses added, "The LORD will give you meat to eat in the evening and bread to satisfy you in the morning, for he has heard all your complaints against him."

⁹Then Moses said to Aaron, "Announce this to the entire community of Israel: 'Present yourselves before the LORD, for he has heard your complaining.'" ¹⁰And as Aaron spoke to the whole community of Israel, they looked out toward the wilderness. There they could see the awesome glory of the LORD in the cloud.

¹¹Then the LORD said to Moses, ¹²"I have heard the Israelites' complaints. Now tell them, 'In the evening you will have meat to eat, and in the morning you will have all the bread you want. Then you will know that I am the LORD your God.'"

~ Exodus 16:4-12

GOOD ADVICE

Moses was wearing himself out solving the problems of the Israelites. Jethro told Moses to get help. He listened to his father-in-law and it worked. God never expects us to be lone rangers. Take the support that is offered from fellow believers.

¹³The next day, Moses took his seat to hear the people's disputes against each other. They waited before him from morning till evening. ¹⁴When Moses' father-in-law saw all that Moses was doing for the people, he asked, "What are you really accomplishing here? Why are you trying to do all this alone while everyone stands around you from morning till evening?"

¹⁷"This is not good!" Moses' father-in-law exclaimed. ¹⁸"You're going to wear yourself out—and the people, too. This job is too heavy a burden for you to handle all by yourself. ¹⁹Now listen to me, and let me give you a word of advice, and may God be with you. You should continue to be the people's representative before God, bringing their disputes to him. ²⁰Teach them God's decrees, and give them his instructions. Show them how to conduct their lives. ²¹But select from all the people some capable, honest men who fear God and hate bribes. Appoint them as leaders over groups of one thousand, one hundred, fifty, and ten. ²²They should always be available to solve the people's common disputes, but have them bring the major cases to you. Let the leaders decide the smaller matters themselves. They will help you carry the load, making the task easier for you. ²³If you follow this advice, and if God commands you to do so, then you will be able to endure the pressures, and all these people will go home in peace." ²⁴Moses listened to his father-in-law's advice and followed his suggestions.

~ Exodus 18:13-14, 17-24

THE TEN COMMANDMENTS

The Ten Commandments are for our benefit and they are relevant today. God wants us to live lives that are full of blessing, but in order to do so, we have to live in an orderly manner.

³"You must not have any other god but me.

⁴"You must not make for yourself an idol of any kind or an image of anything in the heavens or on the earth or in the sea. ⁵You must not bow down to them or worship them, for I, the Lᴏʀᴅ your God, am a jealous God who will not tolerate your affection for any other gods. I lay the sins of the parents upon their children; the entire family is affected. ⁶But I lavish unfailing love for a thousand generations on those who love me and obey my commands.

⁷"You must not misuse the name of the Lᴏʀᴅ your God. The Lᴏʀᴅ will not let you go unpunished if you misuse his name.

⁸"Remember to observe the Sabbath day by keeping it holy. ⁹You have six days each week for your ordinary work, ¹⁰but the seventh day is a Sabbath day of rest dedicated to the Lᴏʀᴅ your God. On that day no one in your household may do any work. ¹¹For in six days the Lᴏʀᴅ made the heavens, the earth, the sea, and everything in them; but on the seventh day he rested. That is why the Lᴏʀᴅ blessed the Sabbath day and set it apart as holy.

¹²"Honor your father and mother. Then you will live a long, full life in the land the Lᴏʀᴅ your God is giving you.

¹³"You must not murder. ¹⁴You must not commit adultery. ¹⁵You must not steal. ¹⁶You must not testify falsely against your neighbor. ¹⁷You must not covet your neighbor's house. You must not covet your neighbor's wife, male or female servant, ox or donkey, or anything else that belongs to your neighbor."

~ Exodus 20:3-17

THE GOLDEN CALF

The Israelites became impatient waiting for Moses. They built a golden calf and worshipped it. God hates idolatry – it could be sport, money, fame or work. God was furious but, because of Moses' prayers, He refrained from destroying the Israelites. What a merciful God we serve.

¹When the people saw how long it was taking Moses to come back down the mountain, they gathered around Aaron. "Come on," they said, "make us some gods who can lead us."

⁷The Lord told Moses, "Quick! Go down the mountain! Your people whom you brought from the land of Egypt have corrupted themselves. ⁸How quickly they have turned away from the way I commanded them to live! They have melted down gold and made a calf, and they have bowed down and sacrificed to it. They are saying, 'These are your gods, O Israel, who brought you out of the land of Egypt.'"

⁹Then the Lord said, "I have seen how stubborn and rebellious these people are." ¹⁰Now leave me alone so my fierce anger can blaze against them, and I will destroy them.

¹¹But Moses tried to pacify the Lord his God. "O Lord!" he said. "Why are you so angry with your own people whom you brought from the land of Egypt with such great power and such a strong hand? ¹³Remember your servants Abraham, Isaac, and Jacob. You bound yourself with an oath to them, saying, 'I will make your descendants as numerous as the stars of heaven. And I will give them all of this land that I have promised to your descendants, and they will possess it forever.'"

¹⁴So the Lord changed his mind about the terrible disaster he had threatened to bring on his people.

~ Exodus 32:1, 7-11, 13-14

JANUARY 25
OUR GOD IS HOLY

God is a holy God and He cannot look upon sin. The people of Israel offered up animals as living sacrifices to the Lord for their sins. These were the scapegoats. The ultimate scapegoat is the Lord Jesus Christ. He took the punishment for our sins on Himself when He died on the cross. Praise Him for His great sacrifice.

¹Then the LORD said to Moses, ²"Suppose one of you sins against your associate and is unfaithful to the LORD. Suppose you cheat in a deal involving a security deposit, or you steal or commit fraud, ³or you find lost property and lie about it, or you lie while swearing to tell the truth, or you commit any other such sin.

⁴If you have sinned in any of these ways, you are guilty. You must give back whatever you stole, or the money you took by extortion, or the security deposit, or the lost property you found, ⁵or anything obtained by swearing falsely. You must make restitution by paying the full price plus an additional 20 percent to the person you have harmed. On the same day you must present a guilt offering.

⁶As a guilt offering to the LORD, you must bring to the priest your own ram with no defects, or you may buy one of equal value. ⁷Through this process, the priest will purify you before the LORD, making you right with him, and you will be forgiven for any of these sins you have committed."

~ Leviticus 6:1-7

THE FEAST OF TABERNACLES

The Feast of Tabernacles, or Festival of Shelters, reminds Jewish people that the Lord took care of them. The feast lasts seven days and they spend that time rejoicing and thanking God for His care. We need to spend time with the Lord every day thanking Him for all He does for us.

³³And the LORD said to Moses, ³⁴"Give the following instructions to the people of Israel. Begin celebrating the Festival of Shelters on the fifteenth day of the appointed month—five days after the Day of Atonement. This festival to the LORD will last for seven days. ³⁵On the first day of the festival you must proclaim an official day for holy assembly, when you do no ordinary work. ³⁶For seven days you must present special gifts to the LORD. The eighth day is another holy day on which you present your special gifts to the LORD. This will be a solemn occasion, and no ordinary work may be done that day.

³⁹"Remember that this seven-day festival to the LORD— the Festival of Shelters—begins on the fifteenth day of the appointed month, after you have harvested all the produce of the land. The first day and the eighth day of the festival will be days of complete rest. ⁴⁰On the first day gather branches from magnificent trees—palm fronds, boughs from leafy trees, and willows that grow by the streams. Then celebrate with joy before the LORD your God for seven days. ⁴¹You must observe this festival to the LORD for seven days every year."

~ Leviticus 23:33-36, 39-41

A PRIESTLY BLESSING

What a wonderful blessing to pray over your children and loved ones. What a privilege to know that God is not a man that He should lie, and what He has promised He will accomplish. His blessing is one of peace, grace and protection. Pray this blessing over your family. God always answers the prayer of faith.

¹⁸"Then the Nazirites will shave their heads at the entrance of the Tabernacle. They will take the hair that had been dedicated and place it on the fire beneath the peace-offering sacrifice. ¹⁹After the Nazirite's head has been shaved, the priest will take for each of them the boiled shoulder of the ram, and he will take from the basket a cake and a wafer made without yeast. He will put them all into the Nazirite's hands. ²⁰Then the priest will lift them up as a special offering before the Lord. These are holy portions for the priest, along with the breast of the special offering and the thigh of the sacred offering that are lifted up before the Lord. After this ceremony the Nazirites may again drink wine.

²¹"This is the ritual law of the Nazirites, who vow to bring these offerings to the Lord. They may also bring additional offerings if they can afford it. And they must be careful to do whatever they vowed when they set themselves apart as Nazirites."

²²Then the Lord said to Moses, ²³"Tell Aaron and his sons to bless the people of Israel with this special blessing:
²⁴'May the Lord bless you
and protect you.
²⁵May the Lord smile on you
and be gracious to you.
²⁶May the Lord show you his favor
and give you his peace.'"

~ Numbers 6:18-26

POSITIVE REPORTS

Moses sent twelve spies to the Promised Land. Ten came back with negative reports and only Joshua and Caleb came back with positive reports. These two looked at the size of the land whereas the ten looked at the size of the giants. The question is: Who are you looking at, the problem or the Problem Solver?

[23]When they came to the valley of Eshcol, they cut down a branch with a single cluster of grapes so large that it took two of them to carry it on a pole between them! They also brought back samples of the pomegranates and figs. [24]That place was called the valley of Eshcol (which means "cluster"), because of the cluster of grapes the Israelite men cut there.

[25]After exploring the land for forty days, the men returned [26]to Moses, Aaron, and the whole community of Israel at Kadesh in the wilderness of Paran. They reported to the whole community what they had seen and showed them the fruit they had taken from the land. [27]This was their report to Moses: "We entered the land you sent us to explore, and it is indeed a bountiful country—a land flowing with milk and honey. Here is the kind of fruit it produces. [28]But the people living there are powerful, and their towns are large and fortified. We even saw giants there, the descendants of Anak!"

[30]But Caleb tried to quiet the people as they stood before Moses. "Let's go at once to take the land," he said.

[31]But the other men who had explored the land with him disagreed. "We can't go up against them! They are stronger than we are!"

~ Numbers 13:23-28, 30-31

TIME TO MOVE ON

There comes a time when you have to move on, whether in business, sport or even ministry. God will say when we need to move across and possess the land. It takes a lot of faith and God always honors faithfulness. Keith Green once said, "If you are not moving forward, you are going backwards." We need to go in and possess the land.

⁶"When we were at Mount Sinai, the LORD our God said to us, 'You have stayed at this mountain long enough. ⁷It is time to break camp and move on. Go to the hill country of the Amorites and to all the neighboring regions—the Jordan Valley, the hill country, the western foothills, the Negev, and the coastal plain. Go to the land of the Canaanites and to Lebanon, and all the way to the great Euphrates River. ⁸Look, I am giving all this land to you! Go in and occupy it, for it is the land the LORD swore to give to your ancestors Abraham, Isaac, and Jacob, and to all their descendants.'"

¹⁹"Then, just as the LORD our God commanded us, we left Mount Sinai and traveled through the great and terrifying wilderness, as you yourselves remember, and headed toward the hill country of the Amorites. When we arrived at Kadesh-barnea, ²⁰I said to you, 'You have now reached the hill country of the Amorites that the LORD our God is giving us. ²¹Look! He has placed the land in front of you. Go and occupy it as the LORD, the God of your ancestors, has promised you. Don't be afraid! Don't be discouraged!'"

~ Deuteronomy 1:6-8, 19-21

THE GREATEST COMMANDMENT

Deuteronomy 6:5 contains the greatest commandment in the Bible. If we obey this commandment, the other commandments will just fall into place. Once you meet the Lord in a personal way, it is not difficult to obey His commandments, especially this commandment, because of the love you have for Him. Obedience to God brings joy.

¹"These are the commands, decrees, and regulations that the LORD your God commanded me to teach you. You must obey them in the land you are about to enter and occupy, ²and you and your children and grandchildren must fear the LORD your God as long as you live. If you obey all his decrees and commands, you will enjoy a long life. ³Listen closely, Israel, and be careful to obey. Then all will go well with you, and you will have many children in the land flowing with milk and honey, just as the LORD, the God of your ancestors, promised you.

⁴"Listen, O Israel! The LORD is our God, the LORD alone. ⁵And you must love the LORD your God with all your heart, all your soul, and all your strength. ⁶And you must commit yourselves wholeheartedly to these commands that I am giving you today. ⁷Repeat them again and again to your children. Talk about them when you are at home and when you are on the road, when you are going to bed and when you are getting up. ⁸Tie them to your hands and wear them on your forehead as reminders. ⁹Write them on the doorposts of your house and on your gates.

~ Deuteronomy 6:1-9

CURSES OF DISOBEDIENCE

God not only desires to bless us, but He also punishes those who refuse to obey Him. It is not that God wants to punish us, but He loves us. He does, however, need to follow through on His word. Many people ask why God is punishing them. God is not punishing us; He expects us to live with the consequences of our actions.

¹²"When you begin living in the towns the LORD your God is giving you, you may hear ¹³that scoundrels among you are leading their fellow citizens astray by saying, 'Let us go worship other gods'—gods you have not known before. ¹⁴In such cases, you must examine the facts carefully. If you find that the report is true and such a detestable act has been committed among you, ¹⁵you must attack that town and completely destroy all its inhabitants, as well as all the livestock. ¹⁶Then you must pile all the plunder in the middle of the open square and burn it. Burn the entire town as a burnt offering to the LORD your God. That town must remain a ruin forever; it may never be rebuilt. ¹⁷Keep none of the plunder that has been set apart for destruction. Then the LORD will turn from his fierce anger and be merciful to you. He will have compassion on you and make you a large nation, just as he swore to your ancestors.

¹⁸"The LORD your God will be merciful only if you listen to his voice and keep all his commands that I am giving you today, doing what pleases him."

~ Deuteronomy 13:12-18

FEBRUARY

God desires to bless those who are obedient. It is as if the Lord is waiting eagerly to bless us unconditionally if we would just obey His commandments. I have experienced many of these blessings when I have been obedient to His Word and faithful to what He has said.

¹"If you fully obey the LORD your God and carefully keep all his commands that I am giving you today, the LORD your God will set you high above all the nations of the world. ²You will experience all these blessings if you obey the LORD your God:
³Your towns and your fields
   will be blessed.
⁴Your children and your crops
   will be blessed.
The offspring of your herds and flocks
   will be blessed.
⁵Your fruit baskets and breadboards
   will be blessed.
⁶Wherever you go and whatever you do,
   you will be blessed.
⁷"The LORD will conquer your enemies when they attack you.

⁸"The LORD will guarantee a blessing on everything you do and will fill your storehouses with grain. ⁹If you obey the commands of the LORD your God and walk in his ways, the LORD will establish you as his holy people as he swore he would do. ¹¹The LORD will give you prosperity in the land he swore to your ancestors to give you, blessing you with many children, numerous livestock, and abundant crops. ¹²The LORD will send rain at the proper time from his rich treasury in the heavens and will bless all the work you do."

~ Deuteronomy 28:1-9, 11-12

THE CHOICE

God gives us many choices. He also allows us to make our own choices and gives us the necessary guidance to make the right ones. Choose life today by committing your life to God and by living and obeying Him.

[11]"This command I am giving you today is not too difficult for you to understand, and it is not beyond your reach. [12]It is not kept in heaven, so distant that you must ask, 'Who will go up to heaven and bring it down so we can hear it and obey?' [13]It is not kept beyond the sea, so far away that you must ask, 'Who will cross the sea to bring it to us so we can hear it and obey?' [14]No, the message is very close at hand; it is on your lips and in your heart so that you can obey it.

[15]"Now listen! Today I am giving you a choice between life and death, between prosperity and disaster. [16]For I command you this day to love the LORD your God and to keep his commands, decrees, and regulations by walking in his ways. If you do this, you will live and multiply, and the LORD your God will bless you and the land you are about to enter and occupy.

[17]"But if your heart turns away and you refuse to listen, and if you are drawn away to serve and worship other gods, [18]then I warn you now that you will certainly be destroyed. You will not live a long, good life in the land you are crossing the Jordan to occupy.

[19]"Today I have given you the choice between life and death, between blessings and curses. Now I call on heaven and earth to witness the choice you make. Oh, that you would choose life, so that you and your descendants might live! [20]You can make this choice by loving the LORD your God, obeying him, and committing yourself firmly to him."

~ Deuteronomy 30:11-20

STRONG AND COURAGEOUS

Joshua's responsibility was to lead the Israelites across the Jordan River and into the Promised Land. The Lord continued to remind Joshua to be strong and courageous. It doesn't matter how big the challenge is, God will see us through if we are obedient to Him.

¹After the death of Moses the LORD's servant, the LORD spoke to Joshua son of Nun, Moses' assistant. He said, ²"Moses my servant is dead. Therefore, the time has come for you to lead these people, the Israelites, across the Jordan River into the land I am giving them. ³I promise you what I promised Moses: 'Wherever you set foot, you will be on land I have given you— ⁴from the Negev wilderness in the south to the Lebanon mountains in the north, from the Euphrates River in the east to the Mediterranean Sea in the west, including all the land of the Hittites.' ⁵No one will be able to stand against you as long as you live. For I will be with you as I was with Moses. I will not fail you or abandon you.

⁶"Be strong and courageous, for you are the one who will lead these people to possess all the land I swore to their ancestors I would give them. ⁷Be strong and very courageous. Be careful to obey all the instructions Moses gave you. Do not deviate from them, turning either to the right or to the left. Then you will be successful in everything you do. ⁸Study this Book of Instruction continually. Meditate on it day and night so you will be sure to obey everything written in it. Only then will you prosper and succeed in all you do. ⁹This is my command—be strong and courageous! Do not be afraid or discouraged. For the LORD your God is with you wherever you go."

~ Joshua 1:1-9

Faith has feet. Faith is action. The high priests didn't stand at the river's edge waiting for the waters to part, but walked into the water and the water parted. Don't expect God to open the way before you move. He wants you to step out in faith. He wants to see us trust Him before He parts the waters.

⁹So Joshua told the Israelites, "Come and listen to what the LORD your God says. ¹⁰Today you will know that the living God is among you. He will surely drive out the Canaanites, Hittites, Hivites, Perizzites, Girgashites, Amorites, and Jebusites ahead of you. ¹¹Look, the Ark of the Covenant, which belongs to the Lord of the whole earth, will lead you across the Jordan River! ¹²Now choose twelve men from the tribes of Israel, one from each tribe. ¹³The priests will carry the Ark of the LORD, the Lord of all the earth. As soon as their feet touch the water, the flow of water will be cut off upstream, and the river will stand up like a wall." ¹⁴So the people left their camp to cross the Jordan, and the priests who were carrying the Ark of the Covenant went ahead of them. ¹⁵It was the harvest season, and the Jordan was overflowing its banks. But as soon as the feet of the priests who were carrying the Ark touched the water at the river's edge, ¹⁶the water above that point began backing up a great distance away at a town called Adam, which is near Zarethan. And the water below that point flowed on to the Dead Sea until the riverbed was dry. Then all the people crossed over near the town of Jericho.

¹⁷Meanwhile, the priests who were carrying the Ark of the LORD's Covenant stood on dry ground in the middle of the riverbed as the people passed by. They waited there until the whole nation of Israel had crossed the Jordan on dry ground.

~ Joshua 3:9-17

The Lord undertakes for us in different areas of our lives in different seasons. He provided manna for the Israelites in the wilderness until they could provide for themselves. The Lord will supply what we need, while we need it. As soon as we are able to undertake for ourselves in that area, He will cease to supply in order for us to mature.

³During all this time you have not deserted the other tribes. You have been careful to obey the commands of the LORD your God right up to the present day. ⁴And now the LORD your God has given the other tribes rest, as he promised them. So go back home to the land that Moses, the servant of the LORD, gave you as your possession on the east side of the Jordan River.

⁵But be very careful to obey all the commands and the instructions that Moses gave to you. Love the LORD your God, walk in all his ways, obey his commands, hold firmly to him, and serve him with all your heart and all your soul." ⁶So Joshua blessed them and sent them away, and they went home.

⁷Moses had given the land of Bashan, east of the Jordan River, to the half-tribe of Manasseh. (The other half of the tribe was given land west of the Jordan.) As Joshua sent them away and blessed them, ⁸he said to them, "Go back to your homes with the great wealth you have taken from your enemies—the vast herds of livestock, the silver, gold, bronze, and iron, and the large supply of clothing."

~ Joshua 22:3-8

ME AND MY HOUSE

Joshua's decision to serve the Lord is the reason why God blessed him so much. I would like to challenge all those who head up households, farms, businesses and schools to lead by example. If you are steadfast in what you believe, you might not be liked, but you will be respected.

¹⁴"So fear the LORD and serve him wholeheartedly. Put away forever the idols your ancestors worshiped when they lived beyond the Euphrates River and in Egypt. Serve the LORD alone. ¹⁵But if you refuse to serve the LORD, then choose today whom you will serve. Would you prefer the gods your ancestors served beyond the Euphrates? Or will it be the gods of the Amorites in whose land you now live? But as for me and my family, we will serve the LORD."

¹⁶The people replied, "We would never abandon the LORD and serve other gods. ¹⁷For the LORD our God is the one who rescued us and our ancestors from slavery in the land of Egypt. He performed mighty miracles before our very eyes. As we traveled through the wilderness among our enemies, he preserved us. ¹⁸It was the LORD who drove out the Amorites and the other nations living here in the land. So we, too, will serve the LORD, for he alone is our God."

¹⁹Then Joshua warned the people, "You are not able to serve the LORD, for he is a holy and jealous God. He will not forgive your rebellion and your sins. ²⁰If you abandon the LORD and serve other gods, he will turn against you and destroy you, even though he has been so good to you."

²¹But the people answered Joshua, "No, we will serve the LORD!"

~ Joshua 24:14-21

THE FLEECE

Sometimes you have to make important decisions. It is good to seek God's face in these things. Gideon asked the Lord twice to confirm what he should do and the Lord spoke to him. We never need to be unsure about what to do because God is faithful to guide us.

[14]Then the LORD turned to him and said, "Go with the strength you have, and rescue Israel from the Midianites. I am sending you!"

[17]Gideon replied, "If you are truly going to help me, show me a sign to prove that it is really the LORD speaking to me."

[20]The angel of God said to him, "Place the meat and the unleavened bread on this rock, and pour the broth over it." And Gideon did as he was told. [21]Then the angel of the LORD touched the meat and bread with the tip of the staff in his hand, and fire flamed up from the rock and consumed all he had brought.

[36]Then Gideon said to God, "If you are truly going to use me to rescue Israel as you promised, [37]prove it to me in this way. I will put a wool fleece on the threshing floor tonight. If the fleece is wet with dew in the morning but the ground is dry, then I will know that you are going to help me rescue Israel as you promised." [38]And that is just what happened. When Gideon got up early the next morning, he squeezed the fleece and wrung out a whole bowlful of water.

[39]Then Gideon said to God, "Let me use the fleece for one more test. This time let the fleece remain dry while the ground around it is wet with dew." [40]So that night God did as Gideon asked. The fleece was dry in the morning, but the ground was covered with dew.

~ Judges 6:14, 17, 20-21, 36-40

THREE HUNDRED MEN

Gideon won the battle with 300 men and God was glorified. Gideon was obedient and through his obedience God's greatness was revealed.

[1]So Jerub-baal (that is, Gideon) and his army got up early and went as far as the spring of Harod. The armies of Midian were camped north of them in the valley near the hill of Moreh. [2]The LORD said to Gideon, "You have too many warriors with you. If I let all of you fight the Midianites, the Israelites will boast to me that they saved themselves by their own strength. [3]Therefore, tell the people, 'Whoever is timid or afraid may leave this mountain and go home.'" So 22,000 of them went home, leaving only 10,000 who were willing to fight.

[4]But the LORD told Gideon, "There are still too many! Bring them down to the spring, and I will test them to determine who will go with you and who will not." [5]When Gideon took his warriors down to the water, the LORD told him, "Divide the men into two groups. In one group put all those who cup water in their hands and lap it up with their tongues like dogs. In the other group put all those who kneel down and drink with their mouths in the stream." [6]Only 300 of the men drank from their hands. All the others got down on their knees and drank with their mouths in the stream.

[7]The LORD told Gideon, "With these 300 men I will rescue you and give you victory over the Midianites. Send all the others home." [8]So Gideon sent them home. But he kept the 300 men with him.

The Midianite camp was in the valley just below Gideon. [9]That night the LORD said, "Get up! Go down into the Midianite camp, for I have given you victory over them!"

~ Judges 7:1-9

THE VOW

Jephthah made a promise he regretted. Never make a promise hastily or without intending to keep it.

³¹"I will give to the LORD whatever comes out of my house to meet me when I return in triumph. I will sacrifice it as a burnt offering." ³²So Jephthah led his army against the Ammonites, and the LORD gave him victory. ³³He crushed the Ammonites, devastating about twenty towns from Aroer to an area near Minnith and as far away as Abel-keramim. In this way Israel defeated the Ammonites. ³⁴When Jephthah returned home to Mizpah, his daughter came out to meet him, playing on a tambourine and dancing for joy. She was his one and only child; he had no other sons or daughters. ³⁵When he saw her, he tore his clothes in anguish. "Oh, my daughter!" he cried out. "You have completely destroyed me! You've brought disaster on me! For I have made a vow to the LORD, and I cannot take it back."

³⁶And she said, "Father, if you have made a vow to the LORD, you must do to me what you have vowed, for the LORD has given you a great victory over your enemies, the Ammonites. ³⁷But first let me do this one thing: Let me go up and roam in the hills and weep with my friends for two months, because I will die a virgin."

³⁸"You may go," Jephthah said. And he sent her away for two months. She and her friends went into the hills and wept because she would never have children. ³⁹When she returned home, her father kept the vow he had made, and she died a virgin.

So it has become a custom in Israel ⁴⁰for young Israelite women to go away for four days each year to lament the fate of Jephthah's daughter.

~ Judges 11:31-40

CONSEQUENCES

Samson strayed from God and had to suffer the consequences. God continued to love Samson and showed him mercy, even though he had to live with the results of his actions.

¹⁷Finally, Samson shared his secret with her. "My hair has never been cut," he confessed, "for I was dedicated to God as a Nazirite from birth. If my head were shaved, my strength would leave me, and I would become as weak as anyone else."

¹⁸Delilah realized he had finally told her the truth, so she sent for the Philistine rulers. "Come back one more time," she said, "for he has finally told me his secret." So the Philistine rulers returned with the money in their hands. ¹⁹Delilah lulled Samson to sleep with his head in her lap, and then she called in a man to shave off the seven locks of his hair. In this way she began to bring him down, and his strength left him.

²¹So the Philistines captured him and gouged out his eyes. They took him to Gaza, where he was bound with bronze chains and forced to grind grain in the prison.

²⁸Then Samson prayed to the LORD, "Sovereign LORD, remember me again. O God, please strengthen me just one more time. With one blow let me pay back the Philistines for the loss of my two eyes." ²⁹Then Samson put his hands on the two center pillars that held up the temple. Pushing against them with both hands, ³⁰he prayed, "Let me die with the Philistines." And the temple crashed down on the Philistine rulers and all the people. So he killed more people when he died than he had during his entire lifetime.

~ Judges 16:17-19, 21, 28-30

REWARD FOR FAITHFULNESS

This is a beautiful example of how God rewards faithfulness. God honored Ruth's faithfulness by allowing her to marry Boaz. The Lord blessed Ruth with a son called Obed, who was King David's grandfather. Be faithful to God and He will bless you.

⁵Then Boaz asked his foreman, "Who is that young woman over there? Who does she belong to?"

⁶And the foreman replied, "She is the young woman from Moab who came back with Naomi. ⁷She asked me this morning if she could gather grain behind the harvesters. She has been hard at work ever since, except for a few minutes' rest in the shelter."

¹⁰Ruth fell at his feet and thanked him warmly. "What have I done to deserve such kindness?" she asked. "I am only a foreigner."

¹¹"Yes, I know," Boaz replied. "But I also know about everything you have done for your mother-in-law since the death of your husband. I have heard how you left your father and mother and your own land to live here among complete strangers. ¹²May the LORD, the God of Israel, under whose wings you have come to take refuge, reward you fully for what you have done."

4¹³So Boaz took Ruth into his home, and she became his wife. When he slept with her, the LORD enabled her to become pregnant, and she gave birth to a son. ¹⁴Then the women of the town said to Naomi, "Praise the LORD, who has now provided a redeemer for your family! May this child be famous in Israel. ¹⁵May he restore your youth and care for you in your old age. For he is the son of your daughter-in-law who loves you and has been better to you than seven sons!"

~ Ruth 2:5-7, 10-12; 4:13-15

A MIGHTY PROPHET

Hannah cried out to God for a child and God honored her prayers. Samuel was one of the most faithful and holy prophets in the Old Testament. It is the prayer of faith that moves the hand of God.

¹⁷"In that case," Eli said, "go in peace! May the God of Israel grant the request you have asked of him."

¹⁸"Oh, thank you, sir!" she exclaimed. Then she went back and began to eat again, and she was no longer sad.

¹⁹When Elkanah slept with Hannah, the LORD remembered her plea, ²⁰and in due time she gave birth to a son. She named him Samuel, for she said, "I asked the LORD for him."

²¹The next year Elkanah and his family went on their annual trip to offer a sacrifice to the LORD. ²²But Hannah did not go. She told her husband, "Wait until the boy is weaned. Then I will take him to the Tabernacle and leave him there with the LORD permanently."

²³"Whatever you think is best," Elkanah agreed. "Stay here for now, and may the LORD help you keep your promise." So she stayed home and nursed the boy until he was weaned.

²⁴When the child was weaned, Hannah took him to the Tabernacle in Shiloh. They brought along a three-year-old bull for the sacrifice and a basket of flour and some wine. ²⁵After sacrificing the bull, they brought the boy to Eli. ²⁶"Sir, do you remember me?" Hannah asked. "I am the woman who stood here several years ago praying to the LORD. ²⁷I asked the LORD to give me this boy, and he has granted my request. ²⁸Now I am giving him to the LORD, and he will belong to the LORD his whole life." And they worshiped the LORD there.

~ 1 Samuel 1:17-28

DISOBEDIENT SONS

Eli served the Lord, but he could not discipline his children. His two sons destroyed his whole ministry. When Eli heard the news of his sons' death, he fell off a log and broke his neck. This story dramatically illustrates the need to discipline our children. It is our duty to train up our children in God's ways.

¹¹Then Elkanah returned home to Ramah without Samuel. And the boy served the LORD by assisting Eli the priest. ¹²Now the sons of Eli were scoundrels who had no respect for the LORD ¹³or for their duties as priests. Whenever anyone offered a sacrifice, Eli's sons would send over a servant with a three-pronged fork. While the meat of the sacrificed animal was still boiling, ¹⁴the servant would stick the fork into the pot and demand that whatever it brought up be given to Eli's sons. All the Israelites who came to worship at Shiloh were treated this way. ¹⁵Sometimes the servant would come even before the animal's fat had been burned on the altar. He would demand raw meat before it had been boiled so that it could be used for roasting.

¹⁶The man offering the sacrifice might reply, "Take as much as you want, but the fat must be burned first." Then the servant would demand, "No, give it to me now, or I'll take it by force." ¹⁷So the sin of these young men was very serious in the LORD's sight, for they treated the LORD's offerings with contempt.

~ 1 Samuel 2:11-17

GOD'S LAWS

Samuel confronted Saul about his disobedience. Saul tried to justify what he had done, but he lost his kingship and was rejected by God as king. We need to repent of our sins and turn from our wicked ways, otherwise we have no hope.

¹⁶Then Samuel said to Saul, "Stop! Listen to what the Lord told me last night!" "What did he tell you?" Saul asked.

¹⁷And Samuel told him, "Although you may think little of yourself, are you not the leader of the tribes of Israel? The Lord has anointed you king of Israel. ¹⁸And the Lord sent you on a mission and told you, 'Go and completely destroy the sinners, the Amalekites, until they are all dead.' ¹⁹Why haven't you obeyed the Lord? Why did you rush for the plunder and do what was evil in the Lord's sight?"

²⁰"But I did obey the Lord," Saul insisted. "I carried out the mission he gave me. I brought back King Agag, but I destroyed everyone else. ²¹Then my troops brought in the best of the sheep, goats, cattle, and plunder to sacrifice to the Lord your God in Gilgal."

²²But Samuel replied,

"What is more pleasing to the Lord:
  your burnt offerings and sacrifices
  or your obedience to his voice?
Listen! Obedience is better than sacrifice,
  and submission is better than offering the fat of rams.
²³Rebellion is as sinful as witchcraft,
  and stubbornness as bad as worshiping idols.
So because you have rejected the command of the Lord,
  he has rejected you as king."

~ 1 Samuel 15:16-23

THE HOLY SPIRIT

It must be the worst thing in the world to realize that the Spirit of God has departed from you. That is exactly what happened to Saul. Our Lord is the Holy Spirit. He cannot look upon sin of any degree. Never offend the Holy Spirit, because when He departs from us, our lives will be hopeless and joyless.

¹⁴Now the Spirit of the LORD had left Saul, and the LORD sent a tormenting spirit that filled him with depression and fear.

¹⁵Some of Saul's servants said to him, "A tormenting spirit from God is troubling you. ¹⁶Let us find a good musician to play the harp whenever the tormenting spirit troubles you. He will play soothing music, and you will soon be well again."

¹⁷"All right," Saul said. "Find me someone who plays well, and bring him here."

¹⁸One of the servants said to Saul, "One of Jesse's sons from Bethlehem is a talented harp player. Not only that—he is a brave warrior, a man of war, and has good judgment. He is also a fine-looking young man, and the LORD is with him."

¹⁹So Saul sent messengers to Jesse to say, "Send me your son David, the shepherd." ²⁰Jesse responded by sending David to Saul.

²¹So David went to Saul and began serving him. Saul loved David very much, and David became his armor bearer.

²²Then Saul sent word to Jesse asking, "Please let David remain in my service, for I am very pleased with him."

²³And whenever the tormenting spirit from God troubled Saul, David would play the harp. Then Saul would feel better, and the tormenting spirit would go away.

~ 1 Samuel 16:14-23

STAND UP FOR GOD

Goliath hurled abuse at the God of Israel and this angered David. God was with David and he killed the giant. God honors those who stand up for Him.

⁴⁰He picked up five smooth stones from a stream and put them into his shepherd's bag. Then, armed only with his shepherd's staff and sling, he started across the valley to fight the Philistine.

⁴¹Goliath walked out toward David with his shield bearer ahead of him, ⁴²sneering in contempt at this ruddy-faced boy. ⁴³"Am I a dog," he roared at David, "that you come at me with a stick?" And he cursed David by the names of his gods. ⁴⁴"Come over here, and I'll give your flesh to the birds and wild animals!" Goliath yelled.

⁴⁵David replied to the Philistine, "You come to me with sword, spear, and javelin, but I come to you in the name of the LORD of Heaven's Armies—the God of the armies of Israel, whom you have defied. ⁴⁶Today the LORD will conquer you, and I will kill you and cut off your head. And then I will give the dead bodies of your men to the birds and wild animals, and the whole world will know that there is a God in Israel! ⁴⁷And everyone assembled here will know that the LORD rescues his people, but not with sword and spear. This is the LORD's battle, and he will give you to us!"

⁴⁸As Goliath moved closer to attack, David quickly ran out to meet him. ⁴⁹Reaching into his shepherd's bag and taking out a stone, he hurled it with his sling and hit the Philistine in the forehead. The stone sank in, and Goliath stumbled and fell face down on the ground.

⁵⁰So David triumphed over the Philistine with only a sling and a stone, for he had no sword.

~ 1 Samuel 17:40-50

GOD'S ANOINTED ONES

God is more than capable of dealing with His own servants. David could have killed Saul, but he would not touch God's anointed one. If you know of a man of God who has fallen, pray for him as God's anointed one and help him up again.

⁴"Now's your opportunity!" David's men whispered to him. "Today the Lord is telling you, 'I will certainly put your enemy into your power, to do with as you wish.'" So David crept forward and cut off a piece of the hem of Saul's robe.

⁵But then David's conscience began bothering him because he had cut Saul's robe. ⁶"The Lord knows I shouldn't have done that to my lord the king," he said to his men. "The Lord forbid that I should do this to my lord the king and attack the Lord's anointed one, for the Lord himself has chosen him." ⁷So David restrained his men and did not let them kill Saul.

After Saul had left the cave and gone on his way, ⁸David came out and shouted after him, "My lord the king!" And when Saul looked around, David bowed low before him.

⁹Then he shouted to Saul, "Why do you listen to the people who say I am trying to harm you? ¹⁰This very day you can see with your own eyes it isn't true. For the Lord placed you at my mercy back there in the cave. Some of my men told me to kill you, but I spared you. For I said, 'I will never harm the king—he is the Lord's anointed one.' ¹¹Look, my father, at what I have in my hand. It is a piece of the hem of your robe! I cut it off, but I didn't kill you. This proves that I am not trying to harm you and that I have not sinned against you, even though you have been hunting for me to kill me."

~ 1 Samuel 24:4-11

LIVING BY THE SWORD

The Holy Spirit departed from Saul and he and his three sons died in battle. When a man departs from God, death closes in on all sides. Our relationship with our Savior must be treasured.

⁴Saul groaned to his armor bearer, "Take your sword and kill me before these pagan Philistines come to run me through and taunt and torture me."

But his armor bearer was afraid and would not do it. So Saul took his own sword and fell on it. ⁵When his armor bearer realized that Saul was dead, he fell on his own sword and died beside the king. ⁶So Saul, his three sons, his armor bearer, and his troops all died together that same day.

⁸The next day, when the Philistines went out to strip the dead, they found the bodies of Saul and his three sons on Mount Gilboa. ⁹So they cut off Saul's head and stripped off his armor. Then they proclaimed the good news of Saul's death in their pagan temple and to the people throughout the land of Philistia. ¹⁰They placed his armor in the temple of the Ashtoreths, and they fastened his body to the wall of the city of Beth-shan.

¹¹But when the people of Jabesh-gilead heard what the Philistines had done to Saul, ¹²all their mighty warriors traveled through the night to Beth-shan and took the bodies of Saul and his sons down from the wall. They brought them to Jabesh, where they burned the bodies. ¹³Then they took their bones and buried them beneath the tamarisk tree at Jabesh, and they fasted for seven days.

~ 1 Samuel 31:4-6, 8-13

UNASHAMED

David was so excited when the ark of the covenant was brought to Jerusalem that he danced before the Lord. When Michal rebuked David, he said he would be even more undignified than this for the Lord.

Never be ashamed of your faith, but give God the honor He deserves.

¹⁴And David danced before the Lord with all his might, wearing a priestly garment. ¹⁵So David and all the people of Israel brought up the Ark of the Lord with shouts of joy and the blowing of rams' horns.

¹⁶But as the Ark of the Lord entered the City of David, Michal, the daughter of Saul, looked down from her window. When she saw King David leaping and dancing before the Lord, she was filled with contempt for him.

²⁰When David returned home to bless his own family, Michal, the daughter of Saul, came out to meet him. She said in disgust, "How distinguished the king of Israel looked today, shamelessly exposing himself to the servant girls like any vulgar person might do!"

²¹David retorted to Michal, "I was dancing before the Lord, who chose me above your father and all his family! He appointed me as the leader of Israel, the people of the Lord, so I celebrate before the Lord. ²²Yes, and I am willing to look even more foolish than this, even to be humiliated in my own eyes! But those servant girls you mentioned will indeed think I am distinguished!"

~ 2 Samuel 6:14-16, 20-22

LOYALTY TO A FRIEND

David took care of his good friend Jonathan's disabled son, Mephibosheth. By taking care of him, David was honoring his friendship with Jonathan. Men of God make loyal, trustworthy and reliable friends.

⁶His name was Mephibosheth; he was Jonathan's son and Saul's grandson. When he came to David, he bowed low to the ground in deep respect. David said, "Greetings, Mephibosheth."

Mephibosheth replied, "I am your servant."

⁷"Don't be afraid!" David said. "I intend to show kindness to you because of my promise to your father, Jonathan. I will give you all the property that once belonged to your grandfather Saul, and you will eat here with me at the king's table!"

⁸Mephibosheth bowed respectfully and exclaimed, "Who is your servant, that you should show such kindness to a dead dog like me?"

⁹Then the king summoned Saul's servant Ziba and said, "I have given your master's grandson everything that belonged to Saul and his family. ¹⁰You and your sons and servants are to farm the land for him to produce food for your master's household. But Mephibosheth, your master's grandson, will eat here at my table." (Ziba had fifteen sons and twenty servants.)

¹¹Ziba replied, "Yes, my lord the king; I am your servant, and I will do all that you have commanded." And from that time on, Mephibosheth ate regularly at David's table, like one of the king's own sons.

¹²Mephibosheth had a young son named Mica. From then on, all the members of Ziba's household were Mephibosheth's servants. ¹³And Mephibosheth, who was crippled in both feet, lived in Jerusalem and ate regularly at the king's table.

~ 2 Samuel 9:6-13

DEATH LEADS TO LIFE

David knew about eternal life. He knew that he would go to be with his child. David also knew that he had sinned and that he had to bear the consequences.

¹³ David confessed to Nathan, "I have sinned against the LORD."

Nathan replied, "Yes, but the LORD has forgiven you, and you won't die for this sin. ¹⁴Nevertheless, because you have shown utter contempt for the LORD by doing this, your child will die." ¹⁵After Nathan returned to his home, the LORD sent a deadly illness to the child of David and Uriah's wife. ¹⁶David begged God to spare the child. He went without food and lay all night on the bare ground. ¹⁸Then on the seventh day the child died. David's advisers were afraid to tell him. "He wouldn't listen to reason while the child was ill," they said. "What drastic thing will he do when we tell him the child is dead?"

¹⁹When David saw them whispering, he realized what had happened. "Is the child dead?" he asked.

"Yes," they replied, "he is dead."

²⁰Then David got up from the ground, washed himself, put on lotions, and changed his clothes. He went to the Tabernacle and worshiped the LORD. After that, he returned to the palace and was served food and ate.

²¹His advisers were amazed. "We don't understand you," they told him. "While the child was still living, you wept and refused to eat. But now that the child is dead, you have stopped your mourning and are eating again."

²²David replied, "I fasted and wept while the child was alive, for I said, 'Perhaps the LORD will be gracious to me and let the child live.' ²³But why should I fast when he is dead? Can I bring him back again?"

~ 2 Samuel 12:13-16, 18-23

HONOR YOUR PARENTS

Absalom rebelled against King David. Absalom died a terrible death because of his betrayal. God tells us to honor our father and mother. Now is the time to heal broken family relationships, before it is too late.

¹After this, Absalom bought a chariot and horses, and he hired fifty bodyguards to run ahead of him. ²He got up early every morning and went out to the gate of the city. When people brought a case to the king for judgment, Absalom would ask where in Israel they were from, and they would tell him their tribe. ³Then Absalom would say, "You've really got a strong case here! It's too bad the king doesn't have anyone to hear it. ⁴I wish I were the judge. Then everyone could bring their cases to me for judgment, and I would give them justice!"

⁵When people tried to bow before him, Absalom wouldn't let them. Instead, he took them by the hand and kissed them. ⁶Absalom did this with everyone who came to the king for judgment, and so he stole the hearts of all the people of Israel.

⁷After four years, Absalom said to the king, "Let me go to Hebron to offer a sacrifice to the LORD and fulfill a vow I made to him. ⁸For while your servant was at Geshur in Aram, I promised to sacrifice to the LORD in Hebron if he would bring me back to Jerusalem."

⁹"All right," the king told him. "Go and fulfill your vow."

So Absalom went to Hebron. ¹⁰But while he was there, he sent secret messengers to all the tribes of Israel to stir up a rebellion against the king. "As soon as you hear the ram's horn," his message read, "you are to say, 'Absalom has been crowned king in Hebron.'" ¹¹He took 200 men from Jerusalem with him as guests, but they knew nothing of his intentions.

~ 2 Samuel 15:1-11

DAVID'S MIGHTY MEN

David had thirty-seven mighty men in his elite group. We are to be mighty men and take up our roles as prophet, priest and king in our homes and communities. We can only do this through God's power in us.

⁸These are the names of David's mightiest warriors. The first was Jashobeam the Hacmonite, who was leader of the Three—the three mightiest warriors among David's men. He once used his spear to kill 800 enemy warriors in a single battle.

⁹Next in rank among the Three was Eleazar son of Dodai, a descendant of Ahoah. Once Eleazar and David stood together against the Philistines when the entire Israelite army had fled. ¹⁰He killed Philistines until his hand was too tired to lift his sword, and the LORD gave him a great victory that day.

¹¹Next in rank was Shammah son of Agee from Harar. One time the Philistines gathered at Lehi and attacked the Israelites in a field full of lentils. The Israelite army fled, ¹²but Shammah held his ground in the middle of the field and beat back the Philistines. So the LORD brought about a great victory.

¹³Once during the harvest, when David was at the cave of Adullam, the Philistine army was camped in the valley of Rephaim. The Three (who were among the Thirty—an elite group among David's fighting men) went down to meet him there. ¹⁴David was staying in the stronghold at the time, and a Philistine detachment had occupied the town of Bethlehem.

¹⁵David remarked longingly to his men, "Oh, how I would love some of that good water from the well by the gate in Bethlehem." ¹⁶So the Three broke through the Philistine lines, drew some water from the well by the gate in Bethlehem, and brought it back to David.

~ 2 Samuel 23:8-16

A HEART OF WISDOM

Solomon was the wisest man who ever lived. The Lord asked him what he wanted and he asked for wisdom and discernment. God was so touched by his request that He also gave him riches and honor. If we ask God for wisdom without personal gain as Solomon did, we will be blessed.

⁵That night the LORD appeared to Solomon in a dream, and God said, "What do you want? Ask, and I will give it to you!"

⁶Solomon replied, "You showed faithful love to your servant my father, David, because he was honest and true and faithful to you. And you have continued your faithful love to him today by giving him a son to sit on his throne.

⁷"Now, O LORD my God, you have made me king instead of my father, David, but I am like a little child who doesn't know his way around. ⁸And here I am in the midst of your own chosen people, a nation so great and numerous they cannot be counted! ⁹Give me an understanding heart so that I can govern your people well and know the difference between right and wrong. For who by himself is able to govern this great people of yours?"

¹⁰The Lord was pleased that Solomon had asked for wisdom. ¹¹So God replied, "Because you have asked for wisdom in governing my people with justice and have not asked for a long life or wealth or the death of your enemies— ¹²I will give you what you asked for! I will give you a wise and understanding heart such as no one else has had or ever will have! ¹³And I will also give you what you did not ask for—riches and fame! No other king in all the world will be compared to you for the rest of your life! ¹⁴And if you follow me and obey my decrees and my commands as your father, David, did, I will give you a long life."

~ 1 Kings 3:5-14

FINISH THE JOB

David was not appointed to build the temple, but he did start collecting what was needed for Solomon to build it. It is important to finish a job once we start it and to finish it to the glory of God.

¹It was in midspring, in the month of Ziv, during the fourth year of Solomon's reign, that he began to construct the Temple of the LORD. ²The Temple that King Solomon built for the LORD was 90 feet long, 30 feet wide, and 45 feet high. ³The entry room at the front of the Temple was 30 feet wide, running across the entire width of the Temple. It projected outward 15 feet from the front of the Temple. ⁴Solomon also made narrow recessed windows throughout the Temple.

⁵He built a complex of rooms against the outer walls of the Temple, all the way around the sides and rear of the building. ⁶The complex was three stories high, the bottom floor being 7 1/2 feet wide, the second floor 9 feet wide, and the top floor 10 1/2 feet wide. The rooms were connected to the walls of the Temple by beams resting on ledges built out from the wall. So the beams were not inserted into the walls themselves.

⁷The stones used in the construction of the Temple were finished at the quarry, so there was no sound of hammer, ax, or any other iron tool at the building site.

¹¹Then the LORD gave this message to Solomon: ¹²"Concerning this Temple you are building, if you keep all my decrees and regulations and obey all my commands, I will fulfill through you the promise I made to your father, David. ¹³I will live among the Israelites and will never abandon my people Israel."

¹⁴So Solomon finished building the Temple.

~ 1 Kings 6:1-7, 11-14

SUCCESS

God blessed Solomon for his obedience. The queen of Sheba was overwhelmed by his wisdom and wealth. As believers we must set the example to the world. We will succeed if we walk in the ways of God.

¹When the queen of Sheba heard of Solomon's fame, which brought honor to the name of the LORD, she came to test him with hard questions. ²When she met with Solomon, she talked with him about everything she had on her mind. ³Solomon had answers for all her questions; nothing was too hard for the king to explain to her. ⁴When the queen of Sheba realized how very wise Solomon was, and when she saw the palace he had built, ⁵she was overwhelmed. She was also amazed at the food on his tables, the organization of his officials and their splendid clothing, the cup-bearers, and the burnt offerings Solomon made at the Temple of the LORD.

⁶She exclaimed to the king, "Everything I heard in my country about your achievements and wisdom is true! ⁷I didn't believe what was said until I arrived here and saw it with my own eyes. In fact, I had not heard the half of it! Your wisdom and prosperity are far beyond what I was told. ⁸How happy your people must be! What a privilege for your officials to stand here day after day, listening to your wisdom! ⁹Praise the LORD your God, who delights in you and has placed you on the throne of Israel. Because of the LORD's eternal love for Israel, he has made you king so you can rule with justice and righteousness."

¹⁰Then she gave the king a gift of 9,000 pounds of gold, great quantities of spices, and precious jewels. Never again were so many spices brought in as those the queen of Sheba gave to King Solomon.

~ 1 Kings 10:1-10

GOD HONORS FAITH

Elijah was an exceptional man of faith. He told King Ahab that it would not rain on the land for three and a half years and it did not rain on the land for three and a half years, until he prayed again for rain. God always honors faith.

¹Now Elijah, who was from Tishbe in Gilead, told King Ahab, "As surely as the LORD, the God of Israel, lives—the God I serve—there will be no dew or rain during the next few years until I give the word!"

²Then the LORD said to Elijah, ³"Go to the east and hide by Kerith Brook, near where it enters the Jordan River. ⁴Drink from the brook and eat what the ravens bring you, for I have commanded them to bring you food."

⁵So Elijah did as the LORD told him and camped beside Kerith Brook, east of the Jordan.

⁶The ravens brought him bread and meat each morning and evening, and he drank from the brook.

⁷But after a while the brook dried up, for there was no rainfall anywhere in the land.

~ 1 Kings 17:1-7

FIRE FROM HEAVEN

Elijah had incredible faith in God. He allowed the prophets of Baal to perform their ceremony. Elijah called down fire from heaven and not only did the sacrifice burn, the altar did as well. We have nothing to fear if we trust in Him.

[30]Then Elijah called to the people, "Come over here!" They all crowded around him as he repaired the altar of the LORD that had been torn down. [31]He took twelve stones, one to represent each of the tribes of Israel, [32]and he used the stones to rebuild the altar in the name of the LORD. Then he dug a trench around the altar large enough to hold about three gallons. [33]He piled wood on the altar, cut the bull into pieces, and laid the pieces on the wood. Then he said, "Fill four large jars with water, and pour the water over the offering and the wood."

[34]After they had done this, he said, "Do the same thing again!" And when they were finished, he said, "Now do it a third time!" So they did as he said, [35]and the water ran around the altar and even filled the trench.

[36]At the usual time for offering the evening sacrifice, Elijah the prophet walked up to the altar and prayed, "O LORD, God of Abraham, Isaac, and Jacob, prove today that you are God in Israel and that I am your servant. Prove that I have done all this at your command. [37]O LORD, answer me! Answer me so these people will know that you, O LORD, are God."

[38]Immediately the fire of the LORD flashed down from heaven and burned up the young bull, the wood, the stones, and the dust. It even licked up all the water in the trench! [39]And when all the people saw it, they fell face down on the ground and cried out, "The LORD—he is God! Yes, the LORD is God!"

~ 1 Kings 18:30-39

THE STILL, SMALL VOICE

So often in life, we try to hear from God in large gospel meetings or TV broadcasts, but often the Lord speaks to us through that still, small voice. Just like with Elijah, God didn't speak through the earthquake, wind or fire, but through a gentle whisper.

[10]Elijah replied, "I have zealously served the LORD God Almighty. But the people of Israel have broken their covenant with you, torn down your altars, and killed every one of your prophets. I am the only one left, and now they are trying to kill me, too." [11]"Go out and stand before me on the mountain," the LORD told him. And as Elijah stood there, the LORD passed by, and a mighty windstorm hit the mountain. It was such a terrible blast that the rocks were torn loose, but the LORD was not in the wind. After the wind there was an earthquake, but the LORD was not in the earthquake. [12]And after the earthquake there was a fire, but the LORD was not in the fire. And after the fire there was the sound of a gentle whisper. [13]When Elijah heard it, he wrapped his face in his cloak and went out and stood at the entrance of the cave.

And a voice said, "What are you doing here, Elijah?"

[14]He replied again, "I have zealously served the LORD God Almighty. But the people of Israel have broken their covenant with you, torn down your altars, and killed every one of your prophets. I am the only one left, and now they are trying to kill me, too."

[15]Then the LORD told him, "Go back the same way you came, and travel to the wilderness of Damascus. When you arrive there, anoint Hazael to be king of Aram."

~ 1 Kings 19:10-15

MARCH

A DOUBLE PORTION

Elisha was unwilling to let go of Elijah until he received a double portion of God's blessing. Due to his persistence and determination, he received Elijah's cloak and performed exactly double the number of miracles Elijah performed.

[7]Fifty men from the group of prophets also went and watched from a distance as Elijah and Elisha stopped beside the Jordan River. [8]Then Elijah folded his cloak together and struck the water with it. The river divided, and the two of them went across on dry ground! [9]When they came to the other side, Elijah said to Elisha, "Tell me what I can do for you before I am taken away."

And Elisha replied, "Please let me inherit a double share of your spirit and become your successor." [10]"You have asked a difficult thing," Elijah replied. "If you see me when I am taken from you, then you will get your request. But if not, then you won't." [11]As they were walking along and talking, suddenly a chariot of fire appeared, drawn by horses of fire. It drove between the two men, separating them, and Elijah was carried by a whirlwind into heaven. [12]Elisha saw it and cried out, "My father! My father! I see the chariots and charioteers of Israel!" And as they disappeared from sight, Elisha tore his clothes in distress.

[13]Elisha picked up Elijah's cloak, which had fallen when he was taken up. Then Elisha returned to the bank of the Jordan River. [14]He struck the water with Elijah's cloak and cried out, "Where is the LORD, the God of Elijah?" Then the river divided, and Elisha went across. [15]When the group of prophets from Jericho saw from a distance what happened, they exclaimed, "Elijah's spirit rests upon Elisha!" And they went to meet him and bowed to the ground before him.

~ 2 Kings 2:7-15

HEALING THROUGH HUMILITY

Naaman was the commander of the army of Syria and he had leprosy. He expected Elisha to heal him instantly. Naaman had to humble himself and do what the prophet told him to do before he could be healed.

⁹So Naaman went with his horses and chariots and waited at the door of Elisha's house. ¹⁰But Elisha sent a messenger out to him with this message: "Go and wash yourself seven times in the Jordan River. Then your skin will be restored, and you will be healed of your leprosy."

¹¹But Naaman became angry and stalked away. "I thought he would certainly come out to meet me!" he said. "I expected him to wave his hand over the leprosy and call on the name of the LORD his God and heal me! ¹²Aren't the rivers of Damascus, the Abana and the Pharpar, better than any of the rivers of Israel? Why shouldn't I wash in them and be healed?" So Naaman turned and went away in a rage.

¹³But his officers tried to reason with him and said, "Sir, if the prophet had told you to do something very difficult, wouldn't you have done it? So you should certainly obey him when he says simply, 'Go and wash and be cured!'" ¹⁴So Naaman went down to the Jordan River and dipped himself seven times, as the man of God had instructed him. And his skin became as healthy as the skin of a young child's, and he was healed!

~ 2 Kings 5:9-14

MARCH 3
GREED

When Gehazi heard that his master would not receive anything for Naaman's healing, he ran after Naaman. He lied and said Elisha wanted the gifts. As a result of his dishonesty, Gehazi received the leprosy that Naaman had been healed of. Greed leads to death.

²⁰But Gehazi, the servant of Elisha, the man of God, said to himself, "My master should not have let this Aramean get away without accepting any of his gifts. As surely as the Lord lives, I will chase after him and get something from him." ²¹So Gehazi set off after Naaman. When Naaman saw Gehazi running after him, he climbed down from his chariot and went to meet him. "Is everything all right?" Naaman asked. ²²"Yes," Gehazi said, "but my master has sent me to tell you that two young prophets from the hill country of Ephraim have just arrived. He would like 75 pounds of silver and two sets of clothing to give to them." ²³"By all means, take twice as much silver," Naaman insisted. He gave him two sets of clothing, tied up the money in two bags, and sent two of his servants to carry the gifts for Gehazi. ²⁴But when they arrived at the citadel, Gehazi took the gifts from the servants and sent the men back. Then he went and hid the gifts inside the house. ²⁵When he went in to his master, Elisha asked him, "Where have you been, Gehazi?"

"I haven't been anywhere," he replied.

²⁷"Because you have done this, you and your descendants will suffer from Naaman's leprosy forever." When Gehazi left the room, he was covered with leprosy; his skin was white as snow.

~ 2 Kings 5:20-25, 27

THE CENSUS

David started in the Spirit but ended in the flesh. He called Joab to count the people. This made God angry because David was trying to win the battle in the flesh. If we start in the Spirit, we must finish in the Spirit, otherwise we bring no glory to the Lord.

²So David said to Joab and the commanders of the army, "Take a census of all the people of Israel." ³But Joab replied, "May the LORD increase the number of his people a hundred times over! But why, my lord the king, do you want to do this? Are they not all your servants? Why must you cause Israel to sin?"

⁴But the king insisted that they take the census, so Joab traveled throughout all Israel to count the people. Then he returned to Jerusalem ⁵and reported the number of people to David. There were 1,100,000 warriors in all Israel who could handle a sword, and 470,000 in Judah. ⁶But Joab did not include the tribes of Levi and Benjamin in the census because he was so distressed at what the king had made him do.

⁷God was very displeased with the census, and he punished Israel for it. ⁸Then David said to God, "I have sinned greatly by taking this census. Please forgive my guilt for doing this foolish thing." ⁹Then the LORD spoke to Gad, David's seer. This was the message: ¹⁰"Go and say to David, 'This is what the LORD says: I will give you three choices. Choose one of these punishments, and I will inflict it on you.'"

~ 1 Chronicles 21:2-10

DUTIES

The Lord told David to instruct his son to build the temple of God. God gives each one of us specific work to do. One man ploughs, one man waters, one man harvests, but God adds the increase.

²David rose to his feet and said: "My brothers and my people! It was my desire to build a temple where the Ark of the LORD's Covenant, God's footstool, could rest permanently. I made the necessary preparations for building it, ³but God said to me, 'You must not build a temple to honor my name, for you are a warrior and have shed much blood.'

⁴"Yet the LORD, the God of Israel, has chosen me from among all my father's family to be king over Israel forever. For he has chosen the tribe of Judah to rule, and from among the families of Judah he chose my father's family. And from among my father's sons the LORD was pleased to make me king over all Israel. ⁶He said to me, 'Your son Solomon will build my Temple and its courtyards, for I have chosen him as my son, and I will be his father. ⁷And if he continues to obey my commands and regulations as he does now, I will make his kingdom last forever.'

⁸"So now, with God as our witness, and in the sight of all Israel—the LORD's assembly—I give you this charge. Be careful to obey all the commands of the LORD your God, so that you may continue to possess this good land and leave it to your children as a permanent inheritance. ⁹And Solomon, my son, learn to know the God of your ancestors intimately. Worship and serve him with your whole heart and a willing mind. For the LORD sees every heart and knows every plan and thought. If you seek him, you will find him."

~ 1 Chronicles 28:2-4, 6-9

MARCH 6
HEAL THE LAND

God says if we do what He has called us to, He will forgive our sins and heal the land. He will watch over us and listen to us. We need to humble ourselves before the Lord our God. If we do this, He will bestow His blessing upon us.

¹²Then one night the LORD appeared to Solomon and said, "I have heard your prayer and have chosen this Temple as the place for making sacrifices. ¹³At times I might shut up the heavens so that no rain falls, or command grasshoppers to devour your crops, or send plagues among you. ¹⁴Then if my people who are called by my name will humble themselves and pray and seek my face and turn from their wicked ways, I will hear from heaven and will forgive their sins and restore their land. ¹⁵My eyes will be open and my ears attentive to every prayer made in this place. ¹⁶For I have chosen this Temple and set it apart to be holy—a place where my name will be honored forever. I will always watch over it, for it is dear to my heart.

¹⁷"As for you, if you faithfully follow me as David your father did, obeying all my commands, decrees, and regulations, ¹⁸then I will establish the throne of your dynasty. For I made this covenant with your father, David, when I said, 'One of your descendants will always rule over Israel.'

¹⁹"But if you or your descendants abandon me and disobey the decrees and commands I have given you, and if you serve and worship other gods, ²⁰then I will uproot the people from this land that I have given them. I will reject this Temple that I have made holy to honor my name. I will make it an object of mockery and ridicule among the nations."

~ 2 Chronicles 7:12-20

ARE YOU TRUSTWORTHY?

The Lord is looking for people He can trust. He is not concerned about our abilities or gifts, but whether we are trustworthy. We need to be loyal to Jesus and He will use us in great ways in these last days.

³"Let there be a treaty between you and me like the one between your father and my father. See, I am sending you silver and gold. Break your treaty with King Baasha of Israel so that he will leave me alone."

⁴Ben-hadad agreed to King Asa's request and sent the commanders of his army to attack the towns of Israel. They conquered the towns of Ijon, Dan, Abel-beth-maacah, and all the store cities in Naphtali. ⁵As soon as Baasha of Israel heard what was happening, he abandoned his project of fortifying Ramah and stopped all work on it. ⁶Then King Asa called out all the men of Judah to carry away the building stones and timbers that Baasha had been using to fortify Ramah. Asa used these materials to fortify the towns of Geba and Mizpah.

⁷At that time Hanani the seer came to King Asa and told him, "Because you have put your trust in the king of Aram instead of in the LORD your God, you missed your chance to destroy the army of the king of Aram. ⁸Don't you remember what happened to the Ethiopians and Libyans and their vast army, with all of their chariots and charioteers? At that time you relied on the LORD, and he handed them over to you. ⁹The eyes of the LORD search the whole earth in order to strengthen those whose hearts are fully committed to him. What a fool you have been! From now on you will be at war."

~ 2 Chronicles 16:3-9

MARCH 8

REMAIN HUMBLE

King Uzziah was successful and proud. He believed he could do anything, even burn incense on the altar. This was a task reserved for the high priest and Uzziah was struck with leprosy. We need to remain humble, lest God withdraws His blessing from us.

¹⁶But when he had become powerful, he also became proud, which led to his downfall. He sinned against the LORD his God by entering the sanctuary of the LORD's Temple and personally burning incense on the incense altar. ¹⁷Azariah the high priest went in after him with eighty other priests of the LORD, all brave men. ¹⁸They confronted King Uzziah and said, "It is not for you, Uzziah, to burn incense to the LORD. That is the work of the priests alone, the descendants of Aaron who are set apart for this work. Get out of the sanctuary, for you have sinned. The LORD God will not honor you for this!"

¹⁹Uzziah, who was holding an incense burner, became furious. But as he was standing there raging at the priests before the incense altar in the LORD's Temple, leprosy suddenly broke out on his forehead. ²⁰When Azariah the high priest and all the other priests saw the leprosy, they rushed him out. And the king himself was eager to get out because the LORD had struck him. ²¹So King Uzziah had leprosy until the day he died. He lived in isolation in a separate house, for he was excluded from the Temple of the LORD. His son Jotham was put in charge of the royal palace, and he governed the people of the land.

~ 2 Chronicles 26:16-21

TEAMWORK

As believers, we need to work together for the glory of God. Just as the Israelites worked together to rebuild the altar of God, so we should also work together in building God's kingdom here on earth. People need to know that Jesus is our only Lord and Savior and that He wants us to draw near to Him.

¹In early autumn, when the Israelites had settled in their towns, all the people assembled in Jerusalem with a unified purpose. ²Then Jeshua son of Jehozadak joined his fellow priests and Zerubbabel son of Shealtiel with his family in rebuilding the altar of the God of Israel. They wanted to sacrifice burnt offerings on it, as instructed in the Law of Moses, the man of God. ³Even though the people were afraid of the local residents, they rebuilt the altar at its old site. Then they began to sacrifice burnt offerings on the altar to the LORD each morning and evening.

⁴They celebrated the Festival of Shelters as prescribed in the Law, sacrificing the number of burnt offerings specified for each day of the festival. ⁵They also offered the regular burnt offerings and the offerings required for the new moon celebrations and the annual festivals as prescribed by the LORD. The people also gave voluntary offerings to the LORD. ⁶Fifteen days before the Festival of Shelters began, the priests had begun to sacrifice burnt offerings to the LORD. This was even before they had started to lay the foundation of the LORD's Temple.

~ Ezra 3:1-6

REMAIN STEADFAST

The Lord instructed Nehemiah to rebuild the walls of Jerusalem and that is what he did, even though he was faced with great opposition. Whatever God calls us to do might be accompanied by opposition and resistance. If we remain steadfast like Nehemiah, we shall succeed. Let us complete our calling with joy.

¹Sanballat, Tobiah, Geshem the Arab, and the rest of our enemies found out that I had finished rebuilding the wall and that no gaps remained—though we had not yet set up the doors in the gates. ²So Sanballat and Geshem sent a message asking me to meet them at one of the villages in the plain of Ono.

But I realized they were plotting to harm me, ³so I replied by sending this message to them: "I am engaged in a great work, so I can't come."

⁴Four times they sent the same message, and each time I gave the same reply. ⁵The fifth time, Sanballat's servant came with an open letter in his hand, ⁶and this is what it said: "There is a rumor among the surrounding nations, and Geshem tells me it is true, that you and the Jews are planning to rebel and that is why you are building the wall. According to his reports, you plan to be their king. "You can be very sure that this report will get back to the king, so I suggest that you come and talk it over with me."

⁸I replied, "There is no truth in any part of your story. You are making up the whole thing." ⁹They were just trying to intimidate us, imagining that they could discourage us and stop the work. So I continued the work with even greater determination.

~ Nehemiah 6:1-6, 8-9

A TIME SUCH AS THIS

Esther realized that she had to do something. She understood that God had made her queen for exactly this reason. She risked her life to save her people. God places us in the right place at the right time. We need to act for Him where He has placed us.

⁸Mordecai gave Hathach a copy of the decree issued in Susa that called for the death of all Jews. He asked Hathach to show it to Esther and explain the situation to her. He also asked Hathach to direct her to go to the king to beg for mercy and plead for her people. ⁹So Hathach returned to Esther with Mordecai's message. ¹⁰Then Esther told Hathach to go back and relay this message to Mordecai: ¹¹"All the king's officials and even the people in the provinces know that anyone who appears before the king in his inner court without being invited is doomed to die unless the king holds out his gold scepter. And the king has not called for me to come to him for thirty days." ¹²So Hathach gave Esther's message to Mordecai.

¹³Mordecai sent this reply to Esther: "Don't think for a moment that because you're in the palace you will escape when all other Jews are killed. ¹⁴If you keep quiet at a time like this, deliverance and relief for the Jews will arise from some other place, but you and your relatives will die. Who knows if perhaps you were made queen for just such a time as this?"

¹⁵Then Esther sent this reply to Mordecai: ¹⁶"Go and gather together all the Jews of Susa and fast for me. Do not eat or drink for three days, night or day. My maids and I will do the same. And then, though it is against the law, I will go in to see the king. If I must die, I must die." ¹⁷So Mordecai went away and did everything as Esther had ordered him.

~ Esther 4:8-17

EXTREME FAITH

Job was a godly man. He loved and obeyed God. The devil tested him, thinking that Job would turn away from God. Let us have a faith as firm as Job's.

¹There once was a man named Job who lived in the land of Uz. He was blameless—a man of complete integrity. He feared God and stayed away from evil. ²He had seven sons and three daughters. ³He owned 7,000 sheep, 3,000 camels, 500 teams of oxen, and 500 female donkeys. He also had many servants. He was, in fact, the richest person in that entire area.

⁶One day the members of the heavenly court came to present themselves before the Lord, and the Accuser, Satan, came with them. ⁷"Where have you come from?" the Lord asked Satan.

Satan answered the Lord, "I have been patrolling the earth, watching everything that's going on."

⁸Then the Lord asked Satan, "Have you noticed my servant Job? He is the finest man in all the earth. He is blameless—a man of complete integrity. He fears God and stays away from evil."

⁹Satan replied to the Lord, "Yes, but Job has good reason to fear God. ¹⁰You have always put a wall of protection around him and his home and his property. You have made him prosper in everything he does. Look how rich he is! ¹¹But reach out and take away everything he has, and he will surely curse you!"

¹²"All right, you may test him," the Lord said to Satan. "Do whatever you want with everything he possesses, but don't harm him physically." So Satan left the Lord's presence.

~ Job 1:1-3, 6-12

JOB'S THREE FRIENDS

How often does it happen that we talk of "Job's comforters"? Instead of comforting their dear friend, they actually condemned him. We need to be careful who we listen to – rather ignore the "Job comforters" and listen to our Lord Jesus Christ.

³Then the LORD asked Satan, "Have you noticed my servant Job? He is the finest man in all the earth. He fears God and stays away from evil. And he has maintained his integrity, even though you urged me to harm him without cause."

⁴Satan replied to the LORD, "Skin for skin! A man will give up everything he has to save his life. ⁵But reach out and take away his health, and he will surely curse you to your face!"

⁶"All right, do with him as you please," the LORD said to Satan. "But spare his life." ⁷So Satan left the LORD's presence, and he struck Job with terrible boils from head to foot.

⁸Job scraped his skin with a piece of broken pottery as he sat among the ashes. ⁹His wife said to him, "Are you still trying to maintain your integrity? Curse God and die."

¹⁰But Job replied, "You talk like a foolish woman. Should we accept only good things from the hand of God and never anything bad?" So in all this, Job said nothing wrong.

¹¹When three of Job's friends heard of the tragedy he had suffered, they got together and traveled from their homes to comfort and console him. ¹²When they saw Job from a distance, they scarcely recognized him. Wailing loudly, they tore their robes and threw dust into the air over their heads to show their grief. ¹³Then they sat on the ground with him for seven days and nights. No one said a word to Job, for they saw that his suffering was too great for words.

~ Job 2:3-13

NO OTHER HOPE

Job had been through so much pain and suffering, yet he remained faithful. Job still loved the Lord even though he lost everything. We so often complain to God when things do not go according to plan. Instead, we should trust the Lord with all our heart, soul and mind.

¹³"Be silent now and leave me alone.
   Let me speak, and I will face the consequences.
¹⁴Yes, I will take my life in my hands
   and say what I really think.
¹⁵God might kill me, but I have no other hope.
   I am going to argue my case with him.
¹⁶But this is what will save me—I am not godless.
   If I were, I could not stand before him.

¹⁷"Listen closely to what I am about to say.
   Hear me out.
¹⁸I have prepared my case;
   I will be proved innocent.
¹⁹Who can argue with me over this?
   And if you prove me wrong, I will remain silent and die."

~ Job 13:13-19

TRUST

Even though Job went through very dark and trying times, he could still say, "I know that my Redeemer lives." Here is a man who had such a personal relationship with God, that when those closest to him had turned their backs on him, Job still trusted the Lord. Have faith in God's Word and promises.

²³"Oh, that my words could be recorded.
   Oh, that they could be inscribed on a monument,
²⁴carved with an iron chisel and filled with lead,
   engraved forever in the rock.

²⁵"But as for me, I know that my Redeemer lives,
   and he will stand upon the earth at last.
²⁶And after my body has decayed,
   yet in my body I will see God!
²⁷I will see him for myself.
   Yes, I will see him with my own eyes.
   I am overwhelmed at the thought!

²⁸"How dare you go on persecuting me,
   saying, 'It's his own fault'?
²⁹You should fear punishment yourselves,
   for your attitude deserves punishment.
   Then you will know that there is indeed a judgment."

~ Job 19:23-29

WISDOM

Where can wisdom be found? Right at the end of this passage is a verse that is worth memorizing: "The fear of the Lord is true wisdom; to forsake evil is real understanding" (v. 28). We cannot learn wisdom at university or gain understanding from human intellect. True wisdom comes from God alone.

[19]"Precious peridot from Ethiopia cannot be exchanged for it.
  It's worth more than the purest gold.
[20]"But do people know where to find wisdom?
  Where can they find understanding?
[21]It is hidden from the eyes of all humanity.
  Even the sharp-eyed birds in the sky cannot discover it.
[22]Destruction and Death say,
  'We've heard only rumors of where wisdom can be found.'
[23]"God alone understands the way to wisdom;
  he knows where it can be found,
[24]for he looks throughout the whole earth
  and sees everything under the heavens.
[25]He decided how hard the winds should blow
  and how much rain should fall.
[26]He made the laws for the rain
  and laid out a path for the lightning.
[27]Then he saw wisdom and evaluated it.
  He set it in place and examined it thoroughly.
[28]And this is what he says to all humanity:
'The fear of the Lord is true wisdom;
  to forsake evil is real understanding.'"

~ Job 28:19-28

WISDOM AND AGE

In this Scripture, a young man admits he is not very old, but he says that great men are not always wise, nor do the aged understand justice. Just because a man has white hair does not mean he is wise. Don't judge a man's wisdom by his age, but by God's Word.

⁶Elihu son of Barakel the Buzite said,
"I am young and you are old,
    so I held back from telling you what I think.
⁷I thought, 'Those who are older should speak,
    for wisdom comes with age.'
⁸But there is a spirit within people,
    the breath of the Almighty within them,
    that makes them intelligent.
⁹Sometimes the elders are not wise.
    Sometimes the aged do not understand justice.
¹⁰So listen to me,
    and let me tell you what I think.
¹¹"I have waited all this time,
    listening very carefully to your arguments,
    listening to you grope for words.
¹²I have listened,
    but not one of you has refuted Job
    or answered his arguments.
¹³And don't tell me, 'He is too wise for us.
    Only God can convince him.'
¹⁴If Job had been arguing with me,
    I would not answer with your kind of logic!"

~ Job 32:6-14

OUR CREATOR GOD

In this passage, God asks Job where he was when He created the world. It clearly extols God as the great Creator. The earth was formed by His mighty word. When we realize who we are and who God is, there is nothing more to say than, "God have mercy on us."

¹Then the LORD answered Job from the whirlwind:
²"Who is this that questions my wisdom
  with such ignorant words?
³Brace yourself like a man,
  because I have some questions for you,
  and you must answer them.

⁴"Where were you when I laid the foundations of the earth?
  Tell me, if you know so much.
⁵Who determined its dimensions
  and stretched out the surveying line?
⁶What supports its foundations,
  and who laid its cornerstone
⁷as the morning stars sang together
  and all the angels shouted for joy?

⁸"Who kept the sea inside its boundaries
  as it burst from the womb,
⁹and as I clothed it with clouds
  and wrapped it in thick darkness?
¹⁰For I locked it behind barred gates,
  limiting its shores."

~ Job 38:1-10

GOD'S REWARD

The Lord restored to Job and gave him everything that was taken from him, and more. God is not a taker, but a giver. Job stood firm in the test and God honored him for that. Job lived a long and full life. This book encourages us to run the race to the end and trust God no matter what the situation.

¹Then Job replied to the LORD:

²"I know that you can do anything, and no one can stop you. ³You asked, 'Who is this that questions my wisdom with such ignorance?' It is I—and I was talking about things I knew nothing about, things far too wonderful for me.

⁴You said, 'Listen and I will speak! I have some questions for you, and you must answer them.'

⁵I had only heard about you before, but now I have seen you with my own eyes.

⁶I take back everything I said, and I sit in dust and ashes to show my repentance."

⁷After the LORD had finished speaking to Job, he said to Eliphaz the Temanite: "I am angry with you and your two friends, for you have not spoken accurately about me, as my servant Job has. ⁸So take seven bulls and seven rams and go to my servant Job and offer a burnt offering for yourselves. My servant Job will pray for you, and I will accept his prayer on your behalf. I will not treat you as you deserve, for you have not spoken accurately about me, as my servant Job has." ⁹So Eliphaz the Temanite, Bildad the Shuhite, and Zophar the Naamathite did as the LORD commanded them, and the LORD accepted Job's prayer.

~ Job 42:1-9

THE RIGHTEOUS SUCCEED

Those who walk with God survive even through times of drought and suffering. The Lord says our roots will be planted by rivers of living waters so that when the going gets tough, we shall survive. We need to drink from God's Word daily to grow in Him.

¹Oh, the joys of those who do not
　　follow the advice of the wicked,
　　or stand around with sinners,
　　or join in with mockers.
²But they delight in the law of the LORD,
　　meditating on it day and night.
³They are like trees planted along the riverbank,
　　bearing fruit each season.
Their leaves never wither,
　　and they prosper in all they do.
⁴But not the wicked!
　　They are like worthless chaff, scattered by the wind.
⁵They will be condemned at the time of judgment.
　　Sinners will have no place among the godly.
⁶For the LORD watches over the path of the godly,
　　but the path of the wicked leads to destruction.

~ Psalm 1:1-6

TRUST IN HIM

Those who mock God will definitely come off second best. In fact, this psalm tells us that the Lord literally laughs at those who challenge Him. He also says that if His sons ask, He will give them the nations. If we acknowledge God, we will succeed and God will get all the glory.

²The kings of the earth prepare for battle;
    the rulers plot together
against the Lord
    and against his anointed one.
³"Let us break their chains," they cry,
    "and free ourselves from slavery to God."
⁴But the one who rules in heaven laughs.
    The Lord scoffs at them.
⁵Then in anger he rebukes them,
    terrifying them with his fierce fury.
⁶For the Lord declares, "I have placed my chosen king on the throne in Jerusalem, on my holy mountain."
⁷The king proclaims the Lord's decree:
"The Lord said to me, 'You are my son.
    Today I have become your Father.
⁸Only ask, and I will give you the nations as your inheritance,
    the whole earth as your possession.
⁹You will break them with an iron rod
    and smash them like clay pots.'"
¹⁰Now then, you kings, act wisely!
    Be warned, you rulers of the earth!

~ Psalm 2:2-10

GOD'S OWN

This psalm was written by David when he fled from his son Absalom. It is easier to fight evil from the outside, but when it comes from your own family, it is extremely hard. Yet the Lord comes through for us just as He did for David. We must trust Him.

¹O LORD, I have so many enemies;
   so many are against me.
²So many are saying,
   "God will never rescue him!"
³But you, O LORD, are a shield around me;
   you are my glory, the one who holds my head high.
⁴I cried out to the LORD,
   and he answered me from his holy mountain.
⁵I lay down and slept,
   yet I woke up in safety,
   for the LORD was watching over me.
⁶I am not afraid of ten thousand enemies
   who surround me on every side.
⁷Arise, O LORD!
   Rescue me, my God!
Slap all my enemies in the face!
   Shatter the teeth of the wicked!
⁸Victory comes from you, O LORD.
   May you bless your people.

~ Psalm 3:1-8

MAJESTY!

This psalm reminds us of how big God is and how small we are. We must be grateful for the mercy and patience God shows us. Isn't it amazing that our great Creator makes time for us? He even knows the number of hairs on our heads. Even more significantly, He sent His only Son to die for us. God is great!

¹O Lord, our Lord, your majestic name fills the earth!
    Your glory is higher than the heavens.
²You have taught children and infants
    to tell of your strength,
silencing your enemies
    and all who oppose you.
³When I look at the night sky and see the work of your fingers—
    the moon and the stars you set in place—
⁴what are mere mortals that you should think about them,
    human beings that you should care for them?
⁵Yet you made them only a little lower than God
    and crowned them with glory and honor.
⁶You gave them charge of everything you made,
    putting all things under their authority—
⁷the flocks and the herds
    and all the wild animals,
⁸the birds in the sky, the fish in the sea,
    and everything that swims the ocean currents.
⁹O Lord, our Lord, your majestic name fills the earth!

~ Psalm 8:1-9

VICTORY OVER EVIL

The psalmist struggles to understand why the wicked seem to prosper. It is sad to see so many so-called "successful people" mock God's existence. We need to continue to love them and introduce them to a mighty Creator who hates sin, but who is quick to forgive and slow to anger.

¹O LORD, why do you stand so far away?
Why do you hide when I am in trouble?
²The wicked arrogantly hunt down the poor.
Let them be caught in the evil they plan for others.
³For they brag about their evil desires;
they praise the greedy and curse the LORD.
⁴The wicked are too proud to seek God.
They seem to think that God is dead.
⁵Yet they succeed in everything they do.
They do not see your punishment awaiting them.
They sneer at all their enemies.
⁶They think, "Nothing bad will ever happen to us!
We will be free of trouble forever!"
¹⁶The LORD is king forever and ever!
The godless nations will vanish from the land.
¹⁷LORD, you know the hopes of the helpless.
Surely you will hear their cries and comfort them.
¹⁸You will bring justice to the orphans and the oppressed,
so mere people can no longer terrify them.

~ Psalm 10:1-6, 16-18

CHARACTER

There are benefits to leading a life that pleases God. Those who lead blameless lives are allowed to worship in the Lord's sanctuary. Those who are led by the will of God and not society and its trends find favor with the Lord and He will abide with them.

¹Who may worship in your sanctuary, LORD?
  Who may enter your presence on your holy hill?
²Those who lead blameless lives and do what is right,
  speaking the truth from sincere hearts.
³Those who refuse to gossip
  or harm their neighbors
  or speak evil of their friends.
⁴Those who despise flagrant sinners,
  and honor the faithful followers of the LORD,
  and keep their promises even when it hurts.
⁵Those who lend money without charging interest,
  and who cannot be bribed to lie about the innocent.
Such people will stand firm forever.

~ Psalm 15:1-5

DAVID'S PRAYER

David was a man after God's own heart. He sinned many times, but there is not a man in the Bible who knew how to genuinely repent and turn from his wicked ways as David did. His sincere remorse is the reason why God loved him so much.

[1]O Lord, hear my plea for justice.
     Listen to my cry for help.
Pay attention to my prayer,
     for it comes from honest lips.
[2]Declare me innocent,
     for you see those who do right.
[3]You have tested my thoughts and examined my heart in the night.
     You have scrutinized me and found nothing wrong.
     I am determined not to sin in what I say.
[4]I have followed your commands,
     which keep me from following cruel and evil people.
[5]My steps have stayed on your path;
     I have not wavered from following you.
[6]I am praying to you because I know you will answer, O God.
     Bend down and listen as I pray.
[7]Show me your unfailing love in wonderful ways.
     By your mighty power you rescue
     those who seek refuge from their enemies.
[8]Guard me as you would guard your own eyes.
     Hide me in the shadow of your wings.
[9]Protect me from wicked people who attack me,
     from murderous enemies who surround me.

~ Psalm 17:1-9

GUARD YOUR MOUTH

Words can have a positive or a negative effect, which is why we should ask the Lord to place a guard before our mouths. Before you speak to others today, ask the Lord to place a guard before your mouth.

8The commandments of the LORD are right,
  bringing joy to the heart.
The commands of the LORD are clear,
  giving insight for living.
9Reverence for the LORD is pure,
  lasting forever.
The laws of the LORD are true;
  each one is fair.
10They are more desirable than gold,
  even the finest gold.
They are sweeter than honey,
  even honey dripping from the comb.
11They are a warning to your servant,
  a great reward for those who obey them.
12How can I know all the sins lurking in my heart?
  Cleanse me from these hidden faults.
13Keep your servant from deliberate sins!
  Don't let them control me.
Then I will be free of guilt
  and innocent of great sin.
14May the words of my mouth
  and the meditation of my heart
be pleasing to you,
  O LORD, my rock and my redeemer.

~ Psalm 19:8-14

SUCCESS

We tend to attempt solving our problems on our own and in our own strength. Every time we try something on our own, it ultimately fails. We need to turn to God in times of hardship and despair. With Him on our side, we will succeed.

¹In times of trouble, may the LORD answer your cry.
    May the name of the God of Jacob keep you safe from all harm.
²May he send you help from his sanctuary
    and strengthen you from Jerusalem.
³May he remember all your gifts
    and look favorably on your burnt offerings.
⁴May he grant your heart's desires
    and make all your plans succeed.
⁵May we shout for joy when we hear of your victory
    and raise a victory banner in the name of our God.
May the LORD answer all your prayers.
⁶Now I know that the LORD rescues his anointed king.
    He will answer him from his holy heaven
    and rescue him by his great power.
⁷Some nations boast of their chariots and horses,
    but we boast in the name of the LORD our God.
⁸Those nations will fall down and collapse,
    but we will rise up and stand firm.
⁹Give victory to our king, O LORD!
    Answer our cry for help.

~ Psalm 20:1-9

THE SHEPHERD

The psalmist says that the Lord is his shepherd and that he shall not want. If the Lord is our Shepherd, there is nothing on this earth that we have to be afraid of or shall be in need of. He can fulfill every single one of our needs.

¹The LORD is my shepherd;
    I have all that I need.
²He lets me rest in green meadows;
    he leads me beside peaceful streams.
³He renews my strength.
He guides me along right paths,
    bringing honor to his name.
⁴Even when I walk
    through the darkest valley,
I will not be afraid,
    for you are close beside me.
Your rod and your staff
    protect and comfort me.
⁵You prepare a feast for me
    in the presence of my enemies.
You honor me by anointing my head with oil.
    My cup overflows with blessings.
⁶Surely your goodness and unfailing love will pursue me
    all the days of my life,
and I will live in the house of the LORD
    forever.

~ Psalm 23:1-6

THE SINNER'S FRIEND

Without the grace of our loving Father, not one of us has clean hands or a pure heart. Only through Jesus Christ and the cross do we have access, not only to His presence but also to be called His sons. What an amazing gift from God!

²For he laid the earth's foundation on the seas
   and built it on the ocean depths.
³Who may climb the mountain of the LORD?
   Who may stand in his holy place?
⁴Only those whose hands and hearts are pure,
   who do not worship idols
   and never tell lies.
⁵They will receive the LORD's blessing
   and have a right relationship with God their savior.
⁶Such people may seek you
   and worship in your presence, O God of Jacob.
⁷Open up, ancient gates!
   Open up, ancient doors,
   and let the King of glory enter.
⁸Who is the King of glory?
   The LORD, strong and mighty;
   the LORD, invincible in battle.
⁹Open up, ancient gates!
   Open up, ancient doors,
   and let the King of glory enter.
¹⁰Who is the King of glory?
   The LORD of Heaven's Armies—
   he is the King of glory.

~ Psalm 24:2-10

AMAZING GRACE

Jesus Christ is the Friend of sinners. He desires one thing from us: repentance. When we repent of our sins and show true remorse, the Lord will forgive us and make us new people. He will never reject anyone who is truly remorseful and repentant. Isn't it wonderful to know that God gives His grace to sinners?

¹O LORD, I give my life to you. ²I trust in you, my God!
³No one who trusts in you will ever be disgraced, but disgrace comes to those who try to deceive others.
⁴Show me the right path, O LORD; point out the road for me to follow. ⁵Lead me by your truth and teach me, for you are the God who saves me. All day long I put my hope in you.
⁶Remember, O LORD, your compassion and unfailing love,
　　which you have shown from long ages past.
⁷Do not remember the rebellious sins of my youth.
　　Remember me in the light of your unfailing love,
　　for you are merciful, O LORD.
⁸The LORD is good and does what is right; he shows the proper path to those who go astray.
⁹He leads the humble in doing right, teaching them his way.
¹⁰The LORD leads with unfailing love and faithfulness
　　all who keep his covenant and obey his demands.
¹¹For the honor of your name, O LORD, forgive my many, many sins. ¹²Who are those who fear the LORD?
　　He will show them the path they should choose.
¹³They will live in prosperity,
　　and their children will inherit the land.
¹⁴The LORD is a friend to those who fear him.
　　He teaches them his covenant.

~ Psalm 25:1-14

APRIL

WAIT ON THE LORD

If Christ is with us, we have nothing to fear. We just have to ensure that our lives are in right standing with God. We often try pleasing those around us instead of spending time with God. David reminds us to wait on the Lord because He will be our strength.

¹The LORD is my light and my salvation—
    so why should I be afraid?
The LORD is my fortress, protecting me from danger,
    so why should I tremble?
²When evil people come to devour me,
    when my enemies and foes attack me,
    they will stumble and fall.
³Though a mighty army surrounds me,
    my heart will not be afraid.
Even if I am attacked,
    I will remain confident.
⁴The one thing I ask of the LORD—
    the thing I seek most—
is to live in the house of the LORD all the days of my life,
    delighting in the LORD's perfections
    and meditating in his Temple.
⁵For he will conceal me there when troubles come;
    he will hide me in his sanctuary.
    He will place me out of reach on a high rock.
⁶Then I will hold my head high
    above my enemies who surround me.
At his sanctuary I will offer sacrifices with shouts of joy,
    singing and praising the LORD with music.

~ Psalm 27:1-6

JOY IN THE MORNING

Even though we may go through times of mourning, stress, pain and fear, joy always comes in the morning. We can trust the Lord to comfort us in our trials, no matter how bad things may seem. Never turn your back on God, because He is the only one who can help you.

¹I will exalt you, LORD, for you rescued me.
    You refused to let my enemies triumph over me.
²O LORD my God, I cried to you for help,
    and you restored my health.
³You brought me up from the grave, O LORD.
    You kept me from falling into the pit of death.
⁴Sing to the LORD, all you godly ones!
    Praise his holy name.
⁵For his anger lasts only a moment,
    but his favor lasts a lifetime!
Weeping may last through the night,
    but joy comes with the morning.
⁶When I was prosperous, I said,
    "Nothing can stop me now!"
⁷Your favor, O LORD, made me as secure as a mountain.
    Then you turned away from me, and I was shattered.
⁸I cried out to you, O LORD.
    I begged the Lord for mercy, saying,
⁹"What will you gain if I die,
    if I sink into the grave?
Can my dust praise you?
    Can it tell of your faithfulness?"

~ Psalm 30:1-9

FORGIVENESS

Our God is a compassionate and merciful God. Like a bird set free from a cage, He sets us free from our sin. Confess your sins, repent and then live your life to the full and to the glory of God.

¹Oh, what joy for those
   whose disobedience is forgiven,
   whose sin is put out of sight!
²Yes, what joy for those
   whose record the LORD has cleared of guilt,
   whose lives are lived in complete honesty!
³When I refused to confess my sin,
   my body wasted away,
   and I groaned all day long.
⁴Day and night your hand of discipline was heavy on me.
   My strength evaporated like water in the summer heat.
⁵Finally, I confessed all my sins to you
   and stopped trying to hide my guilt.
I said to myself, "I will confess my rebellion to the LORD."
   And you forgave me! All my guilt is gone.
⁶Therefore, let all the godly pray to you while there is still time,
   that they may not drown in the floodwaters of judgment.
⁷For you are my hiding place;
   you protect me from trouble.
   You surround me with songs of victory.
⁸ The LORD says, "I will guide you along the best pathway for your life.
   I will advise you and watch over you."

~ Psalm 32:1-8

BY HIS WORD

The Lord spoke one word and everything that we see came into being. God's amazing creation surrounds us every day and it is a shame that many people don't take time to enjoy it. This world was made by an artistic and sensitive God who spoke and it came into being.

¹Let the godly sing for joy to the LORD;
  it is fitting for the pure to praise him.
²Praise the LORD with melodies on the lyre;
  make music for him on the ten-stringed harp.
³Sing a new song of praise to him;
  play skillfully on the harp, and sing with joy.
⁴For the word of the LORD holds true,
  and we can trust everything he does.
⁵He loves whatever is just and good;
  the unfailing love of the LORD fills the earth.
⁶The LORD merely spoke,
  and the heavens were created.
He breathed the word,
  and all the stars were born.
⁷He assigned the sea its boundaries
  and locked the oceans in vast reservoirs.
⁸Let the whole world fear the LORD,
  and let everyone stand in awe of him.
⁹For when he spoke, the world began!
  It appeared at his command.

~ Psalm 33:1-9

TRUST

Irrespective of what we are going through, we need to trust the Lord. He will never abandon us. He is dependable and trustworthy. He has a perfect track record. Put your trust not in money, your career, even family, but in Jesus Christ. He will give you the desires of your heart.

¹I will praise the LORD at all times.
   I will constantly speak his praises.
²I will boast only in the LORD;
   let all who are helpless take heart.
³Come, let us tell of the LORD's greatness;
   let us exalt his name together.
⁴I prayed to the LORD, and he answered me.
   He freed me from all my fears.
⁵Those who look to him for help will be radiant with joy;
   no shadow of shame will darken their faces.
⁶In my desperation I prayed, and the LORD listened;
   he saved me from all my troubles.
⁷For the angel of the LORD is a guard;
   he surrounds and defends all who fear him.
⁸Taste and see that the LORD is good.
   Oh, the joys of those who take refuge in him!
⁹Fear the LORD, you his godly people,
   for those who fear him will have all they need.

~ Psalm 34:1-9

AFFLICTION

Believers are not exempt from affliction, in fact they seem to become more. The day I gave my heart to Jesus, the war intensified. The devil does not enjoy what we do, but the comfort lies in knowing that our Lord has already won the battle.

¹²Does anyone want to live a life
  that is long and prosperous?
¹³Then keep your tongue from speaking evil
  and your lips from telling lies!
¹⁴Turn away from evil and do good.
  Search for peace, and work to maintain it.
¹⁵The eyes of the LORD watch over those who do right;
  his ears are open to their cries for help.
¹⁶But the LORD turns his face against those who do evil;
  he will erase their memory from the earth.
¹⁷The LORD hears his people when they call to him for help.
  He rescues them from all their troubles.
¹⁸The LORD is close to the brokenhearted;
  he rescues those whose spirits are crushed.
¹⁹The righteous person faces many troubles,
  but the LORD comes to the rescue each time.
²⁰For the LORD protects the bones of the righteous;
  not one of them is broken!
²¹Calamity will surely overtake the wicked,
  and those who hate the righteous will be punished.
²²But the LORD will redeem those who serve him.
  No one who takes refuge in him will be condemned.

~ Psalm 34:12-22

THE AVENGER

There are some people who are determined to be the judge and executioner of those who have caused hurt or injustice. We need to make sure our lives are pleasing to God instead of judging others. Let us leave revenge to God and rather pray for those whom God will judge.

[1]O Lord, oppose those who oppose me.
  Fight those who fight against me.
[2]Put on your armor, and take up your shield.
  Prepare for battle, and come to my aid.
[3]Lift up your spear and javelin
  against those who pursue me.
Let me hear you say,
  "I will give you victory!"
[4]Bring shame and disgrace on those trying to kill me;
  turn them back and humiliate those who want to harm me.
[5]Blow them away like chaff in the wind—
  a wind sent by the angel of the Lord.
[6]Make their path dark and slippery,
  with the angel of the Lord pursuing them.
[7]I did them no wrong, but they laid a trap for me.
  I did them no wrong, but they dug a pit to catch me.
[8]So let sudden ruin come upon them!
  Let them be caught in the trap they set for me!
  Let them be destroyed in the pit they dug for me.
[9]Then I will rejoice in the Lord.
  I will be glad because he rescues me.

~ Psalm 35:1-9

DO NOT WORRY

Many great men of God have turned to this psalm. George Müller stood on verse 4 as he started his homes for children. David Livingstone chose to keep verse 5 close to his heart when he ministered in Africa. Why not try to memorize this psalm today?

¹Don't worry about the wicked
   or envy those who do wrong.
²For like grass, they soon fade away.
   Like spring flowers, they soon wither.
³Trust in the LORD and do good.
   Then you will live safely in the land and prosper.
⁴Take delight in the LORD,
   and he will give you your heart's desires.
⁵Commit everything you do to the LORD.
   Trust him, and he will help you.
⁶He will make your innocence radiate like the dawn,
   and the justice of your cause will shine like the noonday sun.
⁷Be still in the presence of the LORD,
   and wait patiently for him to act.
Don't worry about evil people who prosper
   or fret about their wicked schemes.
⁸Stop being angry!
   Turn from your rage!
Do not lose your temper—
   it only leads to harm.
⁹For the wicked will be destroyed,
   but those who trust in the LORD will possess the land.

~ Psalm 37:1-9

HE'LL DO THE REST

When we serve the Lord with all our hearts and live a life that is pleasing to God, He will do the rest. If we keep our side of the bargain and live holy lives pleasing to the Lord, not only will He undertake for us, but for our loved ones as well.

18Day by day the LORD takes care of the innocent,
  and they will receive an inheritance that lasts forever.
19They will not be disgraced in hard times;
  even in famine they will have more than enough.
20 But the wicked will die.
  The LORD's enemies are like flowers in a field—
  they will disappear like smoke.
21 The wicked borrow and never repay,
  but the godly are generous givers.
22 Those the LORD blesses will possess the land,
  but those he curses will die.
23 The LORD directs the steps of the godly.
  He delights in every detail of their lives.
24 Though they stumble, they will never fall,
  for the LORD holds them by the hand.
25 Once I was young, and now I am old.
  Yet I have never seen the godly abandoned
  or their children begging for bread.
26 The godly always give generous loans to others,
  and their children are a blessing.

~ Psalm 37:18-26

HOPE IN GOD

Life is far too short to spend it worrying about whether or not others like you. What we should do is live lives that are pleasing to God and that glorify His name. If we do this, we will experience peace like never before.

¹ I said to myself, "I will watch what I do
and not sin in what I say.
I will hold my tongue
when the ungodly are around me."
² But as I stood there in silence—
not even speaking of good things—
the turmoil within me grew worse.
³ The more I thought about it,
the hotter I got,
igniting a fire of words:
⁴ "LORD, remind me how brief my time on earth will be.
Remind me that my days are numbered—
how fleeting my life is.
⁵ You have made my life no longer than the width of my hand.
My entire lifetime is just a moment to you;
at best, each of us is but a breath."
⁶ We are merely moving shadows,
and all our busy rushing ends in nothing.
We heap up wealth,
not knowing who will spend it.
⁷ And so, Lord, where do I put my hope?
My only hope is in you.

~ Psalm 39:1-7

HE CARES FOR US

In life we experience wonderful, prosperous times but, unfortunately, we also experience less pleasant times. In difficult times we mustn't question God, but cast our cares on Him. Follow in David's footsteps as he praises God for His care and faithfulness.

¹I waited patiently for the Lord to help me,
  and he turned to me and heard my cry.
²He lifted me out of the pit of despair,
  out of the mud and the mire.
He set my feet on solid ground
  and steadied me as I walked along.
³He has given me a new song to sing,
  a hymn of praise to our God.
Many will see what he has done and be amazed.
  They will put their trust in the Lord.
⁴Oh, the joys of those who trust the Lord,
  who have no confidence in the proud
  or in those who worship idols.
⁵O Lord my God, you have performed many wonders for us.
  Your plans for us are too numerous to list.
  You have no equal.
If I tried to recite all your wonderful deeds,
  I would never come to the end of them.
⁶You take no delight in sacrifices or offerings.
  Now that you have made me listen, I finally understand—
  you don't require burnt offerings or sin offerings.

~ Psalm 40:1-6

THIRST

This is one of my favorite psalms. Being a farmer, I can really understand how a deer longs for water. When things are tough, people in the world often ask, "Where is your God?" The truth is, He will never leave us nor forsake us. The psalmist asks, "Why am I discouraged? I will put my hope in God!" (v. 11).

¹As the deer longs for streams of water,
　　so I long for you, O God.
²I thirst for God, the living God.
　　When can I go and stand before him?
³Day and night I have only tears for food,
　　while my enemies continually taunt me, saying,
　　"Where is this God of yours?"
⁴My heart is breaking
　　as I remember how it used to be:
I walked among the crowds of worshipers,
　　leading a great procession to the house of God,
singing for joy and giving thanks
　　amid the sound of a great celebration!
⁵ Why am I discouraged?
　　Why is my heart so sad?
I will put my hope in God!
　　I will praise him again—
　　my Savior and ⁶ my God!
Now I am deeply discouraged,
　　but I will remember you—
even from distant Mount Hermon, the source of the Jordan,
　　from the land of Mount Mizar.

~ Psalm 42:1-6

OUR REFUGE

Living in an age of extreme uncertainty and fear, we need to be still and know that He is God. He will be exalted in the earth. He is our refuge. No matter how tough the going gets, He will not let us down. We just need to be still and know that He is God.

³Let the oceans roar and foam.
　　Let the mountains tremble as the waters surge!
⁴A river brings joy to the city of our God,
　　the sacred home of the Most High.
⁵God dwells in that city; it cannot be destroyed.
　　From the very break of day, God will protect it.
⁶The nations are in chaos,
　　and their kingdoms crumble!
God's voice thunders,
　　and the earth melts!
⁷The Lord of Heaven's Armies is here among us;
　　the God of Israel is our fortress.
⁸Come, see the glorious works of the Lord:
　　See how he brings destruction upon the world.
⁹He causes wars to end throughout the earth.
　　He breaks the bow and snaps the spear;
　　he burns the shields with fire.
¹⁰"Be still, and know that I am God!
　　I will be honored by every nation.
　　I will be honored throughout the world."
¹¹The Lord of Heaven's Armies is here among us;
　　the God of Israel is our fortress.

~ Psalm 46:3-11

THE RULER OF EARTH

No matter how much people may brag about their accomplishments, no person or nation will ever rule the earth. That privilege and honor is reserved for God. He will protect His people irrespective of what happens. We have nothing to fear if we put our trust in the Lord.

¹Come, everyone! Clap your hands!
    Shout to God with joyful praise!
²For the Lord Most High is awesome.
    He is the great King of all the earth.
³He subdues the nations before us,
    putting our enemies beneath our feet.
⁴He chose the Promised Land as our inheritance,
    the proud possession of Jacob's descendants, whom he loves.
⁵God has ascended with a mighty shout.
    The Lord has ascended with trumpets blaring.
⁶Sing praises to God, sing praises;
    sing praises to our King, sing praises!
⁷For God is the King over all the earth.
    Praise him with a psalm.
⁸God reigns above the nations,
    sitting on his holy throne.
⁹The rulers of the world have gathered together
    with the people of the God of Abraham.
For all the kings of the earth belong to God.
    He is highly honored everywhere.

~ Psalm 47:1-9

GOD IS PRAISEWORTHY

We need to praise God unconditionally, because He is worthy. He is worthy because of who He Is. He Is almighty, His love lasts forever and He will be with us even in the darkest of times. Whenever you feel overwhelmed by your circumstances, just think of what God did for you, and praise Him!

¹How great is the LORD,
    how deserving of praise,
in the city of our God,
    which sits on his holy mountain!
²It is high and magnificent;
    the whole earth rejoices to see it!
Mount Zion, the holy mountain,
    is the city of the great King!
³God himself is in Jerusalem's towers,
    revealing himself as its defender.
⁴The kings of the earth joined forces
    and advanced against the city.
⁵But when they saw it, they were stunned;
    they were terrified and ran away.
⁶They were gripped with terror
    and writhed in pain like a woman in labor.
⁷You destroyed them like the mighty ships of Tarshish
    shattered by a powerful east wind.
⁸We had heard of the city's glory,
    but now we have seen it ourselves—
    the city of the LORD of Heaven's Armies.
It is the city of our God;
    he will make it safe forever.

~ Psalm 48:1-8

CONFIDENCE OF THE WISE

My confidence is in God, not in man. The psalmist says man will die like the beasts of the field. He may build empires and do well in worldly terms, but eventually all that will pass away – yet the Word of the Lord remains forever.

¹Listen to this, all you people!
    Pay attention, everyone in the world!
²High and low,
    rich and poor—listen!
³For my words are wise,
    and my thoughts are filled with insight.
⁴I listen carefully to many proverbs
    and solve riddles with inspiration from a harp.
⁵Why should I fear when trouble comes,
    when enemies surround me?
⁶They trust in their wealth
    and boast of great riches.
⁷Yet they cannot redeem themselves from death
    by paying a ransom to God.
⁸Redemption does not come so easily,
    for no one can ever pay enough
⁹to live forever
    and never see the grave.
¹⁰Those who are wise must finally die,
    just like the foolish and senseless,
    leaving all their wealth behind.

~ Psalm 49:1-10

REPENTANCE

This is a psalm of true repentance. The psalmist asks for forgiveness and a new start. God is the God of forgiveness and new beginnings. He will never desert us, even if we sin. All He requires of us is that we repent, turn from our wicked ways and follow Him.

¹Have mercy on me, O God,
   because of your unfailing love.
Because of your great compassion,
   blot out the stain of my sins.
²Wash me clean from my guilt.
   Purify me from my sin.
³For I recognize my rebellion;
   it haunts me day and night.
⁴Against you, and you alone, have I sinned;
   I have done what is evil in your sight.
You will be proved right in what you say,
   and your judgment against me is just.
⁵For I was born a sinner—
   yes, from the moment my mother conceived me.
⁶But you desire honesty from the womb,
   teaching me wisdom even there.
⁷Purify me from my sins, and I will be clean;
   wash me, and I will be whiter than snow.
⁸Oh, give me back my joy again;
   you have broken me—
   now let me rejoice.
⁹Don't keep looking at my sins.
   Remove the stain of my guilt.

~ Psalm 51:1-9

THE FOOLISH UNBELIEVER

To say there is no God is absolute foolishness. All around us there is evidence of His existence, whether it is in a small flower or a majestic tree. We are blessed to have met God through Jesus Christ. He is our refuge and salvation. How can we not believe in Him?

¹Only fools say in their hearts,
  "There is no God."
They are corrupt, and their actions are evil;
  not one of them does good!
²God looks down from heaven
  on the entire human race;
he looks to see if anyone is truly wise,
  if anyone seeks God.
³But no, all have turned away;
  all have become corrupt.
No one does good,
  not a single one!
⁴Will those who do evil never learn?
  They eat up my people like bread
  and wouldn't think of praying to God.
⁵Terror will grip them,
  terror like they have never known before.
God will scatter the bones of your enemies.
  You will put them to shame, for God has rejected them.
⁶Who will come from Mount Zion to rescue Israel?
  When God restores his people,
  Jacob will shout with joy, and Israel will rejoice.

~ Psalm 53:1-6

GOD IS OUR REFUGE

There are so many people who have been let down by life. Companies, organizations and even fellow Christians have let them down. This psalm addresses this issue by directing us to the Lord. Rest assured that He will never disappoint us. Put your hope in the Lord, because He cannot be untrue to His word.

¹I wait quietly before God,
    for my victory comes from him.
²He alone is my rock and my salvation,
    my fortress where I will never be shaken.
³So many enemies against one man—
    all of them trying to kill me.
To them I'm just a broken-down wall
    or a tottering fence.
⁴They plan to topple me from my high position.
    They delight in telling lies about me.
They praise me to my face
    but curse me in their hearts.
⁵Let all that I am wait quietly before God,
    for my hope is in him.
⁶He alone is my rock and my salvation,
    my fortress where I will not be shaken.
⁷My victory and honor come from God alone.
    He is my refuge, a rock where no enemy can reach me.
⁸O my people, trust in him at all times.
    Pour out your heart to him,
    for God is our refuge.

~ Psalm 62:1-8

GOD FIRST

If we put God first, the rest will fall into place. If you can't sleep at night, don't waste time counting sheep, but meditate on the Word of God. Before you know it, you will be peacefully asleep.

You will find that if you start your day with God, your day will be successful.

[1]O God, you are my God;
  I earnestly search for you.
My soul thirsts for you;
  my whole body longs for you
in this parched and weary land
  where there is no water.
[2]I have seen you in your sanctuary
  and gazed upon your power and glory.
[3]Your unfailing love is better than life itself;
  how I praise you!
[4]I will praise you as long as I live,
  lifting up my hands to you in prayer.
[5]You satisfy me more than the richest feast.
  I will praise you with songs of joy.
[6]I lie awake thinking of you,
  meditating on you through the night.
[7]Because you are my helper,
  I sing for joy in the shadow of your wings.
[8]I cling to you;
  your strong right hand holds me securely.

~ Psalm 63:1-8

ALL WILL BE REVEALED

We need to understand one thing: our sins will find us out. The Lord reminds us that He knows our innermost thoughts and our hearts. We cannot hide anything from the Lord, because He knows everything. It is therefore important that we live pure and honest lives to the glory of God.

¹O God, listen to my complaint.
   Protect my life from my enemies' threats.
²Hide me from the plots of this evil mob,
   from this gang of wrongdoers.
³They sharpen their tongues like swords
   and aim their bitter words like arrows.
⁴They shoot from ambush at the innocent,
   attacking suddenly and fearlessly.
⁵They encourage each other to do evil
   and plan how to set their traps in secret.
   "Who will ever notice?" they ask.
⁶As they plot their crimes, they say,
   "We have devised the perfect plan!"
   Yes, the human heart and mind are cunning.
⁷But God himself will shoot them with his arrows,
   suddenly striking them down.
⁸Their own tongues will ruin them,
   and all who see them will shake their heads in scorn.
⁹Then everyone will be afraid;
   they will proclaim the mighty acts of God
   and realize all the amazing things he does.

~ Psalm 64:1-9

A FIRM FOOTING

The Lord says that He will not allow us to stumble. He will always watch over us and make sure that we are taken care of. Even when life takes a difficult turn, He will be there. We never have to fear anything, because with God on our side, we will be as firm as a rock.

¹Shout joyful praises to God, all the earth!
²Sing about the glory of his name!
    Tell the world how glorious he is.
³Say to God, "How awesome are your deeds!
    Your enemies cringe before your mighty power.
⁴Everything on earth will worship you;
    they will sing your praises,
    shouting your name in glorious songs."
⁵Come and see what our God has done,
    what awesome miracles he performs for people!
⁶He made a dry path through the Red Sea,
    and his people went across on foot.
    There we rejoiced in him.
⁷For by his great power he rules forever.
    He watches every movement of the nations;
    let no rebel rise in defiance.
⁸Let the whole world bless our God
    and loudly sing his praises.
⁹Our lives are in his hands,
    and he keeps our feet from stumbling.

~ Psalm 66:1-9

OUT OF THE MIRE

We need to concentrate on pleasing God, not men. Men will never be totally satisfied, no matter how hard we try to please them, but God is slow to anger and quick to forgive. Be honest with God; tell Him of your sorrows and confess your sins. Honor God and He will honor you.

¹Save me, O God,
    for the floodwaters are up to my neck.
²Deeper and deeper I sink into the mire;
    I can't find a foothold.
I am in deep water,
    and the floods overwhelm me.
³I am exhausted from crying for help;
    my throat is parched.
My eyes are swollen with weeping,
    waiting for my God to help me.
⁴Those who hate me without cause
    outnumber the hairs on my head.
Many enemies try to destroy me with lies,
    demanding that I give back what I didn't steal.
⁵O God, you know how foolish I am;
    my sins cannot be hidden from you.
⁶Don't let those who trust in you be ashamed because of me,
    O Sovereign LORD of Heaven's Armies.
Don't let me cause them to be humiliated,
    O God of Israel.
⁷For I endure insults for your sake;
    humiliation is written all over my face.

~ Psalm 69:1-7

GOD IS DEPENDABLE

God's amazing faithfulness surrounds us every day. From our youth to old age, God is always with us. When life's storms threaten to overwhelm us, He is there. There is nowhere that God has not been and nothing that He has not seen. God is real and He will never fail us.

¹O Lord, I have come to you for protection;
    don't let me be disgraced.
²Save me and rescue me,
    for you do what is right.
Turn your ear to listen to me,
    and set me free.
³Be my rock of safety
    where I can always hide.
Give the order to save me,
    for you are my rock and my fortress.
⁴My God, rescue me from the power of the wicked,
    from the clutches of cruel oppressors.
⁵O Lord, you alone are my hope.
    I've trusted you, O Lord, from childhood.
⁶Yes, you have been with me from birth;
    from my mother's womb you have cared for me.
    No wonder I am always praising you!
⁷My life is an example to many,
    because you have been my strength and protection.
⁸That is why I can never stop praising you;
    I declare your glory all day long.

~ Psalm 71:1-8

A GATEKEEPER

Wouldn't it be wonderful to dwell in the house of the Lord? The psalmist says that he would rather be a gatekeeper in God's house than live a life of luxury with the wicked. Instead of pursuing fame and fortune, look to the Lord and live a life pleasing to Him, so that you can one day dwell with Him.

⁴What joy for those who can live in your house,
    always singing your praises.
⁵What joy for those whose strength comes from the Lord,
who have set their minds on a pilgrimage to Jerusalem.
⁶When they walk through the Valley of Weeping,
    it will become a place of refreshing springs.
    The autumn rains will clothe it with blessings.
⁷They will continue to grow stronger,
    and each of them will appear before God in Jerusalem.
⁸O Lord God of Heaven's Armies, hear my prayer.
    Listen, O God of Jacob.
⁹O God, look with favor upon the king, our shield!
    Show favor to the one you have anointed.
¹⁰A single day in your courts
    is better than a thousand anywhere else!
I would rather be a gatekeeper in the house of my God
    than live the good life in the homes of the wicked.
¹¹For the Lord God is our sun and our shield.
    He gives us grace and glory.
The Lord will withhold no good thing
    from those who do what is right.

~ Psalm 84:4-11

DESPONDENCY

Here is a prime example of the psalmist confiding in God. It is always good to share your dreams, doubts and heartache with God. Do not be afraid to tell God exactly how you are feeling in your heart of hearts. He will help us if we ask Him to.

¹O Lᴏʀᴅ, God of my salvation,
    I cry out to you by day.
    I come to you at night.
²Now hear my prayer;
    listen to my cry.
³For my life is full of troubles,
    and death draws near.
⁴I am as good as dead,
    like a strong man with no strength left.
⁵They have left me among the dead,
    and I lie like a corpse in a grave.
I am forgotten,
    cut off from your care.
⁶You have thrown me into the lowest pit,
    into the darkest depths.
⁷Your anger weighs me down;
    with wave after wave you have engulfed me.
⁸You have driven my friends away
    by making me repulsive to them.
I am in a trap with no way of escape.

~ Psalm 88:1-8

LIFE IS SHORT

Today's Scripture passage highlights the fragility and brevity of life and how eternal God is. The psalmist warns us to make each day count. Life is too short to waste time on meaningless and frivolous things that rob us of our valuable time on earth. Rather, we should focus our thoughts on eternal things.

¹Lord, through all the generations
   you have been our home!
²Before the mountains were born,
   before you gave birth to the earth and the world,
   from beginning to end, you are God.
³You turn people back to dust, saying,
   "Return to dust, you mortals!"
⁴For you, a thousand years are as a passing day,
   as brief as a few night hours.
⁵You sweep people away like dreams that disappear.
   They are like grass that springs up in the morning.
⁶In the morning it blooms and flourishes,
   but by evening it is dry and withered.
⁷We wither beneath your anger;
   we are overwhelmed by your fury.
⁸You spread out our sins before you—
   our secret sins—and you see them all.
⁹We live our lives beneath your wrath,
   ending our years with a groan.
¹²Teach us to realize the brevity of life,
   so that we may grow in wisdom.

~ Psalm 90:1-9, 12

START LIVING

In today's uncertain times, remember that the Lord is our refuge and fortress and we must put our trust in Him. As long as we love the Lord with our whole heart, He will carry us through any and every situation. Call on Him and He will answer you and give you a long and fulfilling life.

¹Those who live in the shelter of the Most High
    will find rest in the shadow of the Almighty.
²This I declare about the LORD:
He alone is my refuge, my place of safety;
    he is my God, and I trust him.
³For he will rescue you from every trap
    and protect you from deadly disease.
⁴He will cover you with his feathers.
    He will shelter you with his wings.
    His faithful promises are your armor and protection.
⁵Do not be afraid of the terrors of the night,
    nor the arrow that flies in the day.
⁶Do not dread the disease that stalks in darkness,
    nor the disaster that strikes at midday.
⁷Though a thousand fall at your side,
    though ten thousand are dying around you,
    these evils will not touch you.
⁸Just open your eyes,
    and see how the wicked are punished.
⁹If you make the LORD your refuge,
    if you make the Most High your shelter,
no evil will conquer you.

~ Psalm 91:1-9

PRAISE THE LORD

Make time to praise God every day. Praise Him for the big things He has done for you. But praise Him also for the small things. We should praise God for all that He has given us, for never forsaking us, and for the assurance that our future is secure in Him.

¹It is good to give thanks to the LORD,
   to sing praises to the Most High.
²It is good to proclaim your unfailing love in the morning,
   your faithfulness in the evening,
³accompanied by the ten-stringed harp
   and the melody of the lyre.
⁴You thrill me, LORD, with all you have done for me!
   I sing for joy because of what you have done.
⁵O LORD, what great works you do!
   And how deep are your thoughts.
⁶Only a simpleton would not know,
   and only a fool would not understand this:
⁷Though the wicked sprout like weeds
   and evildoers flourish,
   they will be destroyed forever.
⁸But you, O LORD, will be exalted forever.
⁹Your enemies, LORD, will surely perish;
   all evildoers will be scattered.
¹⁰But you have made me as strong as a wild ox.
   You have anointed me with the finest oil.

~ Psalm 92:1-10

OUR GOD REIGNS

Psalm 93 reminds us that our God reigns forever. He is mightier than all the storms that could ever rage against us. What a comfort it is to know that God is in control and that His love for us never ends. His reign is holy forever and ever.

¹The LORD is king! He is robed in majesty.
    Indeed, the LORD is robed in majesty and armed with
    strength.
The world stands firm
    and cannot be shaken.
²Your throne, O LORD, has stood from time immemorial.
    You yourself are from the everlasting past.
³The floods have risen up, O LORD.
    The floods have roared like thunder;
    the floods have lifted their pounding waves.
⁴But mightier than the violent raging of the seas,
    mightier than the breakers on the shore—
    the LORD above is mightier than these!
⁵Your royal laws cannot be changed.
    Your reign, O LORD, is holy forever and ever.

~ Psalm 93:1-5

MAY

HOLY GOD

God is holy and He expects us to be holy as well. When we obey Him, we live holy lives. We shouldn't get too familiar with God. He is not "the man upstairs" or a "buddy next door." He is the sovereign and holy God. Yes, He wants us to speak to Him as to a friend, but we mustn't forget who He is and who we are.

¹The LORD is king!
  Let the nations tremble!
He sits on his throne between the cherubim.
  Let the whole earth quake!
²The LORD sits in majesty in Jerusalem,
  exalted above all the nations.
³Let them praise your great and awesome name.
  Your name is holy!
⁴Mighty King, lover of justice,
  you have established fairness.
You have acted with justice
  and righteousness throughout Israel.
⁵Exalt the LORD our God!
  Bow low before his feet, for he is holy!
⁶Moses and Aaron were among his priests;
  Samuel also called on his name.
They cried to the LORD for help,
  and he answered them.
⁷He spoke to Israel from the pillar of cloud,
  and they followed the laws and decrees he gave them.

~ Psalm 99:1-7

A JOYFUL NOISE

We have every reason to shout and make a joyful noise because we serve a mighty and faithful God. We have done nothing to deserve His love, yet He leads us and loves us like a father loves his child. Let us praise God today with all of our heart, because our Father will never abandon His children.

¹Shout with joy to the Lᴏʀᴅ, all the earth!
²Worship the Lᴏʀᴅ with gladness.
  Come before him, singing with joy.
³Acknowledge that the Lᴏʀᴅ is God!
  He made us, and we are his.
  We are his people, the sheep of his pasture.
⁴Enter his gates with thanksgiving;
  go into his courts with praise.
  Give thanks to him and praise his name.
⁵For the Lᴏʀᴅ is good.
  His unfailing love continues forever,
  and his faithfulness continues to each generation.

~ Psalm 100:1-5

STRIVE FOR EXCELLENCE

David says that he will do his utmost to live a life pleasing to God. He strives to lead a life of integrity, rejects anything vile and vulgar, and stays away from evil. We need to separate ourselves from gossip, and from people who speak negatively. We only need to concentrate on loving God.

¹I will sing of your love and justice, Lord.
    I will praise you with songs.
²I will be careful to live a blameless life—
    when will you come to help me?
I will lead a life of integrity
    in my own home.
³I will refuse to look at
    anything vile and vulgar.
I hate all who deal crookedly;
    I will have nothing to do with them.
⁴I will reject perverse ideas
    and stay away from every evil.
⁵I will not tolerate people who slander their neighbors.
    I will not endure conceit and pride.
⁶I will search for faithful people
    to be my companions.
Only those who are above reproach
    will be allowed to serve me.
⁷I will not allow deceivers to serve in my house,
    and liars will not stay in my presence.
⁸My daily task will be to ferret out the wicked
    and free the city of the Lord from their grip.

~ Psalm 101:1-8

USE YOUR TIME WELL

Don't waste time on frivolous things. God has given us a certain number of days to live on earth and we must live them to the full. Commit your life to God today. Love others today. Forgive today. Repair those broken relationships. Get up in the morning and spend quiet time with God. Give Him all the praise and honor, because He is worthy.

¹²But you, O Lord, will sit on your throne forever.
Your fame will endure to every generation.
¹³You will arise and have mercy on Jerusalem—
and now is the time to pity her,
now is the time you promised to help.
¹⁴For your people love every stone in her walls
and cherish even the dust in her streets.
¹⁵Then the nations will tremble before the Lord.
The kings of the earth will tremble before his glory.
¹⁶For the Lord will rebuild Jerusalem.
He will appear in his glory.
¹⁷He will listen to the prayers of the destitute.
He will not reject their pleas.
¹⁸Let this be recorded for future generations,
so that a people not yet born will praise the Lord.
¹⁹Tell them the Lord looked down
from his heavenly sanctuary.
He looked down to earth from heaven
²⁰to hear the groans of the prisoners,
to release those condemned to die.
²¹And so the Lord's fame will be celebrated in Zion,
his praises in Jerusalem,

~ Psalm 102:12-21

THE LORD'S MERCIES

Do you trust God for divine healing? The number of medicines that people take nowadays is disconcerting. There is nothing wrong with consulting a doctor, but we need to look to the Lord first and foremost for healing. He forgives all our sins and heals all our diseases. He redeems us from death. The Lord crowns us with love and tender mercies. God is good!

¹Let all that I am praise the LORD;
    with my whole heart, I will praise his holy name.
²Let all that I am praise the LORD;
    may I never forget the good things he does for me.
³He forgives all my sins
    and heals all my diseases.
⁴He redeems me from death
    and crowns me with love and tender mercies.
⁵He fills my life with good things.
    My youth is renewed like the eagle's!
⁶The LORD gives righteousness
    and justice to all who are treated unfairly.
⁷He revealed his character to Moses
    and his deeds to the people of Israel.
⁸The LORD is compassionate and merciful,
    slow to get angry and filled with unfailing love.
⁹He will not constantly accuse us,
    nor remain angry forever.
¹⁰He does not punish us for all our sins;
    he does not deal harshly with us, as we deserve.

~ Psalm 103:1-10

GOD'S UNFAILING LOVE

So often people paint a picture of God as an oppressor. He is exactly the opposite! He has compassion for all His children and He loves them with unending love. He is quick to forgive and slow to anger. He does not deal with us as we deserve, but chooses to see the best in us.

¹¹For his unfailing love toward those who fear him
   is as great as the height of the heavens above the earth.
¹²He has removed our sins as far from us
   as the east is from the west.
¹³The Lᴏʀᴅ is like a father to his children,
   tender and compassionate to those who fear him.
¹⁴For he knows how weak we are;
   he remembers we are only dust.
¹⁵Our days on earth are like grass;
   like wildflowers, we bloom and die.
¹⁶The wind blows, and we are gone—
   as though we had never been here.
¹⁷But the love of the Lᴏʀᴅ remains forever
   with those who fear him.
His salvation extends to the children's children
¹⁸of those who are faithful to his covenant,
   of those who obey his commandments!
¹⁹The Lᴏʀᴅ has made the heavens his throne;
   from there he rules over everything.
²⁰Praise the Lᴏʀᴅ, you angels,
   you mighty ones who carry out his plans,
   listening for each of his commands.

~ Psalm 103:11-20

MIGHTY THINGS

If we put our trust in God, He will give us victory. If we are in Christ, we are triumphant; therefore, we must go out and proclaim His greatness. God will help us do mighty things in His name, if we only believe.

¹My heart is confident in you, O God;
　　no wonder I can sing your praises with all my heart!
²Wake up, lyre and harp!
　　I will wake the dawn with my song.
³I will thank you, LORD, among all the people.
　　I will sing your praises among the nations.
⁴For your unfailing love is higher than the heavens.
　　Your faithfulness reaches to the clouds.
⁵Be exalted, O God, above the highest heavens.
　　May your glory shine over all the earth.
⁶Now rescue your beloved people.
　　Answer and save us by your power.
⁷God has promised this by his holiness:
"I will divide up Shechem with joy.
　　I will measure out the valley of Succoth."
¹³With God's help we will do mighty things,
　　for he will trample down our foes.

~ Psalm 108:1-7, 13

THE POWER OF GOD

God is omnipotent! The psalmist captures the power of God so well when he says that the sea saw God's people, Israel, coming, and fled. He is the Creator and in His presence all things tremble. Why do we run around seeking help and counsel when the Creator is only one prayer away? Trust in the Lord!

¹When the Israelites escaped from Egypt—
    when the family of Jacob left that foreign land—
²the land of Judah became God's sanctuary,
    and Israel became his kingdom.
³The Red Sea saw them coming and hurried out of their way!
    The water of the Jordan River turned away.
⁴The mountains skipped like rams,
    the hills like lambs!
⁵What's wrong, Red Sea, that made you hurry out of their way?
    What happened, Jordan River, that you turned away?
⁶Why, mountains, did you skip like rams?
    Why, hills, like lambs?
⁷Tremble, O earth, at the presence of the Lord,
    at the presence of the God of Jacob.
⁸He turned the rock into a pool of water;
    yes, a spring of water flowed from solid rock.

~ Psalm 114:1-8

ONE TRUE GOD

Why do some people worship idols? They can't speak, smell, walk or talk, yet men look to them for help! Idols are not always statues: Many people idolize money; their families; education; sport; or achievements. Look only to God for your security. There is only one God and to His holy name goes all the glory. He is your helper and your shield.

¹Not to us, O LORD, not to us,
　　but to your name goes all the glory
　　for your unfailing love and faithfulness.
²Why let the nations say,
　　"Where is their God?"
³Our God is in the heavens,
　　and he does as he wishes.
⁴Their idols are merely things of silver and gold,
　　shaped by human hands.
⁵They have mouths but cannot speak,
　　and eyes but cannot see.
⁶They have ears but cannot hear,
　　and noses but cannot smell.
⁷They have hands but cannot feel,
　　and feet but cannot walk,
　　and throats but cannot make a sound.
⁸And those who make idols are just like them,
　　as are all who trust in them.
⁹O Israel, trust the LORD!
　　He is your helper and your shield.

~ Psalm 115:1-9

DEATH'S STING

This psalm is a great source of comfort for those who have lost a loved one. Because for those who believe in Jesus there is no death. Someone once said that soon people will read in the newspaper that He has died, but He hasn't died, He just changed his address. That is our hope.

⁸He has saved me from death,
　　my eyes from tears,
　　my feet from stumbling.
⁹And so I walk in the Lord's presence
　　as I live here on earth!
¹⁰I believed in you, so I said,
　　"I am deeply troubled, Lord."
¹¹In my anxiety I cried out to you,
　　"These people are all liars!"
¹²What can I offer the Lord
　　for all he has done for me?
¹³I will lift up the cup of salvation
　　and praise the Lord's name for saving me.
¹⁴I will keep my promises to the Lord
　　in the presence of all his people.
¹⁵The Lord cares deeply
　　when his loved ones die.
¹⁶O Lord, I am your servant;
　　yes, I am your servant, born into your household;
　　you have freed me from my chains.
¹⁷I will offer you a sacrifice of thanksgiving
　　and call on the name of the Lord.

~ Psalm 116:8-17

DISCIPLINE

Here is a mandate about discipline. The psalmist says that before God disciplined him, he wandered off. That's why we need to discipline our children so that they will not go astray, so that they will grow up to be responsible citizens. We need to enable them to follow instructions and give instructions with love. God disciplines us because He loves us.

[65]You have done many good things for me, Lord,
just as you promised.
[66]I believe in your commands;
now teach me good judgment and knowledge.
[67]I used to wander off until you disciplined me;
but now I closely follow your word.
[68]You are good and do only good;
teach me your decrees.
[69]Arrogant people smear me with lies,
but in truth I obey your commandments with all my heart.
[70]Their hearts are dull and stupid,
but I delight in your instructions.
[71]My suffering was good for me,
for it taught me to pay attention to your decrees.
[72]Your instructions are more valuable to me
than millions in gold and silver.

~ Psalm 119:65-72

THE LORD'S STRENGTH

The psalmist says that those who trust in the Lord are like mountains. Mountains are secure, immoveable and strong. This is exactly what happens when we trust in the Lord. Then God will surround us with His love, like the mountains surround Jerusalem.

¹Those who trust in the Lord are as secure as Mount Zion;
   they will not be defeated but will endure forever.
²Just as the mountains surround Jerusalem,
   so the Lord surrounds his people, both now and forever.
³The wicked will not rule the land of the godly,
   for then the godly might be tempted to do wrong.
⁴O Lord, do good to those who are good,
   whose hearts are in tune with you.
⁵But banish those who turn to crooked ways, O Lord.
   Take them away with those who do evil.
May Israel have peace!

~ Psalm 125:1-5

REAP IN JOY

David Livingstone, a well-known missionary in Africa, was one of the men who opened up Africa to the gospel. Yet it is believed that he only ever led one man, Chief Sechele, to Jesus. Livingstone sowed in tears, but firmly believed that those after him would reap the harvest. If we trust God and His will for us, our efforts will never be in vain.

¹When the Lord brought back his exiles to Jerusalem,
   it was like a dream!
²We were filled with laughter,
   and we sang for joy.
And the other nations said,
   "What amazing things the Lord has done for them."
³Yes, the Lord has done amazing things for us!
   What joy!
⁴Restore our fortunes, Lord,
   as streams renew the desert.
⁵Those who plant in tears
   will harvest with shouts of joy.
⁶They weep as they go to plant their seed,
   but they sing as they return with the harvest.

~ Psalm 126:1-6

A GODLY FOUNDATION

A good idea is not always a God idea. A need does not justify a call. If God is not building the house, the work of the builders is in vain. We need God's blessing before starting any project. With His blessing, anything will succeed. But remember that hard work is required in order to make your efforts succeed.

¹Unless the LORD builds a house,
　　the work of the builders is wasted.
Unless the LORD protects a city,
　　guarding it with sentries will do no good.
²It is useless for you to work so hard
　　from early morning until late at night,
anxiously working for food to eat;
　　for God gives rest to his loved ones.
³Children are a gift from the LORD;
　　they are a reward from him.
⁴Children born to a young man
　　are like arrows in a warrior's hands.
⁵How joyful is the man whose quiver is full of them!
　　He will not be put to shame when he confronts his accusers at the city gates.

~ Psalm 127:1-5

FEAR OF THE LORD

The Lord tells us that if we follow His ways, we will enjoy the fruits of our work. Our families will be fruitful and the very heart of our homes will be filled with joy. But respect and reverence toward God is essential. If we fear and respect Him, He will bless us.

¹How joyful are those who fear the LORD—
     all who follow his ways!
²You will enjoy the fruit of your labor.
     How joyful and prosperous you will be!
³Your wife will be like a fruitful grapevine,
     flourishing within your home.
Your children will be like vigorous young olive trees
     as they sit around your table.
⁴That is the LORD's blessing
     for those who fear him.
⁵May the LORD continually bless you from Zion.
     May you see Jerusalem prosper as long as you live.
⁶May you live to enjoy your grandchildren.
     May Israel have peace!

~ Psalm 128:1-6

ARROGANT ONES

One thing that the Lord really dislikes is a proud person. There is no place in the kingdom of God for arrogance and pride. David said that he calmed himself, because when he humbled himself and quieted his soul, then God strengthened him to perform miracles in His name.

¹Lᴏʀᴅ, my heart is not proud;
    my eyes are not haughty.
I don't concern myself with matters too great
    or too awesome for me to grasp.
²Instead, I have calmed and quieted myself,
    like a weaned child who no longer cries for its mother's milk.
    Yes, like a weaned child is my soul within me.
³O Israel, put your hope in the Lᴏʀᴅ—
    now and always.

~ Psalm 131:1-3

GIVE THANKS ALWAYS

In His mercy and grace, God delivered His people from slavery in Egypt, divided the Red Sea, fed the multitudes in the wilderness for forty years, and protected them all the way. He defeated enemies on their behalf. He will do the same for you and me. Therefore, give thanks to God all the time.

⁴Give thanks to him who alone does mighty miracles.
His faithful love endures forever.
⁵Give thanks to him who made the heavens so skillfully.
His faithful love endures forever.
⁶Give thanks to him who placed the earth among the waters.
His faithful love endures forever.
⁷Give thanks to him who made the heavenly lights—
His faithful love endures forever.
⁸the sun to rule the day,
His faithful love endures forever.
⁹and the moon and stars to rule the night.
His faithful love endures forever.
¹⁰Give thanks to him who killed the firstborn of Egypt.
His faithful love endures forever.
¹¹He brought Israel out of Egypt.
His faithful love endures forever.
¹²He acted with a strong hand and powerful arm.
His faithful love endures forever.
¹³Give thanks to him who parted the Red Sea.
His faithful love endures forever.

~ Psalm 136:4-13

OUR HEAVENLY HOME

Don't become too comfortable here on earth. Remind yourself that this is not your eternal home and that you are only a sojourner. Look around you. Do you put more effort into your temporary dwelling than your eternal home? Spend time on things of eternal value – on God.

¹Beside the rivers of Babylon, we sat and wept
    as we thought of Jerusalem.
²We put away our harps,
    hanging them on the branches of poplar trees.
³For our captors demanded a song from us.
    Our tormentors insisted on a joyful hymn:
    "Sing us one of those songs of Jerusalem!"
⁴But how can we sing the songs of the LORD
    while in a pagan land?
⁵If I forget you, O Jerusalem,
    let my right hand forget how to play the harp.
⁶May my tongue stick to the roof of my mouth
    if I fail to remember you,
    if I don't make Jerusalem my greatest joy.
⁷O LORD, remember what the Edomites did
    on the day the armies of Babylon captured Jerusalem.
"Destroy it!" they yelled.
    "Level it to the ground!"
⁸O Babylon, you will be destroyed.
    Happy is the one who pays you back
    for what you have done to us.

~ Psalm 137:1-8

GOD KNOWS BEST

The Lord knows us better than anyone else. In fact, He knows us better than we know ourselves. Because He created you, you can't fool God. Listen to His counsel, because He knows what is best for you. Start doing things according to His will and see how God will make you prosper.

¹O LORD, you have examined my heart
    and know everything about me.
²You know when I sit down or stand up.
    You know my thoughts even when I'm far away.
³You see me when I travel
    and when I rest at home.
    You know everything I do.
⁴You know what I am going to say
    even before I say it, LORD.
⁵You go before me and follow me.
    You place your hand of blessing on my head.
⁶Such knowledge is too wonderful for me,
    too great for me to understand!
⁷I can never escape from your Spirit!
    I can never get away from your presence!
⁸If I go up to heaven, you are there;
    if I go down to the grave, you are there.
⁹If I ride the wings of the morning,
    if I dwell by the farthest oceans,
¹⁰even there your hand will guide me,
    and your strength will support me.

~ Psalm 139:1-10

GOD IS OUR CONFIDENCE

The closer we walk with God, the less we have to fear the world. God will give us the right words to speak when we need them. He will deliver us from evil and its practices. God is your Protector, so do not fear the things of the world.

¹O LORD, rescue me from evil people.
   Protect me from those who are violent,
²those who plot evil in their hearts
   and stir up trouble all day long.
³Their tongues sting like a snake;
   the venom of a viper drips from their lips.
⁴O LORD, keep me out of the hands of the wicked.
   Protect me from those who are violent,
   for they are plotting against me.
⁵The proud have set a trap to catch me;
   they have stretched out a net;
   they have placed traps all along the way.
⁶I said to the LORD, "You are my God!"
   Listen, O LORD, to my cries for mercy!
⁷O Sovereign LORD, the strong one who rescued me,
   you protected me on the day of battle.
⁸LORD, do not let evil people have their way.
   Do not let their evil schemes succeed,
   or they will become proud.

~ Psalm 140:1-8

OUR ROLE MODEL

No one is as righteous as the Lord. In fact, Jesus Christ is the only Righteous Person who has ever lived. That is why we should look to Him as our Mentor, Example and Redeemer. We need to put our trust in Him, not people, for guidance.

[1]Hear my prayer, O LORD; listen to my plea!

Answer me because you are faithful and righteous.

[2]Don't put your servant on trial,

for no one is innocent before you.

[3]My enemy has chased me.

He has knocked me to the ground

and forces me to live in darkness like those in the grave.

[4]I am losing all hope; I am paralyzed with fear.

[5]I remember the days of old. I ponder all your great works and think about what you have done.

[6]I lift my hands to you in prayer.

I thirst for you as parched land thirsts for rain.

[7]Come quickly, LORD, and answer me, for my depression deepens. Don't turn away from me, or I will die.

[8]Let me hear of your unfailing love each morning,

for I am trusting you.

Show me where to walk, for I give myself to you.

[9]Rescue me from my enemies, LORD;

I run to you to hide me.

[10]Teach me to do your will, for you are my God.

May your gracious Spirit lead me forward

on a firm footing.

[11]For the glory of your name, O LORD, preserve my life.

Because of your faithfulness, bring me out of this distress.

~ Psalm 143:1-11

WHAT IS HUMANKIND?

With the psalmist we wonder, "What are mere mortals that You think about us, Lord?" Why does the Lord, who is praised by all creation, bother with us? We are so small and insignificant, a mere breath of air. Yet the Master still cares for us. Give thanks to our mighty Creator who allows us to call Him Father.

³O LORD, what are human beings that you should notice them,
  mere mortals that you should think about them?
⁴For they are like a breath of air;
  their days are like a passing shadow.
⁵Open the heavens, LORD, and come down.
  Touch the mountains so they billow smoke.
⁶Hurl your lightning bolts and scatter your enemies!
  Shoot your arrows and confuse them!
⁷Reach down from heaven and rescue me;
  rescue me from deep waters,
  from the power of my enemies.
⁸Their mouths are full of lies;
  they swear to tell the truth, but they lie instead.
⁹I will sing a new song to you, O God!
  I will sing your praises with a ten-stringed harp.
¹⁵Joyful are those who live like this!
  Joyful indeed are those whose God is the LORD.

~ Psalm 144:3-9, 15

WORSHIP GOD

The Lord is worthy of praise. There is nothing else in this world that deserves our praise as much as our heavenly Father. He created the heavens and the earth and He sustains us. Let us praise Him with thankful hearts. Praise God simply because He is God.

¹Praise the LORD!
Praise God in his sanctuary;
    praise him in his mighty heaven!
²Praise him for his mighty works;
    praise his unequaled greatness!
³Praise him with a blast of the ram's horn;
    praise him with the lyre and harp!
⁴Praise him with the tambourine and dancing;
    praise him with strings and flutes!
⁵Praise him with a clash of cymbals;
    praise him with loud clanging cymbals.
⁶ Let everything that breathes sing praises to the LORD!
Praise the LORD!

~ Psalm 150:1-6

WISDOM

In this passage, King Solomon, a very wise man, writes about the importance of gaining wisdom. Wisdom cannot be bought or obtained by attending a university or college. True and lasting wisdom comes from God. The more time we spend with Him, the wiser we will become. Ask God today to grant you wisdom. He'll surely answer you.

¹My child, listen to what I say,
and treasure my commands.
²Tune your ears to wisdom,
and concentrate on understanding.
³Cry out for insight,
and ask for understanding.
⁴Search for them as you would for silver;
seek them like hidden treasures.
⁵Then you will understand what it means to fear the Lord,
and you will gain knowledge of God.
⁶For the Lord grants wisdom!
From his mouth come knowledge and understanding.
⁷He grants a treasure of common sense to the honest.
He is a shield to those who walk with integrity.
⁸He guards the paths of the just
and protects those who are faithful to him.
⁹Then you will understand what is right, just, and fair,
and you will find the right way to go.
¹⁰For wisdom will enter your heart,
and knowledge will fill you with joy.
¹¹Wise choices will watch over you.
Understanding will keep you safe.

~ Proverbs 2:1-11

FOLLOW GOD'S INSTRUCTION

If we trust God with all our hearts and we don't try to work things out in our own way, then God can undertake for us. The Lord wants only what is best for us. He gives us instructions and rules to protect and guide us. As His children, we must obey His instructions – it is for our own good.

¹My child, never forget the things I have taught you.
    Store my commands in your heart.
²If you do this, you will live many years,
    and your life will be satisfying.
³Never let loyalty and kindness leave you!
    Tie them around your neck as a reminder.
    Write them deep within your heart.
⁴Then you will find favor with both God and people,
    and you will earn a good reputation.
⁵Trust in the LORD with all your heart;
    do not depend on your own understanding.
⁶Seek his will in all you do,
    and he will show you which path to take.
⁷Don't be impressed with your own wisdom.
    Instead, fear the LORD and turn away from evil.
⁸Then you will have healing for your body
    and strength for your bones.
⁹Honor the LORD with your wealth
    and with the best part of everything you produce.
¹⁰Then he will fill your barns with grain,
    and your vats will overflow with good wine.

~ Proverbs 3:1-10

THE LORD'S DISCIPLINE

The Lord loves us, therefore He disciplines us when we make mistakes. If we are not corrected, we will keep on making the same mistakes and never learn from them. Discipline is used to correct and train. As parents, it is our responsibility to raise our children correctly in the ways of the Lord.

¹¹My child, don't reject the LORD's discipline,
　　and don't be upset when he corrects you.
¹²For the LORD corrects those he loves,
　　just as a father corrects a child in whom he delights.
¹³Joyful is the person who finds wisdom,
　　the one who gains understanding.
¹⁴For wisdom is more profitable than silver,
　　and her wages are better than gold.
¹⁵Wisdom is more precious than rubies;
　　nothing you desire can compare with her.
¹⁶She offers you long life in her right hand,
　　and riches and honor in her left.
¹⁷She will guide you down delightful paths;
　　all her ways are satisfying.
¹⁸Wisdom is a tree of life to those who embrace her;
　　happy are those who hold her tightly.

~ Proverbs 3:11-18

GUARD YOUR HEART

The Lord is very clear that if we listen to His instruction and walk in His ways, we will have peace of mind. The Lord tells us to guard our hearts, because it is the wellspring of life. A farmer knows how important it is to guard a wellspring of water. The Lord warns us to guard our hearts, as it determines the course of our lives.

¹⁴Don't do as the wicked do,
  and don't follow the path of evildoers.
¹⁵Don't even think about it; don't go that way.
  Turn away and keep moving.
¹⁸The way of the righteous is like the first gleam of dawn,
  which shines ever brighter until the full light of day.
¹⁹But the way of the wicked is like total darkness.
  They have no idea what they are stumbling over.
²⁰My child, pay attention to what I say.
  Listen carefully to my words.
²¹Don't lose sight of them.
  Let them penetrate deep into your heart,
²²for they bring life to those who find them,
  and healing to their whole body.
²³Guard your heart above all else,
  for it determines the course of your life.
²⁴Avoid all perverse talk;
  stay away from corrupt speech.
²⁵Look straight ahead,
  and fix your eyes on what lies before you.
²⁶Mark out a straight path for your feet;
  stay on the safe path.

~ Proverbs 4:14-15, 18-26

A STERN WARNING

In this passage, Solomon warns us against the dangers of sexual promiscuity. Not only is this kind of behavior against God's will, it can also lead to broken relationships and all kinds of diseases. God cares for us, therefore He warns us against the dangers of such behavior. Look to God for help – He is all you need.

³For the lips of an immoral woman are as sweet as honey,
  and her mouth is smoother than oil.
⁴But in the end she is as bitter as poison,
  as dangerous as a double-edged sword.
⁵Her feet go down to death;
  her steps lead straight to the grave.
⁶For she cares nothing about the path to life.
  She staggers down a crooked trail and doesn't realize it.
⁷So now, my sons, listen to me.
  Never stray from what I am about to say:
⁸Stay away from her!
  Don't go near the door of her house!
⁹If you do, you will lose your honor
  and will lose to merciless people all you have achieved.
¹⁰Strangers will consume your wealth,
  and someone else will enjoy the fruit of your labor.
¹¹In the end you will groan in anguish
  when disease consumes your body.
¹²You will say, "How I hated discipline!
  If only I had not ignored all the warnings!"

~ Proverbs 5:3-12

NO SURETY

This is a very important instruction from God. The Lord says that you will be trapped by your agreement if you've put up security for a friend's debt. Sooner or later it will backfire. Don't stand surety for anybody, quite simply because it is dangerous and also an instruction from God.

[1]My child, if you have put up security for a friend's debt
   or agreed to guarantee the debt of a stranger—
[2]if you have trapped yourself by your agreement
   and are caught by what you said—
[3]follow my advice and save yourself,
   for you have placed yourself at your friend's mercy.
Now swallow your pride;
   go and beg to have your name erased.
[4]Don't put it off; do it now!
   Don't rest until you do.
[5]Save yourself like a gazelle escaping from a hunter,
   like a bird fleeing from a net.

~ Proverbs 6:1-5

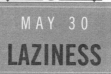

LAZINESS

The writer of Proverbs not only condemns laziness, he also points out that it has consequences. He says that we should learn from ants. They work hard so that they will have enough food stored up when winter comes. As children of God, we need to work to the best of our abilities, not only to avoid the consequence of being lazy, but to glorify God with our lives.

[6]Take a lesson from the ants, you lazybones.
   Learn from their ways and become wise!
[7]Though they have no prince
   or governor or ruler to make them work,
[8]they labor hard all summer,
   gathering food for the winter.
[9]But you, lazybones, how long will you sleep?
   When will you wake up?
[10]A little extra sleep, a little more slumber,
   a little folding of the hands to rest—
[11]then poverty will pounce on you like a bandit;
   scarcity will attack you like an armed robber.

~ Proverbs 6:6-11

WICKEDNESS

Today's passage describes a wicked man as a liar, arrogant and proud. The Lord does not approve of such a person. There is no future in wickedness. We need to humble ourselves and come to God. He will give us a game plan that will never fail.

[12]What are worthless and wicked people like?
   They are constant liars,
[13]signaling their deceit with a wink of the eye,
   a nudge of the foot, or the wiggle of fingers.
[14]Their perverted hearts plot evil,
   and they constantly stir up trouble.
[15]But they will be destroyed suddenly,
   broken in an instant beyond all hope of healing.
[16]There are six things the Lord hates—
   no, seven things he detests:
[17]haughty eyes,
   a lying tongue,
   hands that kill the innocent,
[18]a heart that plots evil,
   feet that race to do wrong,
[19]a false witness who pours out lies,
   a person who sows discord in a family.

~ Proverbs 6:12-19

JUNE

THE TONGUE

There is so much power in the tongue: power to create and power to destroy. When we speak wholesome and godly words of encouragement to people, it can build them up. Likewise, negative words can break people down. We should pay careful attention to what we say to others. If you don't have anything good to say, rather say nothing at all.

[19]Too much talk leads to sin.
   Be sensible and keep your mouth shut.
[20]The words of the godly are like sterling silver;
   the heart of a fool is worthless.
[21]The words of the godly encourage many,
   but fools are destroyed by their lack of common sense.
[30] The godly will never be disturbed,
   but the wicked will be removed from the land.
[31] The mouth of the godly person gives wise advice,
   but the tongue that deceives will be cut off.
[32] The lips of the godly speak helpful words,
   but the mouth of the wicked speaks perverse words.

~ Proverbs 10:19-21, 30-32

GODLY INSTRUCTION

The Lord does not approve of wicked behavior and dishonesty. It is important that we strive to live godly lives, not only at home and in church, but also in the workplace. The world desperately needs men of integrity and honesty. Be more concerned about right living than riches.

¹The Lord detests the use of dishonest scales,
  but he delights in accurate weights.
²Pride leads to disgrace,
  but with humility comes wisdom.
³Honesty guides good people;
  dishonesty destroys treacherous people.
⁴Riches won't help on the day of judgment,
  but right living can save you from death.
⁵The godly are directed by honesty;
  the wicked fall beneath their load of sin.
⁶The godliness of good people rescues them;
  the ambition of treacherous people traps them.
⁷When the wicked die, their hopes die with them,
  for they rely on their own feeble strength.
⁸The godly are rescued from trouble,
  and it falls on the wicked instead.

~ Proverbs 11:1-8

A GODLY NATURE

The Lord is well-pleased with people who strive to live godly lives. If we live lives of integrity, honesty and generosity, we will reap the benefits and enjoy lives of prosperity. The opposite, however, is true for the wicked. Remember that as a Christian, you have a responsibility to reflect your Master – other people, especially your children, are watching your every move.

¹⁹Godly people find life;
  evil people find death.
²⁰The LORD detests people with crooked hearts,
  but he delights in those with integrity.
²¹Evil people will surely be punished,
  but the children of the godly will go free.
²²A beautiful woman who lacks discretion
  is like a gold ring in a pig's snout.
²³The godly can look forward to a reward,
  while the wicked can expect only judgment.
²⁴Give freely and become more wealthy;
  be stingy and lose everything.
²⁵The generous will prosper;
  those who refresh others will themselves be refreshed.
²⁶People curse those who hoard their grain,
  but they bless the one who sells in time of need.
²⁷If you search for good, you will find favor;
  but if you search for evil, it will find you!

~ Proverbs 11:19-27

GUARD YOUR HEARTS

The Bible says that a merry heart is like medicine, but a broken spirit literally dries out the bones. We need to seek wisdom and understanding from God daily to deal with situations calmly. We need to speak less and listen more. A person who holds his tongue is wise.

²²A cheerful heart is good medicine,
but a broken spirit saps a person's strength.
²³The wicked take secret bribes
to pervert the course of justice.
²⁴Sensible people keep their eyes glued on wisdom,
but a fool's eyes wander to the ends of the earth.
²⁵Foolish children bring grief to their father
and bitterness to the one who gave them birth.
²⁶It is wrong to punish the godly for being good
or to flog leaders for being honest.
²⁷A truly wise person uses few words;
a person with understanding is even-tempered.
²⁸Even fools are thought wise when they keep silent;
with their mouths shut, they seem intelligent.

~ Proverbs 17:22-28

DISCIPLINE

Today's Scripture passage is a beautiful reminder that the Bible is our best guidebook on raising children. If we raise a child in God's ways, he will not lose his way when he is older. When you discipline your child in love, when he grows older there will be no need for it.

⁶Direct your children onto the right path,
  and when they are older, they will not leave it.
⁷Just as the rich rule the poor,
  so the borrower is servant to the lender.
⁸Those who plant injustice will harvest disaster,
  and their reign of terror will come to an end.
⁹Blessed are those who are generous,
  because they feed the poor.
¹⁰Throw out the mocker, and fighting goes, too.
  Quarrels and insults will disappear.
¹¹Whoever loves a pure heart and gracious speech
  will have the king as a friend.
¹²The LORD preserves those with knowledge,
  but he ruins the plans of the treacherous.
¹³The lazy person claims, "There's a lion out there!
  If I go outside, I might be killed!"
¹⁴The mouth of an immoral woman is a dangerous trap;
  those who make the LORD angry will fall into it.
¹⁵A youngster's heart is filled with foolishness,
  but physical discipline will drive it far away.

~ Proverbs 22:6-15

THE VIRTUOUS WIFE

We so often train up our sons to be good business-men, good engineers, good doctors or farmers, but we don't teach them to seek a virtuous wife. A good wife is a gift from God. As men, we should seek wives that have the qualities that God approves of. If we find such a wife, we should thank God every day.

¹⁰Who can find a virtuous and capable wife?
    She is more precious than rubies.
¹¹Her husband can trust her,
    and she will greatly enrich his life.
¹²She brings him good, not harm,
    all the days of her life.
¹⁷She is energetic and strong,
    a hard worker.
²⁰She extends a helping hand to the poor
    and opens her arms to the needy.
²⁵She is clothed with strength and dignity,
    and she laughs without fear of the future.
²⁶When she speaks, her words are wise,
    and she gives instructions with kindness.
²⁷She carefully watches everything in her household
    and suffers nothing from laziness.
²⁸Her children stand and bless her.
    Her husband praises her:
³⁰Charm is deceptive, and beauty does not last;
    but a woman who fears the Lord will be greatly praised.
³¹Reward her for all she has done.
    Let her deeds publicly declare her praise.

~ Proverbs 31:10-12, 17, 20, 25-28, 30-31

THE RIGHT TIME

With age comes wisdom. You realize that there is absolutely nothing new under the sun. Everything has its season, and the Lord knows exactly what the *right* time is. When we need to make decisions, it is important to consult the Lord, because He has the wisdom to know whether or not it is the right thing at the right time.

¹For everything there is a season,
  a time for every activity under heaven.
²A time to be born and a time to die.
  A time to plant and a time to harvest.
³A time to kill and a time to heal.
  A time to tear down and a time to build up.
⁴A time to cry and a time to laugh.
  A time to grieve and a time to dance.
⁵A time to scatter stones and a time to gather stones.
  A time to embrace and a time to turn away.
⁶A time to search and a time to quit searching.
  A time to keep and a time to throw away.
⁷A time to tear and a time to mend.
  A time to be quiet and a time to speak.
⁸A time to love and a time to hate.
  A time for war and a time for peace.

~ Ecclesiastes 3:1-8

THE PURPOSE OF MAN

The writer of Ecclesiastes tells us that we should fear God and keep His commandments, for this is our purpose. When you love someone, you will want to please them. So it is with Jesus – if we love Him, we will follow His ways and be holy.

¹Don't let the excitement of youth cause you to forget your Creator. Honor him in your youth before you grow old and say, "Life is not pleasant anymore." ²Remember him before the light of the sun, moon, and stars is dim to your old eyes, and rain clouds continually darken your sky. ³Remember him before your legs—the guards of your house—start to tremble; and before your shoulders—the strong men—stoop. Remember him before your teeth—your few remaining servants—stop grinding; and before your eyes—the women looking through the windows—see dimly.

⁴Remember him before the door to life's opportunities is closed and the sound of work fades. Now you rise at the first chirping of the birds, but then all their sounds will grow faint.

⁵Remember him before you become fearful of falling and worry about danger in the streets; before your hair turns white like an almond tree in bloom, and you drag along without energy like a dying grasshopper, and the caperberry no longer inspires sexual desire. Remember him before you near the grave, your everlasting home, when the mourners will weep at your funeral.

⁶Yes, remember your Creator now while you are young, before the silver cord of life snaps and the golden bowl is broken. Don't wait until the water jar is smashed at the spring and the pulley is broken at the well. ⁷For then the dust will return to the earth, and the spirit will return to God who gave it.

~ Ecclesiastes 12:1-7

THE GIFT OF LOVE

God created love between a man and a woman. He gave it to us as a gift, a gift that should be kept pure and holy. Let us show our gratitude for this wonderful gift of love by appreciating our loved ones and honoring God through our actions.

Young Woman

[2]My lover has gone down to his garden,
    to his spice beds,
to browse in the gardens
    and gather the lilies.
[3]I am my lover's, and my lover is mine.
    He browses among the lilies.

Young Man

[4]You are beautiful, my darling,
    like the lovely city of Tirzah.
Yes, as beautiful as Jerusalem,
    as majestic as an army with billowing banners.
[5]Turn your eyes away,
    for they overpower me.
Your hair falls in waves,
    like a flock of goats winding down the slopes of Gilead.
[6]Your teeth are as white as sheep
    that are freshly washed.
Your smile is flawless,
    each tooth matched with its twin.
[7]Your cheeks are like rosy pomegranates
    behind your veil.

~ Song of Songs 6:2-7

It is vital for every believer to hear directly from God, especially if He is going to proclaim the gospel of Jesus Christ. God has a specific task in mind for each and every one of us. Whether you are called to proclaim the gospel or take care of the needy, you can be sure that God will give you what you need to perform your task.

¹It was in the year King Uzziah died that I saw the Lord. He was sitting on a lofty throne, and the train of his robe filled the Temple. ²Attending him were mighty seraphim, each having six wings. With two wings they covered their faces, with two they covered their feet, and with two they flew.

³They were calling out to each other,

"Holy, holy, holy is the LORD of Heaven's Armies!

The whole earth is filled with his glory!"

⁴Their voices shook the Temple to its foundations, and the entire building was filled with smoke.

⁵Then I said, "It's all over! I am doomed, for I am a sinful man. I have filthy lips, and I live among a people with filthy lips. Yet I have seen the King, the LORD of Heaven's Armies."

⁶Then one of the seraphim flew to me with a burning coal he had taken from the altar with a pair of tongs.

⁷He touched my lips with it and said, "See, this coal has touched your lips. Now your guilt is removed, and your sins are forgiven."

⁸Then I heard the Lord asking, "Whom should I send as a messenger to this people? Who will go for us?"

I said, "Here I am. Send me."

~ Isaiah 6:1-8

PEACE

It is through Jesus that we have a future hope, not in any earthly ruler, government or establishment. Our faith, hope and most importantly, our peace, comes from the Prince of Peace.

²The people who walk in darkness
　　will see a great light.
For those who live in a land of deep darkness,
　　a light will shine.
⁴For you will break the yoke of their slavery
　　and lift the heavy burden from their shoulders.
You will break the oppressor's rod,
　　just as you did when you destroyed the army of Midian.
⁵The boots of the warrior
　　and the uniforms bloodstained by war
will all be burned.
　　They will be fuel for the fire.
⁶For a child is born to us,
　　a son is given to us.
The government will rest on his shoulders.
　　And he will be called:
Wonderful Counselor, Mighty God,
　　Everlasting Father, Prince of Peace.
⁷His government and its peace
　　will never end.
He will rule with fairness and justice from the throne of his ancestor David for all eternity.
The passionate commitment of the Lord of Heaven's Armies
　　will make this happen!

~ Isaiah 9:2, 4-7

THE REIGN OF GOD

To think that Isaiah was written before the birth of Christ and yet it is so accurate and detailed. When the Prince of Peace comes, will there be peace on earth. He will make a highway for the believers in the last days just like He did for Israel by the Red Sea. What a comfort to know through all these years, God never changes.

[2]And the Spirit of the LORD will rest on him—
   the Spirit of wisdom and understanding,
the Spirit of counsel and might,
   the Spirit of knowledge and the fear of the LORD.
[6]In that day the wolf and the lamb will live together;
   the leopard will lie down with the baby goat.
The calf and the yearling will be safe with the lion,
   and a little child will lead them all.
[7]The cow will graze near the bear.
   The cub and the calf will lie down together.
   The lion will eat hay like a cow.
[8]The baby will play safely near the hole of a cobra.
   Yes, a little child will put its hand in a nest of deadly snakes
without harm.
[9]Nothing will hurt or destroy in all my holy mountain,
   for as the waters fill the sea,
   so the earth will be filled with people who know the LORD.

~ Isaiah 11:2, 6-9

FAITHFULNESS REWARDED

Perfect peace is found when we concentrate our minds on God. When we trust In Him, nothing in this world can move us. It is through Jehovah that we receive everlasting strength. The Lord is good to those who remain faithful to Him. As long as you keep your eyes on the Lord, you will stand firm.

[3]You will keep in perfect peace
  all who trust in you,
  all whose thoughts are fixed on you!
[4]Trust in the LORD always,
  for the LORD GOD is the eternal Rock.
[7]You are a God who does what is right,
  and you smooth out the path ahead of them.
[8]LORD, we show our trust in you by obeying your laws;
  our heart's desire is to glorify your name.
[12]LORD, you will grant us peace;
  all we have accomplished is really from you.
[15]O LORD, you have made our nation great;
  yes, you have made us great.
You have extended our borders,
  and we give you the glory!

~ Isaiah 26:3-4, 7-8, 12, 15

The Lord tells us that we need to obey Him. If we do that, we will be successful in whatever we put our hand to: in business, in our home and in the day-to-day living of life. The Lord is a good and wise teacher. He knows the best ways for us to go about completing our tasks.

23Listen to me;
   listen, and pay close attention.
24Does a farmer always plow and never sow?
   Is he forever cultivating the soil and never planting?
25Does he not finally plant his seeds—
   black cumin, cumin, wheat, barley, and emmer wheat—
each in its proper way,
   and each in its proper place?
26The farmer knows just what to do,
   for God has given him understanding.
27A heavy sledge is never used to thresh black cumin;
   rather, it is beaten with a light stick.
A threshing wheel is never rolled on cumin;
   instead, it is beaten lightly with a flail.
28Grain for bread is easily crushed,
   so he doesn't keep on pounding it.
He threshes it under the wheels of a cart,
   but he doesn't pulverize it.
29The LORD of Heaven's Armies is a wonderful teacher,
   and he gives the farmer great wisdom.

~ Isaiah 28:23-29

JUNE 15
GODLY GUIDANCE

If we are prepared to wait for the Lord, He will answer us and direct our paths. In verse 21, He says we shall hear a word behind us telling us clearly that this is the right way to walk. Whether we are experiencing adversity or prosperity, God will always be with us to guide and protect us. He is only a prayer away.

¹⁸So the LORD must wait for you to come to him
    so he can show you his love and compassion.
For the LORD is a faithful God.
    Blessed are those who wait for his help.
¹⁹O people of Zion, who live in Jerusalem,
    you will weep no more.
He will be gracious if you ask for help.
    He will surely respond to the sound of your cries.
²⁰Though the Lord gave you adversity for food
    and suffering for drink,
he will still be with you to teach you.
    You will see your teacher with your own eyes.
²¹Your own ears will hear him.
    Right behind you a voice will say,
"This is the way you should go,"
    whether to the right or to the left.

~ Isaiah 30:18-21

TRUST IN GOD ALONE

Never turn to the world or earthly things for guidance or help. You will only find yourself utterly disappointed. Rather turn to God, who is trustworthy, wise and eternal. Unlike the world, He can always be trusted to keep His word.

¹What sorrow awaits those who look to Egypt for help,
  trusting their horses, chariots, and charioteers
and depending on the strength of human armies
  instead of looking to the LORD,
  the Holy One of Israel.
²In his wisdom, the LORD will send great disaster;
  he will not change his mind.
He will rise against the wicked
  and against their helpers.
³For these Egyptians are mere humans, not God!
  Their horses are puny flesh, not mighty spirits!
When the LORD raises his fist against them,
  those who help will stumble,
and those being helped will fall.
  They will all fall down and die together.

~ Isaiah 31:1-3

THE HIGHWAY OF HOLINESS

God will transform the wastelands of your life into a beautiful, fruitful land. No matter how sad, lonely or sinful your past, God can change it. He can transform you and lead you on the Highway of Holiness that leads to heaven.

¹Even the wilderness and desert will be glad in those days.
　　The wasteland will rejoice and blossom with spring crocuses.
²Yes, there will be an abundance of flowers
　　and singing and joy!
The deserts will become as green as the mountains of Lebanon,
　　as lovely as Mount Carmel or the plain of Sharon.
There the LORD will display his glory,
　　the splendor of our God.
³With this news, strengthen those who have tired hands,
　　and encourage those who have weak knees.
⁴Say to those with fearful hearts,
　　"Be strong, and do not fear,
for your God is coming to destroy your enemies.
　　He is coming to save you."
⁸And a great road will go through that once deserted land.
　　It will be named the Highway of Holiness.

~ Isaiah 35:1-4, 8

ASSURANCE

Uncertainty is one of the most unpleasant things to experience. If you know God, however, you can always be certain of this: He will never go back on His word or break a promise. The Word of the Lord stands true forever.

¹"Comfort, comfort my people,"
   says your God.
²"Speak tenderly to Jerusalem.
Tell her that her sad days are gone
   and her sins are pardoned.
Yes, the LORD has punished her twice over
   for all her sins."
³Listen! It's the voice of someone shouting,
"Clear the way through the wilderness
   for the LORD!
Make a straight highway through the wasteland
   for our God!
⁴Fill in the valleys,
   and level the mountains and hills.
Straighten the curves,
   and smooth out the rough places.
⁵Then the glory of the LORD will be revealed,
   and all people will see it together.
   The LORD has spoken!"
⁸"The grass withers and the flowers fade,
   but the word of our God stands forever."

~ Isaiah 40:1-5, 8

NO EQUAL

The Lord has no equal. Nobody can match His wisdom, grace or strength. He knows what's in your heart and what you worry about. Worry no more, because the same God who created the heavens and the earth will give you strength like an eagle when you need it most.

25"To whom will you compare me?
   Who is my equal?" asks the Holy One.
26Look up into the heavens.
   Who created all the stars?
He brings them out like an army, one after another,
   calling each by its name.
Because of his great power and incomparable strength,
   not a single one is missing.
28Have you never heard?
   Have you never understood?
The Lord is the everlasting God,
   the Creator of all the earth.
He never grows weak or weary.
   No one can measure the depths of his understanding.
30Even youths will become weak and tired,
   and young men will fall in exhaustion.
31But those who trust in the Lord will find new strength.
   They will soar high on wings like eagles.
They will run and not grow weary.
   They will walk and not faint.

~ Isaiah 40:25-26, 28, 30-31

MY SERVANT

God chooses His servants. He knows exactly who to choose for which task, and when to choose them. So, if God calls you to perform a certain task, don't be fearful. He will give you what you need to do it.

8"But as for you, Israel my servant,
Jacob my chosen one,
descended from Abraham my friend,
9I have called you back from the ends of the earth,
saying, 'You are my servant.'
For I have chosen you
and will not throw you away.
10Don't be afraid, for I am with you.
Don't be discouraged, for I am your God.
I will strengthen you and help you.
I will hold you up with my victorious right hand.
13For I hold you by your right hand—
I, the LORD your God.
And I say to you,
'Don't be afraid. I am here to help you.'"

~ Isaiah 41:8-10, 13

OUR REDEEMER

The Lord will always come through for us. Whether you are struggling with financial or health problems, know that no obstacle is too big for the Lord. With Him by your side you can make it through even the worst times.

[1]But now, O Jacob, listen to the LORD who created you.
    O Israel, the one who formed you says,
"Do not be afraid, for I have ransomed you.
    I have called you by name; you are mine.
[2]When you go through deep waters,
    I will be with you.
When you go through rivers of difficulty,
    you will not drown.
When you walk through the fire of oppression,
    you will not be burned up;
    the flames will not consume you.
[3]For I am the LORD, your God,
    the Holy One of Israel, your Savior.
I gave Egypt as a ransom for your freedom;
    I gave Ethiopia and Seba in your place."

~ Isaiah 43:1-3

LOOK TO THE FUTURE

The Lord has done remarkable things in the past. The good news is that the future will see even more of His wonderful deeds and miracles. The Lord wants us to remember His past works, but He also wants us to look to the future with hope and anticipation.

¹⁶I am the Lord, who opened a way through the waters,
　　making a dry path through the sea.
¹⁷I called forth the mighty army of Egypt
　　with all its chariots and horses.
I drew them beneath the waves, and they drowned,
　　their lives snuffed out like a smoldering candlewick.
¹⁸"But forget all that—
　　it is nothing compared to what I am going to do.
¹⁹For I am about to do something new.
　　See, I have already begun! Do you not see it?
I will make a pathway through the wilderness.
　　I will create rivers in the dry wasteland.
²⁰The wild animals in the fields will thank me,
　　the jackals and owls, too,
　　for giving them water in the desert.
Yes, I will make rivers in the dry wasteland
　　so my chosen people can be refreshed.
²¹I have made Israel for myself,
　　and they will someday honor me before the whole world."

~ Isaiah 43:16-21

ONLY ONE SAVIOR

There is only one God and He alone can grant us eternal salvation. He is the ruler over all, yet He still cares for us and looks after us. All we need to do is look to Him to save us and lead us in life.

¹⁷But the LORD will save the people of Israel
    with eternal salvation.
Throughout everlasting ages,
    they will never again be humiliated and disgraced.
¹⁸For the LORD is God,
    and he created the heavens and earth
    and put everything in place.
He made the world to be lived in,
    not to be a place of empty chaos.
"I am the LORD," he says,
    "and there is no other.
¹⁹I publicly proclaim bold promises.
    I do not whisper obscurities in some dark corner.
I would not have told the people of Israel to seek me
    if I could not be found.
I, the LORD, speak only what is true
    and declare only what is right."
²²Let all the world look to me for salvation!
    For I am God; there is no other.

~ Isaiah 45:17-19, 22

ALWAYS THE SAME

God reassures us that He has always been God and that He will always be God. He has been there since the beginning of time and He knows everything about us. But, unlike us, He never changes and always remains trustworthy and faithful.

³"Listen to me, descendants of Jacob,
    all you who remain in Israel.
I have cared for you since you were born.
    Yes, I carried you before you were born.
⁴I will be your God throughout your lifetime—
    until your hair is white with age.
I made you, and I will care for you.
    I will carry you along and save you.

⁵"To whom will you compare me?
    Who is my equal?
⁶Some people pour out their silver and gold
    and hire a craftsman to make a god from it.
    Then they bow down and worship it!
⁹Remember the things I have done in the past.
    For I alone am God!
    I am God, and there is none like me.
¹⁰Only I can tell you the future
    before it even happens.
Everything I plan will come to pass,
    for I do whatever I wish."

~ Isaiah 46:3-6, 9-10

THE LAMB OF GOD

Jesus did not come to earth as a king or an important leader. He came to earth as an ordinary, humble man. He chose to be among His people, not above them. He made the ultimate sacrifice when He took our sins upon Himself in order to secure eternal life for us.

⁶All of us, like sheep, have strayed away.
    We have left God's paths to follow our own.
Yet the LORD laid on him
    the sins of us all.
⁷He was oppressed and treated harshly,
    yet he never said a word.
He was led like a lamb to the slaughter.
    And as a sheep is silent before the shearers,
    he did not open his mouth.
⁸Unjustly condemned,
    he was led away.
⁹He had done no wrong
    and had never deceived anyone.
¹⁰But it was the LORD's good plan to crush him
    and cause him grief.
Yet when his life is made an offering for sin,
    he will have many descendants.
He will enjoy a long life,
    and the LORD's good plan will prosper in his hands.

~ Isaiah 53:6-10

THE GUARANTEE

The Word of God guarantees us that no weapon used against us will prosper. We do not have to stand up and defend ourselves, because the Lord says He will defend us. If Christ is for us, we have nothing to fear.

14"You will be secure under a government that is just and fair.
  Your enemies will stay far away.
You will live in peace,
  and terror will not come near.
15If any nation comes to fight you,
  it is not because I sent them.
  Whoever attacks you will go down in defeat.
17But in that coming day
  no weapon turned against you will succeed.
You will silence every voice
  raised up to accuse you.
These benefits are enjoyed by the servants of the LORD;
  their vindication will come from me.
  I, the LORD, have spoken!"

~ Isaiah 54:14-15, 17

GOD'S THOUGHTS

God says that every word that goes out His mouth will not return to Him empty, but it will accomplish what He intends it to. God's Word is powerful and His promises hold true.

[8]"My thoughts are nothing like your thoughts," says the LORD.
   "And my ways are far beyond anything you could imagine.
[9]For just as the heavens are higher than the earth,
   so my ways are higher than your ways
   and my thoughts higher than your thoughts.
[10]"The rain and snow come down from the heavens
   and stay on the ground to water the earth.
They cause the grain to grow,
   producing seed for the farmer
   and bread for the hungry.
[11]It is the same with my word.
   I send it out, and it always produces fruit.
It will accomplish all I want it to,
   and it will prosper everywhere I send it.
[12]You will live in joy and peace.
   The mountains and hills will burst into song,
   and the trees of the field will clap their hands!
[13]Where once there were thorns, cypress trees will grow.
   Where nettles grew, myrtles will sprout up.
These events will bring great honor to the LORD's name;
   they will be an everlasting sign of his power and love."

~ Isaiah 55:8-13

DIRECTIVE FROM THE LORD

This is a very clear directive from the Lord as to how we should live. The kind of fasting He has called us to is: breaking the bonds of wickedness, undoing heavy burdens, freeing the oppressed, and taking care of those in need. He says that if we do this, the Lord will be our guide and when we call He will answer.

⁶"No, this is the kind of fasting I want:
Free those who are wrongly imprisoned;
   lighten the burden of those who work for you.
Let the oppressed go free,
   and remove the chains that bind people.
¹⁰Feed the hungry,
   and help those in trouble.
Then your light will shine out from the darkness,
   and the darkness around you will be as bright as noon.
¹¹The LORD will guide you continually,
   giving you water when you are dry
   and restoring your strength.
¹³"Keep the Sabbath day holy.
   Don't pursue your own interests on that day,
but enjoy the Sabbath
   and speak of it with delight as the LORD's holy day.
¹⁴Then the LORD will be your delight.
   I will give you great honor
and satisfy you with the inheritance I promised to your ancestor Jacob.
   I, the LORD, have spoken!"

~ Isaiah 58:6, 10-11, 13-14

DEFENDER

The Lord is a God of justice. He helps the oppressed and destitute and punishes those who oppress them. The Lord defends those who can't help themselves and who look to Him for help. He will always look out for His children.

¹⁵The Lᴏʀᴅ looked and was displeased
  to find there was no justice.
¹⁶He was amazed to see that no one intervened
  to help the oppressed.
So he himself stepped in to save them with his strong arm,
  and his justice sustained him.
¹⁷He put on righteousness as his body armor
  and placed the helmet of salvation on his head.
He clothed himself with a robe of vengeance
  and wrapped himself in a cloak of divine passion.
¹⁸He will repay his enemies for their evil deeds.
  His fury will fall on his foes.
  He will pay them back even to the ends of the earth.
¹⁹In the west, people will respect the name of the Lᴏʀᴅ;
  in the east, they will glorify him.
For he will come like a raging flood tide
  driven by the breath of the Lᴏʀᴅ.
²⁰"The Redeemer will come to Jerusalem
  to buy back those in Israel
who have turned from their sins,"
  says the Lᴏʀᴅ.
²¹"And this is my covenant with them," says the Lᴏʀᴅ. "My Spirit will not leave them, and neither will these words I have given you."

~ Isaiah 59:15-21

SERVING GOD

We need to thank God for the opportunity He has given us to serve Him and to become His children. We need to arise and let our lights shine in this dark world. Be an ambassador for Christ and spread His Word.

[1]"Arise, Jerusalem! Let your light shine for all to see.
  For the glory of the LORD rises to shine on you.
[2]Darkness as black as night covers all the nations of the earth,
  but the glory of the LORD rises and appears over you.
[3]All nations will come to your light;
  mighty kings will come to see your radiance.

[4]"Look and see, for everyone is coming home!
  Your sons are coming from distant lands;
  your little daughters will be carried home.
[5]Your eyes will shine,
  and your heart will thrill with joy,
for merchants from around the world will come to you.
  They will bring you the wealth of many lands."

~ Isaiah 60:1-5

JULY

THE LORD'S PROMISE

The Lord repeats His promise that He will take care of His people. He doesn't like to see His people treated badly and promises to reward them for their suffering. The Lord will treat us in such a way that everybody will see that He is a gracious and caring God.

8"For I, the LORD, love justice.
    I hate robbery and wrongdoing.
I will faithfully reward my people for their suffering
    and make an everlasting covenant with them.
9Their descendants will be recognized
    and honored among the nations.
Everyone will realize that they are a people
    the LORD has blessed."
10I am overwhelmed with joy in the LORD my God!
    For he has dressed me with the clothing of salvation
    and draped me in a robe of righteousness.
I am like a bridegroom in his wedding suit
    or a bride with her jewels.
11The Sovereign LORD will show his justice to the nations of the world.
    Everyone will praise him!
His righteousness will be like a garden in early spring,
    with plants springing up everywhere.

~ Isaiah 61:8-11

THE CALL

When the Lord calls us, we often come up with excuses: I am too young; I am not educated; I am shy. God uses ordinary people to do His work. When He calls someone, He also equips them. When God calls you, don't make excuses, get started!

[4]The Lord gave me this message:

[5]"I knew you before I formed you in your mother's womb.

Before you were born I set you apart

and appointed you as my prophet to the nations."

[6]"O Sovereign Lord," I said, "I can't speak for you! I'm too young!"

[7]The Lord replied, "Don't say, 'I'm too young,' for you must go wherever I send you and say whatever I tell you. [8]And don't be afraid of the people, for I will be with you and will protect you. I, the Lord, have spoken!" [9]Then the Lord reached out and touched my mouth and said,

"Look, I have put my words in your mouth!

[10]Today I appoint you to stand up

against nations and kingdoms.

Some you must uproot and tear down,

destroy and overthrow.

Others you must build up

and plant."

[11]Then the Lord said to me, "Look, Jeremiah! What do you see?"

And I replied, "I see a branch from an almond tree."

[12]And the Lord said, "That's right, and it means that I am watching, and I will certainly carry out all my plans."

~ Jeremiah 1:4-12

TRUST ONLY IN GOD

When we place our trust in man and the flesh, we will fail. But those who trust the Lord will be blessed in times of recession, political unrest and disaster. The only one who will never let us down or betray our trust is the Lord Jesus Christ. As soon as we surrender our lives to Him, we will prosper.

⁵This is what the LORD says:
"Cursed are those who put their trust in mere humans,
    who rely on human strength
    and turn their hearts away from the LORD.
⁶They are like stunted shrubs in the desert,
    with no hope for the future.
They will live in the barren wilderness,
    in an uninhabited salty land.
⁷"But blessed are those who trust in the LORD
    and have made the LORD their hope and confidence.
⁸They are like trees planted along a riverbank,
    with roots that reach deep into the water.
Such trees are not bothered by the heat
    or worried by long months of drought.
Their leaves stay green,
    and they never stop producing fruit."

~ Jeremiah 17:5-8

THE POTTER

When God sent Jeremiah to the potter's home to watch how he made vessels out of clay, He showed Jeremiah that He is the Potter and we are the clay. He will shape and reshape us until we are the beautiful vessel He wants us to be.

¹The LORD gave another message to Jeremiah. He said, ²"Go down to the potter's shop, and I will speak to you there."

³So I did as he told me and found the potter working at his wheel.

⁴But the jar he was making did not turn out as he had hoped, so he crushed it into a lump of clay again and started over.

⁵Then the LORD gave me this message:

⁶"O Israel, can I not do to you as this potter has done to his clay? As the clay is in the potter's hand, so are you in my hand.

⁷If I announce that a certain nation or kingdom is to be uprooted, torn down, and destroyed, ⁸but then that nation renounces its evil ways, I will not destroy it as I had planned.

⁹And if I announce that I will plant and build up a certain nation or kingdom, ¹⁰but then that nation turns to evil and refuses to obey me, I will not bless it as I said I would.

¹¹"Therefore, Jeremiah, go and warn all Judah and Jerusalem. Say to them, 'This is what the LORD says: I am planning disaster for you instead of good. So turn from your evil ways, each of you, and do what is right.'"

~ Jeremiah 18:1-11

NEVER LOSE HOPE

We must have a passion to tell other people about Jesus. Jeremiah could not hold back because it was like a fire in his heart. Even though he was mocked and ridiculed, he spread God's message of salvation.

[7]O LORD, you misled me,
and I allowed myself to be misled.
You are stronger than I am,
and you overpowered me.
Now I am mocked every day;
everyone laughs at me.
[8]When I speak, the words burst out.
"Violence and destruction!" I shout.
So these messages from the LORD
have made me a household joke.
[9]But if I say I'll never mention the LORD
or speak in his name,
his word burns in my heart like a fire.
It's like a fire in my bones!
I am worn out trying to hold it in!
I can't do it!
[10]I have heard the many rumors about me.
They call me "The Man Who Lives in Terror."
They threaten, "If you say anything, we will report it."
Even my old friends are watching me,
waiting for a fatal slip.
"He will trap himself," they say,
"and then we will get our revenge on him."

~ Jeremiah 20:7-10

FALSE PROPHETS

We should beware of false prophets. There are many people who claim that God speaks to them in some way, when they are actually just making it up as they go along. We must ensure that we are not misled by these false prophets and that we always follow the true Word of God.

[25]"I have heard these prophets say, 'Listen to the dream I had from God last night.' And then they proceed to tell lies in my name. [26]How long will this go on? If they are prophets, they are prophets of deceit, inventing everything they say. [27]By telling these false dreams, they are trying to get my people to forget me, just as their ancestors did by worshiping the idols of Baal.

[28]"Let these false prophets tell their dreams,
    but let my true messengers faithfully proclaim my every word.
    There is a difference between straw and grain!
[29]Does not my word burn like fire?"
    says the LORD.
"Is it not like a mighty hammer
    that smashes a rock to pieces?

[30]"Therefore," says the LORD, "I am against these prophets who steal messages from each other and claim they are from me. [31]I am against these smooth-tongued prophets who say, 'This prophecy is from the LORD!' [32]I am against these false prophets. Their imaginary dreams are flagrant lies that lead my people into sin. I did not send or appoint them, and they have no message at all for my people. I, the LORD, have spoken!"

~ Jeremiah 23:25-32

FOR US

Our God is for us and not against us. Our God will make a place for us even in the times of oppression and even when we feel like we are in a desert. He says that His thoughts toward us are of peace and not of evil. We must continue to call upon Him and He will listen.

⁴This is what the LORD of Heaven's Armies, the God of Israel, says to all the captives he has exiled to Babylon from Jerusalem: ⁵"Build homes, and plan to stay. Plant gardens, and eat the food they produce. ⁶Marry and have children. Then find spouses for them so that you may have many grandchildren. Multiply! Do not dwindle away! ⁷And work for the peace and prosperity of the city where I sent you into exile. Pray to the LORD for it, for its welfare will determine your welfare."

⁸This is what the LORD of Heaven's Armies, the God of Israel, says: "Do not let your prophets and fortune-tellers who are with you in the land of Babylon trick you. Do not listen to their dreams, ⁹because they are telling you lies in my name. I have not sent them," says the LORD.

¹⁰This is what the LORD says: "You will be in Babylon for seventy years. But then I will come and do for you all the good things I have promised, and I will bring you home again. ¹¹For I know the plans I have for you," says the LORD. "They are plans for good and not for disaster, to give you a future and a hope. ¹²In those days when you pray, I will listen. ¹³If you look for me wholeheartedly, you will find me. ¹⁴I will be found by you," says the LORD. "I will end your captivity and restore your fortunes. I will gather you out of the nations where I sent you and will bring you home again to your own land."

~ Jeremiah 29:4-14

JULY 8
CALL ON HIM

We should never be afraid to approach the Lord, because He will listen to those who call on Him. Jeremiah 33:3 is like God's telephone number. He is never too busy and His phone is never engaged. When you call Him, He will show you great and mighty things. Don't hesitate to reach out to the Lord.

¹While Jeremiah was still confined in the courtyard of the guard, the LORD gave him this second message:

²"This is what the LORD says—the LORD who made the earth, who formed and established it, whose name is the LORD:

³Ask me and I will tell you remarkable secrets you do not know about things to come.

¹⁴"The day will come, says the LORD, when I will do for Israel and Judah all the good things I have promised them.

¹⁵"In those days and at that time

I will raise up a righteous descendant from King David's line.

He will do what is just and right throughout the land.

¹⁶In that day Judah will be saved,

and Jerusalem will live in safety.

And this will be its name:

'The LORD Is Our Righteousness.'"

~ Jeremiah 33:1-3, 14-16

GREAT FAITHFULNESS

God's promises and His mercies definitely do not fail. They are new every morning. When we feel like we can't face tomorrow, we wake up in the morning, and the Lord has been our portion and our prayers have been answered. Just trust Him. People often make promises they don't keep. God is not like this. His promises and mercies will never fail.

²²The faithful love of the LORD never ends!
  His mercies never cease.
²³Great is his faithfulness;
  his mercies begin afresh each morning.
²⁴I say to myself, "The LORD is my inheritance;
  therefore, I will hope in him!"
²⁵The LORD is good to those who depend on him,
  to those who search for him.
²⁶So it is good to wait quietly
  for salvation from the LORD.
⁵⁷Yes, you came when I called;
  you told me, "Do not fear."
⁵⁸Lord, you are my lawyer! Plead my case!
  For you have redeemed my life.
⁵⁹You have seen the wrong they have done to me, LORD.
  Be my judge, and prove me right.

~ Lamentations 3:22-26, 57-59

THE WATCHMAN

As believers, we have an obligation to share the gospel with unbelievers. When we see those in dire straits and we do not warn them to turn from their wicked ways, their lives will be upon us.

¹⁶After seven days the LORD gave me a message. He said, ¹⁷"Son of man, I have appointed you as a watchman for Israel. Whenever you receive a message from me, warn people immediately. ¹⁸If I warn the wicked, saying, 'You are under the penalty of death,' but you fail to deliver the warning, they will die in their sins. And I will hold you responsible for their deaths. ¹⁹If you warn them and they refuse to repent and keep on sinning, they will die in their sins. But you will have saved yourself because you obeyed me.

²⁰"If righteous people turn away from their righteous behavior and ignore the obstacles I put in their way, they will die. And if you do not warn them, they will die in their sins. None of their righteous acts will be remembered, and I will hold you responsible for their deaths. ²¹But if you warn righteous people not to sin and they listen to you and do not sin, they will live, and you will have saved yourself, too."

²⁴Then the Spirit came into me and set me on my feet. He spoke to me and said, "Go to your house and shut yourself in. ²⁵There, son of man, you will be tied with ropes so you cannot go out among the people. ²⁷But when I give you a message, I will loosen your tongue and let you speak. Then you will say to them, 'This is what the Sovereign LORD says!' Those who choose to listen will listen, but those who refuse will refuse, for they are rebels."

~ Ezekiel 3:16-21, 24-25, 27

The Lord has no pleasure in unbelievers dying and would rather see them repent and turn from their wicked ways. We must make sure that we truly accept Jesus Christ, so that when we die, we will enter into eternal life. Make things right with the Lord, while you still have time.

¹⁹"What?' you ask. 'Doesn't the child pay for the parent's sins?' No! For if the child does what is just and right and keeps my decrees, that child will surely live. ²⁰The person who sins is the one who will die. The child will not be punished for the parent's sins, and the parent will not be punished for the child's sins. Righteous people will be rewarded for their own righteous behavior, and wicked people will be punished for their own wickedness. ²¹But if wicked people turn away from all their sins and begin to obey my decrees and do what is just and right, they will surely live and not die. ²²All their past sins will be forgotten, and they will live because of the righteous things they have done.

²³"Do you think that I like to see wicked people die? says the Sovereign LORD. Of course not! I want them to turn from their wicked ways and live.

³⁰"Therefore, I will judge each of you, O people of Israel, according to your actions, says the Sovereign LORD. Repent, and turn from your sins. Don't let them destroy you! ³¹Put all your rebellion behind you, and find yourselves a new heart and a new spirit. For why should you die, O people of Israel? ³²I don't want you to die, says the Sovereign LORD. Turn back and live!"

~ Ezekiel 18:19-23, 30-32

JULY 12
WORLDY GOODS

Are you concerned about your investments, your possessions, your achievements in life? The Lord is more important than anything in this world. Never allow worldly goods to become more important than the Lord.

[15]"You were blameless in all you did
   from the day you were created
   until the day evil was found in you.
[16]Your rich commerce led you to violence,
   and you sinned.
So I banished you in disgrace
   from the mountain of God.
I expelled you, O mighty guardian,
   from your place among the stones of fire.
[17]Your heart was filled with pride
   because of all your beauty.
Your wisdom was corrupted
   by your love of splendor."

~ Ezekiel 28:15-17

BE ALERT

As believers, we need to understand that we have an urgent responsibility to warn people of the danger of not knowing God. Like the watchman, we must sound the alarm before it's too late. Be alert, and make sure that you are also ready for eternity.

[2]"Son of man, give your people this message: 'When I bring an army against a country, the people of that land choose one of their own to be a watchman. [3]When the watchman sees the enemy coming, he sounds the alarm to warn the people. [4]Then if those who hear the alarm refuse to take action, it is their own fault if they die. [5]They heard the alarm but ignored it, so the responsibility is theirs. If they had listened to the warning, they could have saved their lives. [6]But if the watchman sees the enemy coming and doesn't sound the alarm to warn the people, he is responsible for their captivity. They will die in their sins, but I will hold the watchman responsible for their deaths.'

[7]"Now, son of man, I am making you a watchman for the people of Israel. Therefore, listen to what I say and warn them for me. [8]If I announce that some wicked people are sure to die and you fail to tell them to change their ways, then they will die in their sins, and I will hold you responsible for their deaths. [9]But if you warn them to repent and they don't repent, they will die in their sins, but you will have saved yourself.

[10]"Son of man, give the people of Israel this message: You are saying, 'Our sins are heavy upon us; we are wasting away! How can we survive?' [11]As surely as I live, says the Sovereign Lord, I take no pleasure in the death of wicked people. I only want them to turn from their wicked ways so they can live. Turn! Turn from your wickedness."

~ Ezekiel 33:2-11

SHEPHERDS

The Lord is very clear that He holds spiritual leaders responsible for caring for their flock. A leader who does not take care of his followers properly will be rebuked by the Lord. If you are responsible for leading a group of believers, be sure that you honor your responsibility.

¹Then this message came to me from the LORD: ²"Son of man, prophesy against the shepherds, the leaders of Israel. Give them this message from the Sovereign LORD: What sorrow awaits you shepherds who feed yourselves instead of your flocks. Shouldn't shepherds feed their sheep? ³You drink the milk, wear the wool, and butcher the best animals, but you let your flocks starve. ⁴You have not taken care of the weak. You have not tended the sick or bound up the injured. You have not gone looking for those who have wandered away and are lost. Instead, you have ruled them with harshness and cruelty. ⁵So my sheep have been scattered without a shepherd, and they are easy prey for any wild animal. ⁶They have wandered through all the mountains and all the hills, across the face of the earth, yet no one has gone to search for them.

⁷"Therefore, you shepherds, hear the word of the LORD: ⁸As surely as I live, says the Sovereign LORD, you abandoned my flock and left them to be attacked by every wild animal. And though you were my shepherds, you didn't search for my sheep when they were lost. You took care of yourselves and left the sheep to starve. ⁹Therefore, you shepherds, hear the word of the LORD. ¹⁰This is what the Sovereign LORD says: I now consider these shepherds my enemies, and I will hold them responsible for what has happened to my flock."

~ Ezekiel 34:1-10

DRY BONES

The Word of God brings life. Just as the dry bones came to life when Ezekiel spoke the Word of God over them, so we will come alive when we hear and truly seek God's Word.

⁴Then he said to me, "Speak a prophetic message to these bones and say, 'Dry bones, listen to the word of the LORD! ⁵This is what the Sovereign LORD says: Look! I am going to put breath into you and make you live again! ⁶I will put flesh and muscles on you and cover you with skin. I will put breath into you, and you will come to life. Then you will know that I am the LORD.'"

⁷So I spoke this message, just as he told me. Suddenly as I spoke, there was a rattling noise all across the valley. The bones of each body came together and attached themselves as complete skeletons. ⁸Then as I watched, muscles and flesh formed over the bones. Then skin formed to cover their bodies, but they still had no breath in them.

⁹Then he said to me, "Speak a prophetic message to the winds, son of man. Speak a prophetic message and say, 'This is what the Sovereign LORD says: Come, O breath, from the four winds! Breathe into these dead bodies so they may live again.'"

¹⁰So I spoke the message as he commanded me, and breath came into their bodies. They all came to life and stood up on their feet—a great army.

¹¹Then he said to me, "Son of man, these bones represent the people of Israel. They are saying, 'We have become old, dry bones—all hope is gone. Our nation is finished.' ¹²Therefore, prophesy to them and say, 'This is what the Sovereign LORD says: O my people, I will open your graves of exile and cause you to rise again. Then I will bring you back to the land of Israel.'"

~ Ezekiel 37:4-12

GOD'S COUNSEL

As instruments of God, it is important that we seek His counsel. Often we seek advice from worldly things, when our only help can come from the Lord. Let us remember at all times that we have God's wisdom at our disposal. All we need to do is ask Him.

¹⁶Daniel went at once to see the king and requested more time to tell the king what the dream meant.

¹⁷Then Daniel went home and told his friends Hananiah, Mishael, and Azariah what had happened. ¹⁸He urged them to ask the God of heaven to show them his mercy by telling them the secret, so they would not be executed along with the other wise men of Babylon. ¹⁹That night the secret was revealed to Daniel in a vision. Then Daniel praised the God of heaven. ²⁰He said,

"Praise the name of God forever and ever,
    for he has all wisdom and power.
²¹He controls the course of world events;
    he removes kings and sets up other kings.
He gives wisdom to the wise
    and knowledge to the scholars.
²²He reveals deep and mysterious things
    and knows what lies hidden in darkness,
    though he is surrounded by light.
²³I thank and praise you, God of my ancestors,
    for you have given me wisdom and strength.
You have told me what we asked of you
    and revealed to us what the king demanded."

~ Daniel 2:16-23

NO COMPROMISE

Shadrach, Meshach and Abednego refused to worship anyone or anything except God. They weren't prepared to make any compromises to save their own lives. In your life, strive to be like these brave men.

⁹They said to King Nebuchadnezzar, "Long live the king! ¹⁰You issued a decree requiring all the people to bow down and worship the gold statue when they hear the sound of the horn, flute, zither, lyre, harp, pipes, and other musical instruments. ¹¹That decree also states that those who refuse to obey must be thrown into a blazing furnace. ¹²But there are some Jews— Shadrach, Meshach, and Abednego. They refuse to serve your gods and do not worship the gold statue you have set up."

¹³Then Nebuchadnezzar flew into a rage and ordered that Shadrach, Meshach, and Abednego be brought before him. When they were brought in, ¹⁴Nebuchadnezzar said to them, "Is it true, Shadrach, Meshach, and Abednego, that you refuse to serve my gods or to worship the gold statue I have set up? ¹⁵I will give you one more chance to bow down and worship the statue I have made when you hear the sound of the musical instruments. But if you refuse, you will be thrown immediately into the blazing furnace. And then what god will be able to rescue you from my power?"

¹⁶Shadrach, Meshach, and Abednego replied, "O Nebuchadnezzar, we do not need to defend ourselves before you. ¹⁷If we are thrown into the blazing furnace, the God whom we serve is able to save us. He will rescue us from your power, Your Majesty. ¹⁸But even if he doesn't, we want to make it clear to you, Your Majesty, that we will never serve your gods or worship the gold statue you have set up."

~ Daniel 3:9-18

GOD HONORS HIS OWN

Daniel's refusal to worship any gods except the God of Israel caused him to land up in the lions' den. God, however, saved him and honored Daniel's strong and immovable faith. God will never forsake those who are willing to take a stand for Him.

¹⁰But when Daniel learned that the law had been signed, he went home and knelt down as usual in his upstairs room, with its windows open toward Jerusalem. He prayed three times a day, just as he had always done, giving thanks to his God. ¹⁶So at last the king gave orders for Daniel to be arrested and thrown into the den of lions. The king said to him, "May your God, whom you serve so faithfully, rescue you."

¹⁷A stone was brought and placed over the mouth of the den. The king sealed the stone with his own royal seal and the seals of his nobles, so that no one could rescue Daniel.

¹⁸Then the king returned to his palace and spent the night fasting. He refused his usual entertainment and couldn't sleep at all that night.

¹⁹Very early the next morning, the king got up and hurried out to the lions' den. ²⁰When he got there, he called out in anguish, "Daniel, servant of the living God! Was your God, whom you serve so faithfully, able to rescue you from the lions?"

²¹Daniel answered, "Long live the king! ²²My God sent his angel to shut the lions' mouths so that they would not hurt me, for I have been found innocent in his sight. And I have not wronged you, Your Majesty."

²³The king was overjoyed and ordered that Daniel be lifted from the den. Not a scratch was found on him, for he had trusted in his God.

~ Daniel 6:10, 16-23

A WONDERFUL PROMISE

This is a wonderful promise from our Lord that if we repent and come to Him, He will forgive our backsliding and love us freely. He promises to renew us and not be angry. Let us understand these things, for the ways of the Lord are right.

² Bring your confessions, and return to the LORD.
  Say to him,
"Forgive all our sins and graciously receive us,
  so that we may offer you our praises."
⁴The LORD says,
"Then I will heal you of your faithlessness;
  my love will know no bounds,
  for my anger will be gone forever.
⁵I will be to Israel
  like a refreshing dew from heaven.
Israel will blossom like the lily;
  it will send roots deep into the soil
  like the cedars in Lebanon.
⁸"O Israel, stay away from idols!
  I am the one who answers your prayers and cares for you.
I am like a tree that is always green;
  all your fruit comes from me."
⁹Let those who are wise understand these things.
  Let those with discernment listen carefully.
The paths of the LORD are true and right,
  and righteous people live by walking in them.
  But in those paths sinners stumble and fall.

~ Hosea 14:2, 4-5, 8-9

REPENTANCE

The Lord wants us to repent from our sinful ways and return to Him. He wants to grant us His grace and favor, but before He can do this, we must return to Him. As soon as we do this, we will experience the Lord's forgiveness and grace.

¹²That is why the LORD says,
   "Turn to me now, while there is time.
Give me your hearts.
   Come with fasting, weeping, and mourning.
¹³Don't tear your clothing in your grief,
   but tear your hearts instead."
Return to the LORD your God,
   for he is merciful and compassionate,
slow to get angry and filled with unfailing love.
   He is eager to relent and not punish.
¹⁸Then the LORD will pity his people
   and jealously guard the honor of his land.
¹⁹The LORD will reply,
"Look! I am sending you grain and new wine and olive oil,
   enough to satisfy your needs.
You will no longer be an object of mockery
   among the surrounding nations."

~ Joel 2:12-13, 18-19

NO ESCAPE

The Lord challenges you and me to depend on Him and Him alone. We should not try to run from Him, but rather repent, return to Him, and give Him total control over our lives.

6Come back to the LORD and live!
7You twist justice, making it a bitter pill for the oppressed.
   You treat the righteous like dirt.
8It is the LORD who created the stars,
   the Pleiades and Orion.
He turns darkness into morning
   and day into night.
He draws up water from the oceans
   and pours it down as rain on the land.
   The LORD is his name!
14Do what is good and run from evil
   so that you may live!
Then the LORD God of Heaven's Armies will be your helper,
   just as you have claimed.
15Hate evil and love what is good;
   turn your courts into true halls of justice.
Perhaps even yet the LORD God of Heaven's Armies
   will have mercy on the remnant of his people.

~ Amos 5:6-8, 14-15

GOD OF JUSTICE

God is a God of justice and righteousness. The sins of the nations will not go unpunished. Now is the time to turn to Him in repentance. Pray for the leaders, husbands and fathers of this nation.

¹³You should not have plundered the land of Israel
  when they were suffering such calamity.
You should not have gloated over their destruction
  when they were suffering such calamity.
You should not have seized their wealth
  when they were suffering such calamity.
¹⁴You should not have stood at the crossroads,
  killing those who tried to escape.
You should not have captured the survivors
  and handed them over in their terrible time of trouble.
¹⁵"The day is near when I, the LORD,
  will judge all godless nations!
As you have done to Israel,
  so it will be done to you.
All your evil deeds will fall back on your own heads.
¹⁶Just as you swallowed up my people
  on my holy mountain,
so you and the surrounding nations
  will swallow the punishment I pour out on you.
Yes, all you nations will drink and stagger
  and disappear from history.
¹⁷"But Jerusalem will become a refuge for those who escape;
  it will be a holy place.
And the people of Israel will come back
  to reclaim their inheritance."

~ Obadiah 1:13-17

MERCY AND FORGIVENESS

Jonah disobeyed God and landed up in a big fish's belly. Jonah did the best thing he could in this predicament: he prayed. God was merciful and forgave Jonah's disobedience. God always hears our prayers.

¹Then Jonah prayed to the LORD his God from inside the fish. ²He said, "I cried out to the LORD in my great trouble, and he answered me. I called to you from the land of the dead, and LORD, you heard me!

³You threw me into the ocean depths, and I sank down to the heart of the sea.

The mighty waters engulfed me; I was buried beneath your wild and stormy waves.

⁴Then I said, 'O LORD, you have driven me from your presence.
    Yet I will look once more toward your holy Temple.'

⁵"I sank beneath the waves, and the waters closed over me.
    Seaweed wrapped itself around my head.

⁶I sank down to the very roots of the mountains. I was imprisoned in the earth, whose gates lock shut forever.

But you, O LORD my God, snatched me from the jaws of death! ⁷As my life was slipping away, I remembered the LORD. And my earnest prayer went out to you in your holy Temple.

⁸Those who worship false gods
    turn their backs on all God's mercies.

⁹But I will offer sacrifices to you with songs of praise,
    and I will fulfill all my vows.

    For my salvation comes from the LORD alone."

¹⁰Then the LORD ordered the fish to spit Jonah out onto the beach.

~ Jonah 2:1-10

LET GOD DO THE REST

When Jonah finally obeyed God, the Ninevites repented and turned from their ways. Jonah became angry at God's mercy. So often in our lives we feel that things are not fair, but we serve a very merciful God, who has forgiven us.

⁴On the day Jonah entered the city, he shouted to the crowds: "Forty days from now Nineveh will be destroyed!" ⁵The people of Nineveh believed God's message.

4This change of plans greatly upset Jonah, and he became very angry. ²So he complained to the LORD about it: "Didn't I say before I left home that you would do this, LORD? That is why I ran away to Tarshish! I knew that you are a merciful and compassionate God, slow to get angry and filled with unfailing love. ³Just kill me now, LORD! I'd rather be dead than alive if what I predicted will not happen."

⁵Then Jonah went out to the east side of the city and made a shelter to sit under. ⁶And the LORD God arranged for a leafy plant to grow there, shading him from the sun. This eased his discomfort, and Jonah was very grateful for the plant.

⁷But God also arranged for a worm! The next morning at dawn the worm ate through the stem of the plant so that it withered away.

⁹Then God said to Jonah, "Is it right for you to be angry because the plant died?"

¹⁰Then the LORD said, "You feel sorry about the plant, though you did nothing to put it there. It came quickly and died quickly.

But Nineveh has more than 120,000 people. Shouldn't I feel sorry for such a great city?"

~ Jonah 3:4-5; 4:1-3, 5-7, 9-10

A LIFE OF HONOR

Micah 6:8 tells us how God expects us to live. As Christian men, husbands and fathers, we must choose right over wrong, mercy over judgment and humility over pride. If we do this, we will honor God and our families.

[3]"O my people, what have I done to you?
   What have I done to make you tired of me? Answer me!
[4]For I brought you out of Egypt and redeemed you from slavery.
   I sent Moses, Aaron, and Miriam to help you.
[5]Don't you remember, my people,
   how King Balak of Moab tried to have you cursed
   and how Balaam son of Beor blessed you instead?
And remember your journey from Acacia Grove to Gilgal,
   when I, the LORD, did everything I could
   to teach you about my faithfulness."
[6]What can we bring to the LORD?
   What kind of offerings should we give him?
Should we bow before God with offerings of yearling calves?
[7]Should we offer him thousands of rams
   and ten thousand rivers of olive oil?
Should we sacrifice our firstborn children to pay for our sins?
[8]No, O people, the LORD has told you what is good,
   and this is what he requires of you: to do what is right, to love mercy, and to walk humbly with your God.

~ Micah 6:3-8

OUR GRACIOUS GOD

Nahum captures God's greatness, righteousness and mercy. How marvelous to know that God, who causes the oceans to dry up and the earth to tremble, hears our prayers and is merciful towards us.

¹This message concerning Nineveh came as a vision to Nahum, who lived in Elkosh.

²The LORD is a jealous God, filled with vengeance and rage.
He takes revenge on all who oppose him
    and continues to rage against his enemies!

³The LORD is slow to get angry, but his power is great,
    and he never lets the guilty go unpunished.
He displays his power in the whirlwind and the storm.
    The billowing clouds are the dust beneath his feet.

⁴At his command the oceans dry up, and the rivers disappear.
The lush pastures of Bashan and Carmel fade,
    and the green forests of Lebanon wither.

⁵In his presence the mountains quake, and the hills melt away;
the earth trembles, and its people are destroyed.

⁶Who can stand before his fierce anger?
    Who can survive his burning fury?
His rage blazes forth like fire,
    and the mountains crumble to dust in his presence.

⁷The LORD is good,
    a strong refuge when trouble comes.
    He is close to those who trust in him.

⁸But he will sweep away his enemies
    in an overwhelming flood.
He will pursue his foes
    into the darkness of night.

~ Nahum 1:1-8

PATIENCE AND FAITH

God will never let us down. Even when everything seems to go wrong, be patient, because at the appointed time He will reveal His plan. Until He does, we need to keep on working together as believers to spread His message to the world.

²How long, O Lord, must I call for help?
 But you do not listen!
"Violence is everywhere!" I cry,
 but you do not come to save.
⁴The law has become paralyzed,
 and there is no justice in the courts.
The wicked far outnumber the righteous,
 so that justice has become perverted.
2 I will climb up to my watchtower
 and stand at my guardpost.
There I will wait to see what the Lord says
 and how he will answer my complaint.
²Then the Lord said to me,
"Write my answer plainly on tablets,
 so that a runner can carry the correct message to others.
³This vision is for a future time.
 It describes the end, and it will be fulfilled.
If it seems slow in coming, wait patiently,
 for it will surely take place.
 It will not be delayed.
⁴"Look at the proud!
 They trust in themselves, and their lives are crooked.
 But the righteous will live by their faithfulness to God."

~ Habakkuk 1:2, 4; 2:1-4

UNCONDITIONAL JOY

Our joy shouldn't depend on material things or on our circumstances. Instead, our joy should be in the Lord. We simply need to rejoice in the Lord, because He is our God, our strength, and our hope.

¹I have heard all about you, LORD.
    I am filled with awe by your amazing works.
In this time of our deep need,
    help us again as you did in years gone by.
And in your anger,
    remember your mercy.
¹⁷Even though the fig trees have no blossoms,
    and there are no grapes on the vines;
even though the olive crop fails,
    and the fields lie empty and barren;
even though the flocks die in the fields,
    and the cattle barns are empty,
¹⁸yet I will rejoice in the LORD!
    I will be joyful in the God of my salvation!
¹⁹The Sovereign LORD is my strength!
    He makes me as surefooted as a deer,
    able to tread upon the heights.

~ Habakkuk 3:1, 17-19

IN GOD'S PRESENCE

The Lord loves us! He doesn't want to see us drift away from Him, which is why He welcomes us back with open arms when we turn from our wicked ways. Because of the Lord's great mercy, we are able to enter into God's presence with no fear of rejection.

[10]"My scattered people who live beyond the rivers of Ethiopia
will come to present their offerings.
[11]On that day you will no longer need to be ashamed,
for you will no longer be rebels against me.
I will remove all proud and arrogant people from among you.
There will be no more haughtiness on my holy mountain.
[12]Those who are left will be the lowly and humble,
for it is they who trust in the name of the LORD.
[13]The remnant of Israel will do no wrong;
they will never tell lies or deceive one another.
They will eat and sleep in safety,
and no one will make them afraid."
[14]Sing, O daughter of Zion;
shout aloud, O Israel!
Be glad and rejoice with all your heart,
O daughter of Jerusalem!
[15]For the LORD will remove his hand of judgment
and will disperse the armies of your enemy.
And the LORD himself, the King of Israel,
will live among you!

~ Zephaniah 3:10-15

FOCUS ON THE TASK

Those who walk in God's ways will have peace and purpose. We need to work hard and serve Him. He will take care of the rest. The Lord has called each one of us to perform a specific task. We should not be concerned about where finance or support will come from, we must only concentrate on our task. Just trust the Lord.

³"Does anyone remember this house—this Temple—in its former splendor? How, in comparison, does it look to you now? It must seem like nothing at all!

⁴But now the LORD says: Be strong, Zerubbabel. Be strong, Jeshua son of Jehozadak, the high priest. Be strong, all you people still left in the land. And now get to work, for I am with you, says the LORD of Heaven's Armies. ⁵My Spirit remains among you, just as I promised when you came out of Egypt. So do not be afraid.'

⁶"For this is what the LORD of Heaven's Armies says: In just a little while I will again shake the heavens and the earth, the oceans and the dry land.

⁷I will shake all the nations, and the treasures of all the nations will be brought to this Temple. I will fill this place with glory, says the LORD of Heaven's Armies. ⁸The silver is mine, and the gold is mine, says the LORD of Heaven's Armies.

⁹The future glory of this Temple will be greater than its past glory, says the LORD of Heaven's Armies. And in this place I will bring peace. I, the LORD of Heaven's Armies, have spoken!"

~ Haggai 2:3-9

ONLY BY THE LORD

"Not by strength, but by My Spirit," says the Lord. We can do everything in our power to make a project work, but we will only succeed if we hand it over to the Lord. He will level our mountains. He is the only one who can truly change lives.

⁵"Don't you know?" the angel asked.

"No, my lord," I replied.

⁶Then he said to me, "This is what the LORD says to Zerubbabel: It is not by force nor by strength, but by my Spirit, says the LORD of Heaven's Armies.

⁷Nothing, not even a mighty mountain, will stand in Zerubbabel's way; it will become a level plain before him! And when Zerubbabel sets the final stone of the Temple in place, the people will shout: 'May God bless it! May God bless it!'"

⁸Then another message came to me from the LORD:

⁹"Zerubbabel is the one who laid the foundation of this Temple, and he will complete it. Then you will know that the LORD of Heaven's Armies has sent me.

¹⁰Do not despise these small beginnings, for the LORD rejoices to see the work begin, to see the plumb line in Zerubbabel's hand."

(The seven lamps represent the eyes of the LORD that search all around the world.)

~ Zechariah 4:5-10

AUGUST

AUGUST 1
DON'T ROB GOD

The Lord is very clear that we must not try to cheat Him by withholding our tithes. We need to give Him a tenth of what we have, cheerfully, and then He will pour out His blessing on us. Give to the Lord to show Him your appreciation, not to gain more.

[6]"I am the LORD, and I do not change. That is why you descendants of Jacob are not already destroyed. [7]Ever since the days of your ancestors, you have scorned my decrees and failed to obey them. Now return to me, and I will return to you," says the LORD of Heaven's Armies.

"But you ask, 'How can we return when we have never gone away?'

[8]"Should people cheat God? Yet you have cheated me!

"But you ask, 'What do you mean? When did we ever cheat you?'

"You have cheated me of the tithes and offerings due to me. [9]You are under a curse, for your whole nation has been cheating me. [10]Bring all the tithes into the storehouse so there will be enough food in my Temple. If you do," says the LORD of Heaven's Armies, "I will open the windows of heaven for you. I will pour out a blessing so great you won't have enough room to take it in! Try it! Put me to the test! [11]Your crops will be abundant, for I will guard them from insects and disease. Your grapes will not fall from the vine before they are ripe," says the LORD of Heaven's Armies. [12]"Then all nations will call you blessed, for your land will be such a delight," says the LORD of Heaven's Armies.

~ Malachi 3:6-12

ON HIS WAY

There is urgency in this Scripture passage. The Lord is on His way! We need to be ready and prepare the way for the Lord, by turning the hearts of fathers to their children and the hearts of children to their fathers.

¹The LORD of Heaven's Armies says, "The day of judgment is coming, burning like a furnace. On that day the arrogant and the wicked will be burned up like straw. They will be consumed— roots, branches, and all.

²"But for you who fear my name, the Sun of Righteousness will rise with healing in his wings. And you will go free, leaping with joy like calves let out to pasture. ³On the day when I act, you will tread upon the wicked as if they were dust under your feet," says the LORD of Heaven's Armies.

⁴"Remember to obey the Law of Moses, my servant—all the decrees and regulations that I gave him on Mount Sinai for all Israel.

⁵"Look, I am sending you the prophet Elijah before the great and dreadful day of the LORD arrives. ⁶His preaching will turn the hearts of fathers to their children, and the hearts of children to their fathers. Otherwise I will come and strike the land with a curse."

~ Malachi 4:1-6

THE BIRTH OF JESUS

Jesus' birth was nothing short of a miracle. First of all, a virgin became pregnant, then God sent an angel to tell Joseph to stay with Mary and that her pregnancy was from the Holy Spirit. Only those who have faith will be able to believe that Jesus is truly our Savior.

[18]This is how Jesus the Messiah was born. His mother, Mary, was engaged to be married to Joseph. But before the marriage took place, while she was still a virgin, she became pregnant through the power of the Holy Spirit. [19]Joseph, her fiancé, was a good man and did not want to disgrace her publicly, so he decided to break the engagement quietly.

[20]As he considered this, an angel of the Lord appeared to him in a dream. "Joseph, son of David," the angel said, "do not be afraid to take Mary as your wife. For the child within her was conceived by the Holy Spirit. [21]And she will have a son, and you are to name him Jesus, for he will save his people from their sins."

[22]All of this occurred to fulfill the Lord's message through his prophet:

[23]"Look! The virgin will conceive a child!
    She will give birth to a son,
and they will call him Immanuel,
    which means 'God is with us.'"

[24]When Joseph woke up, he did as the angel of the Lord commanded and took Mary as his wife. [25]But he did not have sexual relations with her until her son was born. And Joseph named him Jesus.

~ Matthew 1:18-25

TO EGYPT

God looked out for Jesus once again when He sent an angel to tell Joseph to flee to Egypt in order to escape Herod's evil plan. God not only protected Jesus, He also protected us, because Jesus was born to save us from sin.

¹³After the wise men were gone, an angel of the Lord appeared to Joseph in a dream. "Get up! Flee to Egypt with the child and his mother," the angel said. "Stay there until I tell you to return, because Herod is going to search for the child to kill him."

¹⁴That night Joseph left for Egypt with the child and Mary, his mother, ¹⁵and they stayed there until Herod's death. This fulfilled what the Lord had spoken through the prophet: "I called my Son out of Egypt."

¹⁶Herod was furious when he realized that the wise men had outwitted him. He sent soldiers to kill all the boys in and around Bethlehem who were two years old and under, based on the wise men's report of the star's first appearance. ¹⁷Herod's brutal action fulfilled what God had spoken through the prophet Jeremiah:

¹⁸"A cry was heard in Ramah—
   weeping and great mourning.
Rachel weeps for her children,
   refusing to be comforted,
   for they are dead."

~ Matthew 2:13-18

THE BAPTIST

John the Baptist was responsible for preparing the way for Jesus. He baptized those who confessed their sins and repented. Jesus also asked John to baptize Him. Each one of us has a specific task to perform here on earth. Make sure that you follow God's will for you, because then you will successfully complete your task.

¹In those days John the Baptist came to the Judean wilderness and began preaching. His message was, ²"Repent of your sins and turn to God, for the Kingdom of Heaven is near." ³The prophet Isaiah was speaking about John when he said,

"He is a voice shouting in the wilderness,
'Prepare the way for the LORD's coming!
    Clear the road for him!'"

⁴John's clothes were woven from coarse camel hair, and he wore a leather belt around his waist. ⁵People from Jerusalem and from all of Judea and all over the Jordan Valley went out to see and hear John. ⁶And when they confessed their sins, he baptized them in the Jordan River.

¹³Then Jesus went from Galilee to the Jordan River to be baptized by John. ¹⁴But John tried to talk him out of it. "I am the one who needs to be baptized by you," he said, "so why are you coming to me?"

¹⁵But Jesus said, "It should be done, for we must carry out all that God requires." So John agreed to baptize him.

¹⁶After his baptism, as Jesus came up out of the water, the heavens were opened and he saw the Spirit of God descending like a dove and settling on him. ¹⁷And a voice from heaven said, "This is my dearly loved Son, who brings me great joy."

~ Matthew 3:1-6, 13-17

TEMPTATION

There is no sin in being tempted. The sin comes when we yield to temptation. Jesus was also tempted, so He understands how it feels. We are often tempted when doing great things for God. Do not be discouraged, because if the devil tempts us, it must mean we are doing something that annoys him.

¹Then Jesus was led by the Spirit into the wilderness to be tempted there by the devil. ²For forty days and forty nights he fasted and became very hungry.

³During that time the devil came and said to him, "If you are the Son of God, tell these stones to become loaves of bread."

⁴But Jesus told him, "No! The Scriptures say,

'People do not live by bread alone,

but by every word that comes from the mouth of God.'"

⁵Then the devil took him to the holy city, Jerusalem, to the highest point of the Temple, ⁶and said, "If you are the Son of God, jump off! For the Scriptures say,

'He will order his angels to protect you. And they will hold you up with their hands so you won't even hurt your foot on a stone.'"

⁷Jesus responded, "The Scriptures also say, 'You must not test the LORD your God.'"

⁸Next the devil took him to the peak of a very high mountain and showed him all the kingdoms of the world and their glory. ⁹"I will give it all to you," he said, "if you will kneel down and worship me."

¹⁰"Get out of here, Satan," Jesus told him. "For the Scriptures say, 'You must worship the LORD your God and serve only him.'"

¹¹Then the devil went away, and angels came and took care of Jesus.

~ Matthew 4:1-11

THE BEATITUDES

Jesus says that we will be rewarded if we continue to walk in the ways of God. We must rejoice, because our reward is in heaven, where moth and rust cannot destroy it. When you feel discouraged, remember the Lord's promise that your reward awaits you in heaven.

¹One day as he saw the crowds gathering, Jesus went up on the mountainside and sat down. His disciples gathered around him, ²and he began to teach them. ³"God blesses those who are poor and realize their need for him, for the Kingdom of Heaven is theirs.

⁴God blesses those who mourn,
> for they will be comforted.
⁵God blesses those who are humble,
> for they will inherit the whole earth.
⁶God blesses those who hunger and thirst for justice,
> for they will be satisfied.
⁷God blesses those who are merciful,
> for they will be shown mercy.
⁸God blesses those whose hearts are pure,
> for they will see God.
⁹God blesses those who work for peace,
> for they will be called the children of God.
¹⁰God blesses those who are persecuted for doing right,
> for the Kingdom of Heaven is theirs.

¹¹"God blesses you when people mock you and persecute you and lie about you and say all sorts of evil things against you because you are my followers. ¹²Be happy about it! Be very glad! For a great reward awaits you in heaven."

~ Matthew 5:1-12

THE MODEL PRAYER

Someone once said that when men work, men work, but when men pray, God works. In this passage, Jesus gives us the ultimate model prayer. God desires to communicate with us. He wants fellowship with us. Decide today to spend more time in prayer with Him.

⁵"When you pray, don't be like the hypocrites who love to pray publicly on street corners and in the synagogues where everyone can see them. I tell you the truth, that is all the reward they will ever get. ⁶But when you pray, go away by yourself, shut the door behind you, and pray to your Father in private. Then your Father, who sees everything, will reward you.

⁷"When you pray, don't babble on and on as people of other religions do. They think their prayers are answered merely by repeating their words again and again. ⁸Don't be like them, for your Father knows exactly what you need even before you ask him! ⁹Pray like this:

Our Father in heaven,
    may your name be kept holy.
¹⁰May your Kingdom come soon.
May your will be done on earth,
    as it is in heaven.
¹¹Give us today the food we need,
¹²and forgive us our sins,
    as we have forgiven those who sin against us.
¹³And don't let us yield to temptation,
    but rescue us from the evil one.

¹⁴"If you forgive those who sin against you, your heavenly Father will forgive you. ¹⁵But if you refuse to forgive others, your Father will not forgive your sins."

~ Matthew 6:5-15

AUGUST 9
DON'T JUDGE

Jesus was very clear about judgment. We should not judge others. We will be judged in the same way that we judge others. People who live in glass houses shouldn't throw stones. The Word of God says that we should take the log out of our own eye, before taking the speck out of someone else's eye.

[1]"Do not judge others, and you will not be judged.

[2]For you will be treated as you treat others. The standard you use in judging is the standard by which you will be judged.

[3]"And why worry about a speck in your friend's eye when you have a log in your own?

[4]How can you think of saying to your friend, 'Let me help you get rid of that speck in your eye,' when you can't see past the log in your own eye?

[5]Hypocrite! First get rid of the log in your own eye; then you will see well enough to deal with the speck in your friend's eye."

~ Matthew 7:1-5

BUILT ON THE ROCK

We should beware of false teachings. If we disobey God's Word, we will be like the foolish man who built his house on the sand, which eventually collapsed. If we obey God's Word, we will be like the wise man, who built a sturdy, immovable house on the rock that withstands all of the storms of life.

²⁴"Anyone who listens to my teaching and follows it is wise, like a person who builds a house on solid rock.

²⁵Though the rain comes in torrents and the floodwaters rise and the winds beat against that house, it won't collapse because it is built on bedrock.

²⁶But anyone who hears my teaching and doesn't obey it is foolish, like a person who builds a house on sand. ²⁷When the rains and floods come and the winds beat against that house, it will collapse with a mighty crash."

²⁸When Jesus had finished saying these things, the crowds were amazed at his teaching, ²⁹for he taught with real authority—quite unlike their teachers of religious law.

~ Matthew 7:24-29

DO YOU BELIEVE?

This is a classic example of God honoring men because of their persistence. The two blind men believed Jesus could heal them and He did! God requires us to exercise our faith and believe that He can and will answer prayer.

²⁷After Jesus left the girl's home, two blind men followed along behind him, shouting, "Son of David, have mercy on us!"

²⁸They went right into the house where he was staying, and Jesus asked them, "Do you believe I can make you see?"

"Yes, Lord," they told him, "we do."

²⁹Then he touched their eyes and said, "Because of your faith, it will happen."

³⁰Then their eyes were opened, and they could see! Jesus sternly warned them, "Don't tell anyone about this." ³¹But instead, they went out and spread his fame all over the region.

³²When they left, a demon-possessed man who couldn't speak was brought to Jesus.

³³So Jesus cast out the demon, and then the man began to speak. The crowds were amazed. "Nothing like this has ever happened in Israel!" they exclaimed.

³⁴But the Pharisees said, "He can cast out demons because he is empowered by the prince of demons."

~ Matthew 9:27-34

WHO IS MY FAMILY?

This Scripture passage is very serious about obedience. Although Jesus loved His mother and brothers very much, He considers those who obey God's will His mother and brothers. If we obey God's will and live lives that are pleasing to Him, we will become part of His eternal family.

⁴⁶As Jesus was speaking to the crowd, his mother and brothers stood outside, asking to speak to him.

⁴⁷Someone told Jesus, "Your mother and your brothers are outside, and they want to speak to you."

⁴⁸Jesus asked, "Who is my mother? Who are my brothers?" ⁴⁹Then he pointed to his disciples and said, "Look, these are my mother and brothers.

⁵⁰Anyone who does the will of my Father in heaven is my brother and sister and mother!"

~ Matthew 12:46-50

FOCUS ON JESUS

When Peter stepped out of the boat and walked toward Jesus on the water, he kept his eyes on Him. The moment that he looked away, he started to sink and the Lord had to save him. We really need to keep our eyes focused on the Lord if we want to walk on the water with Him.

²²Immediately after this, Jesus insisted that his disciples get back into the boat and cross to the other side of the lake, while he sent the people home. ²³After sending them home, he went up into the hills by himself to pray. Night fell while he was there alone.

²⁴Meanwhile, the disciples were in trouble far away from land, for a strong wind had risen, and they were fighting heavy waves. ²⁵About three o'clock in the morning Jesus came toward them, walking on the water.

²⁷But Jesus spoke to them at once. "Don't be afraid," he said. "Take courage. I am here!"

²⁸Then Peter called to him, "Lord, if it's really you, tell me to come to you, walking on the water."

²⁹"Yes, come," Jesus said.

So Peter went over the side of the boat and walked on the water toward Jesus. ³⁰But when he saw the strong wind and the waves, he was terrified and began to sink. "Save me, Lord!" he shouted.

³¹Jesus immediately reached out and grabbed him. "You have so little faith," Jesus said. "Why did you doubt me?"

³²When they climbed back into the boat, the wind stopped. ³³Then the disciples worshiped him. "You really are the Son of God!" they exclaimed.

~ Matthew 14:22-25, 27-33

OBEY THE LAW

Even the Son of God obeyed the law and paid His taxes. As His children, we should follow His example and do the same. It is not our duty to decide when to pay taxes or who to pay it to or whether the government is worthy to receive it or not. All we must do is obey the law.

[24]On their arrival in Capernaum, the collectors of the Temple tax came to Peter and asked him, "Doesn't your teacher pay the Temple tax?"

[25]"Yes, he does," Peter replied. Then he went into the house.

But before he had a chance to speak, Jesus asked him, "What do you think, Peter? Do kings tax their own people or the people they have conquered?"

[26]"They tax the people they have conquered," Peter replied.

"Well, then," Jesus said, "the citizens are free!

[27]However, we don't want to offend them, so go down to the lake and throw in a line. Open the mouth of the first fish you catch, and you will find a large silver coin. Take it and pay the tax for both of us."

~ Matthew 17:24-27

THE LORD'S PREROGATIVE

The Lord used a beautiful parable here to show people that it is His prerogative to bless. The land owner paid all the workers the same wage, regardless of when they started work that day. Whether a man is saved early or late in his life, our only concern should be that he is saved.

¹"For the Kingdom of Heaven is like the landowner who went out early one morning to hire workers for his vineyard. ²He agreed to pay the normal daily wage and sent them out to work.

³"At nine o'clock in the morning he was passing through the marketplace and saw some people standing around doing nothing. ⁴So he hired them. At noon and again at three o'clock he did the same thing.

⁶"At five o'clock that afternoon he was in town again and saw some more people standing around. The landowner told them, 'Then go out and join the others in my vineyard.'

⁹"When those hired at five o'clock were paid, each received a full day's wage. ¹⁰When those hired first came to get their pay, they assumed they would receive more. But they, too, were paid a day's wage. ¹²'Those people worked only one hour, and yet you've paid them just as much as you paid us who worked all day in the scorching heat.'

¹³"He answered one of them, 'Friend, I haven't been unfair! Didn't you agree to work all day for the usual wage? ¹⁴Take your money and go. I wanted to pay this last worker the same as you. ¹⁵Is it against the law for me to do what I want with my money? Should you be jealous because I am kind to others?'

¹⁶"So those who are last now will be first then, and those who are first will be last."

~ Matthew 20:1-4, 6, 9-10, 12-16

People are constantly trying to predict the end of the world. God is very clear in the Bible that no man knows when the Lord will return, not even Jesus Himself. Only the Father knows. He warns us to be prepared, because we never know when He will come or when we will die. Be ready!

³⁶"However, no one knows the day or hour when these things will happen, not even the angels in heaven or the Son himself. Only the Father knows.

³⁷"When the Son of Man returns, it will be like it was in Noah's day. ³⁸In those days before the flood, the people were enjoying banquets and parties and weddings right up to the time Noah entered his boat. ³⁹People didn't realize what was going to happen until the flood came and swept them all away. That is the way it will be when the Son of Man comes.

⁴⁰"Two men will be working together in the field; one will be taken, the other left. ⁴¹Two women will be grinding flour at the mill; one will be taken, the other left.

⁴²"So you, too, must keep watch! For you don't know what day your Lord is coming. ⁴³Understand this: If a homeowner knew exactly when a burglar was coming, he would keep watch and not permit his house to be broken into. ⁴⁴You also must be ready all the time, for the Son of Man will come when least expected."

~ Matthew 24:36-44

IN THE GARDEN

Jesus was deeply troubled about what lay before Him. He knew the suffering that lay ahead, yet He said that God's will must be done. Praise God for saving us through Jesus' sacrifice.

³⁶Then Jesus went with them to the olive grove called Gethsemane, and he said, "Sit here while I go over there to pray." ³⁷He took Peter and Zebedee's two sons, James and John, and he became anguished and distressed. ³⁸He told them, "My soul is crushed with grief to the point of death. Stay here and keep watch with me."

³⁹He went on a little farther and bowed with his face to the ground, praying, "My Father! If it is possible, let this cup of suffering be taken away from me. Yet I want your will to be done, not mine."

⁴⁰Then he returned to the disciples and found them asleep. He said to Peter, "Couldn't you watch with me even one hour? ⁴¹Keep watch and pray, so that you will not give in to temptation. For the spirit is willing, but the body is weak!"

⁴²Then Jesus left them a second time and prayed, "My Father! If this cup cannot be taken away unless I drink it, your will be done." ⁴³When he returned to them again, he found them sleeping, for they couldn't keep their eyes open.

⁴⁴So he went to pray a third time, saying the same things again. ⁴⁵Then he came to the disciples and said, "Go ahead and sleep. Have your rest. But look—the time has come. The Son of Man is betrayed into the hands of sinners. ⁴⁶Up, let's be going. Look, my betrayer is here!"

~ Matthew 26:36-46

JESUS' SACRIFICE

If Jesus hadn't gone through with God's plan, we would all have been lost. Jesus went through terrible pain and suffering for us. He was tortured, forced to carry His own cross and ridiculed. Will we ever be able to grasp the love that the Lord has for us?

³²Along the way, they came across a man named Simon, who was from Cyrene, and the soldiers forced him to carry Jesus' cross. ³³And they went out to a place called Golgotha (which means "Place of the Skull"). ³⁴The soldiers gave him wine mixed with bitter gall, but when he had tasted it, he refused to drink it.

³⁵After they had nailed him to the cross, the soldiers gambled for his clothes by throwing dice. ³⁶Then they sat around and kept guard as he hung there. ³⁷A sign was fastened above Jesus' head, announcing the charge against him. It read: "This is Jesus, the King of the Jews." ³⁸Two revolutionaries were crucified with him, one on his right and one on his left.

³⁹The people passing by shouted abuse, shaking their heads in mockery. ⁴⁰"Look at you now!" they yelled at him. "You said you were going to destroy the Temple and rebuild it in three days. Well then, if you are the Son of God, save yourself and come down from the cross!"

⁴¹The leading priests, the teachers of religious law, and the elders also mocked Jesus. ⁴²"He saved others," they scoffed, "but he can't save himself! So he is the King of Israel, is he? Let him come down from the cross right now, and we will believe in him! ⁴³He trusted God, so let God rescue him now if he wants him! For he said, 'I am the Son of God.'" ⁴⁴Even the revolutionaries who were crucified with him ridiculed him in the same way.

~ Matthew 27:32-44

DEATH ON THE CROSS

What is most touching here is that the people who were faithfully standing by the cross were the womenfolk. Thank God for women – Mary Magdalene, Mary the mother of James and the mother of the Zebedee sons. We also, in this late hour, need to stand up for the Lord even if it means persecution.

⁴⁵At noon, darkness fell across the whole land until three o'clock. ⁴⁶At about three o'clock, Jesus called out with a loud voice, "Eli, Eli, lema sabachthani?" which means "My God, my God, why have you abandoned me?"

⁴⁷Some of the bystanders misunderstood and thought he was calling for the prophet Elijah. ⁴⁸One of them ran and filled a sponge with sour wine, holding it up to him on a reed stick so he could drink. ⁴⁹But the rest said, "Wait! Let's see whether Elijah comes to save him."

⁵⁰Then Jesus shouted out again, and he released his spirit. ⁵¹At that moment the curtain in the sanctuary of the Temple was torn in two, from top to bottom. The earth shook, rocks split apart, ⁵²and tombs opened. The bodies of many godly men and women who had died were raised from the dead. ⁵³They left the cemetery after Jesus' resurrection, went into the holy city of Jerusalem, and appeared to many people.

⁵⁴The Roman officer and the other soldiers at the crucifixion were terrified by the earthquake and all that had happened. They said, "This man truly was the Son of God!"

⁵⁵And many women who had come from Galilee with Jesus to care for him were watching from a distance. ⁵⁶Among them were Mary Magdalene, Mary (the mother of James and Joseph), and the mother of James and John, the sons of Zebedee.

~ Matthew 27:45-56

JESUS IS BURIED

Joseph of Arimathea and Nicodemus, two followers of Jesus, took Him off the cross and buried Him according to Jewish custom. This was a very sad time for Jesus' followers. We, however, do not need to be sad when someone passes away, because Jesus, through His death, has made eternal life a reality for all who believe.

⁵⁷As evening approached, Joseph, a rich man from Arimathea who had become a follower of Jesus, ⁵⁸went to Pilate and asked for Jesus' body. And Pilate issued an order to release it to him. ⁵⁹Joseph took the body and wrapped it in a long sheet of clean linen cloth. ⁶⁰He placed it in his own new tomb, which had been carved out of the rock. Then he rolled a great stone across the entrance and left. ⁶¹Both Mary Magdalene and the other Mary were sitting across from the tomb and watching.

~ Matthew 27:57-61

THE GREAT COMMISSION

This is a victorious chapter in the Bible. Jesus is raised from the dead! He gives us a serious and sincere commission – to go into the world and preach the gospel to every person, baptizing them in the name of the Father, the Son and the Holy Spirit. He promised that He will be with us until the end. What a blessing!

[5] "I know you are looking for Jesus, who was crucified. [6]He isn't here! He is risen from the dead, just as he said would happen. Come, see where his body was lying. [7]And now, go quickly and tell his disciples that he has risen from the dead, and he is going ahead of you to Galilee. You will see him there. Remember what I have told you."

[8]The women ran quickly from the tomb. They were very frightened but also filled with great joy, and they rushed to give the disciples the angel's message. [9]And as they went, Jesus met them and greeted them. And they ran to him, grasped his feet, and worshiped him. [10]Then Jesus said to them, "Don't be afraid! Go tell my brothers to leave for Galilee, and they will see me there."

[16]Then the eleven disciples left for Galilee, going to the mountain where Jesus had told them to go. [17]When they saw him, they worshiped him—but some of them doubted!

[18]Jesus came and told his disciples, "I have been given all authority in heaven and on earth. [19]Therefore, go and make disciples of all the nations, baptizing them in the name of the Father and the Son and the Holy Spirit. [20]Teach these new disciples to obey all the commands I have given you. And be sure of this: I am with you always, even to the end of the age."

~ Matthew 28:5-10, 16-20

THE SABBATH

In this Scripture passage, Jesus explains to the Pharisees that the Sabbath is there for man and not man
for the Sabbath. We must never allow the law and
traditions to become more important than people.
Follow Jesus' example and do good every day.

²³One Sabbath day as Jesus was walking through some grain-
fields, his disciples began breaking off heads of grain to eat.
²⁴But the Pharisees said to Jesus, "Look, why are they breaking
the law by harvesting grain on the Sabbath?"

²⁵Jesus said to them, "Haven't you ever read in the Scriptures
what David did when he and his companions were hungry?
²⁶He went into the house of God (during the days when Abiathar
was high priest) and broke the law by eating the sacred loaves
of bread that only the priests are allowed to eat. He also gave
some to his companions."

²⁷Then Jesus said to them, "The Sabbath was made to meet
the needs of people, and not people to meet the requirements
of the Sabbath. ²⁸So the Son of Man is Lord, even over the
Sabbath!"

~ Mark 2:23-28

REJECTED AT HOME

Jesus wasn't accepted and loved everywhere He went. The people of His hometown, Nazareth, rejected Him. Still, Jesus carried on doing the work that God had sent Him to do. We shouldn't get discouraged when we are met with opposition, even when it is by those closest to us. We need to keep going and complete our godly task.

[31] Then Jesus' mother and brothers came to see him. They stood outside and sent word for him to come out and talk with them. [32] There was a crowd sitting around Jesus, and someone said, "Your mother and your brothers are outside asking for you."

[33] Jesus replied, "Who is my mother? Who are my brothers?" [34] Then he looked at those around him and said, "Look, these are my mother and brothers. [35] Anyone who does God's will is my brother and sister and mother."

~ Mark 3:31-35

THE MIRACLE WORKER

This Scripture passage is of great encouragement to farmers. There have been many instances of miracles on farms, where God turned back a fire or brought renewing rain. All you need to do is humble yourself and pray. God is indeed the miracle worker.

35As evening came, Jesus said to his disciples, "Let's cross to the other side of the lake." 36So they took Jesus in the boat and started out, leaving the crowds behind (although other boats followed).

37But soon a fierce storm came up. High waves were breaking into the boat, and it began to fill with water.

38Jesus was sleeping at the back of the boat with his head on a cushion. The disciples woke him up, shouting, "Teacher, don't you care that we're going to drown?"

39When Jesus woke up, he rebuked the wind and said to the waves, "Silence! Be still!" Suddenly the wind stopped, and there was a great calm.

40Then he asked them, "Why are you afraid? Do you still have no faith?"

41The disciples were absolutely terrified. "Who is this man?" they asked each other. "Even the wind and waves obey him!"

~ Mark 4:35-41

BLIND BARTIMAEUS

Bartimaeus knew he only had one chance to catch Jesus' attention. He persisted until Jesus heard him and never doubted that Jesus could heal him. Jesus saw his faith and granted his request. We need to be more persistent when asking God for a miracle.

⁴⁶Then they reached Jericho, and as Jesus and his disciples left town, a large crowd followed him. A blind beggar named Bartimaeus (son of Timaeus) was sitting beside the road. ⁴⁷When Bartimaeus heard that Jesus of Nazareth was nearby, he began to shout, "Jesus, Son of David, have mercy on me!"

⁴⁸"Be quiet!" many of the people yelled at him.

But he only shouted louder, "Son of David, have mercy on me!"

⁴⁹When Jesus heard him, he stopped and said, "Tell him to come here."

So they called the blind man. "Cheer up," they said. "Come on, he's calling you!" ⁵⁰Bartimaeus threw aside his coat, jumped up, and came to Jesus.

⁵¹"What do you want me to do for you?" Jesus asked.

"My rabbi," the blind man said, "I want to see!"

⁵²And Jesus said to him, "Go, for your faith has healed you." Instantly the man could see, and he followed Jesus down the road.

~ Mark 10:46-52

THE GREATEST LAW

The Lord says clearly that the greatest commandment is that you must love the Lord your God with your all your heart, soul and might. He also said that it was just as important to love your neighbor as yourself. These two commandments form God's mandate for us.

²⁸One of the teachers of religious law was standing there listening to the debate. He realized that Jesus had answered well, so he asked, "Of all the commandments, which is the most important?"

²⁹Jesus replied, "The most important commandment is this: 'Listen, O Israel! The LORD our God is the one and only LORD. ³⁰And you must love the LORD your God with all your heart, all your soul, all your mind, and all your strength.' ³¹The second is equally important: 'Love your neighbor as yourself.' No other commandment is greater than these."

³²The teacher of religious law replied, "Well said, Teacher. You have spoken the truth by saying that there is only one God and no other. ³³And I know it is important to love him with all my heart and all my understanding and all my strength, and to love my neighbor as myself. This is more important than to offer all of the burnt offerings and sacrifices required in the law."

³⁴Realizing how much the man understood, Jesus said to him, "You are not far from the Kingdom of God." And after that, no one dared to ask him any more questions.

~ Mark 12:28-34

JESUS NEVER FORGETS

The passage about Christ's resurrection touches us so deeply. The Lord knew that because Peter denied Him three times, he probably felt wretched. But the Lord said, "Tell the disciples and Peter that I will meet them in Galilee." The Lord will never forget you. It does not matter what you have done, if you repent like Peter did, God will forgive you.

¹Saturday evening, when the Sabbath ended, Mary Magdalene, Mary the mother of James, and Salome went out and purchased burial spices so they could anoint Jesus' body. ²Very early on Sunday morning, just at sunrise, they went to the tomb. ³On the way they were asking each other, "Who will roll away the stone for us from the entrance to the tomb?" ⁴But as they arrived, they looked up and saw that the stone, which was very large, had already been rolled aside.

⁵When they entered the tomb, they saw a young man clothed in a white robe sitting on the right side. The women were shocked, ⁶but the angel said, "Don't be alarmed. You are looking for Jesus of Nazareth, who was crucified. He isn't here! He is risen from the dead! Look, this is where they laid his body. ⁷Now go and tell his disciples, including Peter, that Jesus is going ahead of you to Galilee. You will see him there, just as he told you before he died."

⁸The women fled from the tomb, trembling and bewildered, and they said nothing to anyone because they were too frightened. Then they briefly reported all this to Peter and his companions. Afterward Jesus himself sent them out from east to west with the sacred and unfailing message of salvation that gives eternal life. Amen.

~ Mark 16:1-8

THE ELEMENTS OBEY HIM

The disciples were petrified and worried that their boat would sink. They woke Jesus, who was asleep in the boat. Jesus rebuked the wind and immediately the sea was calm. The disciples were amazed! Our God is so powerful that even the elements obey Him.

²²One day Jesus said to his disciples, "Let's cross to the other side of the lake." So they got into a boat and started out.

²³As they sailed across, Jesus settled down for a nap. But soon a fierce storm came down on the lake. The boat was filling with water, and they were in real danger.

²⁴The disciples went and woke him up, shouting, "Master, Master, we're going to drown!"

When Jesus woke up, he rebuked the wind and the raging waves. Suddenly the storm stopped and all was calm.

²⁵Then he asked them, "Where is your faith?"

The disciples were terrified and amazed. "Who is this man?" they asked each other. "When he gives a command, even the wind and waves obey him!"

~ Luke 8:22-25

TAKE UP YOUR CROSS

There is a price to pay to be a follower of Jesus. There are some people who want to serve the Lord on their own terms, without committing, and that is not possible. The whole meaning of the cross is dying to self. If we want to follow Him, we need to deny ourselves, take up our cross and follow Him.

23Then he said to the crowd, "If any of you wants to be my follower, you must turn from your selfish ways, take up your cross daily, and follow me. 24If you try to hang on to your life, you will lose it. But if you give up your life for my sake, you will save it. 25And what do you benefit if you gain the whole world but are yourself lost or destroyed? 26If anyone is ashamed of me and my message, the Son of Man will be ashamed of that person when he returns in his glory and in the glory of the Father and the holy angels. 27I tell you the truth, some standing here right now will not die before they see the Kingdom of God."

~ Luke 9:23-27

THE WORDS TO SAY

Jesus warned the disciples that persecution was coming. He said that they should not worry about what to say when they have to speak, because He would give them the right words. The same is true for us. When we are unsure of what to do or say, we need not worry, because the Lord will guide us.

³Now go, and remember that I am sending you out as lambs among wolves.

⁵"Whenever you enter someone's home, first say, 'May God's peace be on this house.' ⁶If those who live there are peaceful, the blessing will stand; if they are not, the blessing will return to you. ⁷Don't move around from home to home. Stay in one place, eating and drinking what they provide. Don't hesitate to accept hospitality, because those who work deserve their pay.

⁸"If you enter a town and it welcomes you, eat whatever is set before you. ⁹Heal the sick, and tell them, 'The Kingdom of God is near you now.'"

¹⁶Then he said to the disciples, "Anyone who accepts your message is also accepting me. And anyone who rejects you is rejecting me. And anyone who rejects me is rejecting God, who sent me."

¹⁷When the seventy-two disciples returned, they joyfully reported to him, "Lord, even the demons obey us when we use your name!" ¹⁸"Yes," he told them, "I saw Satan fall from heaven like lightning! ¹⁹Look, I have given you authority over all the power of the enemy, and you can walk among snakes and scorpions and crush them. Nothing will injure you. ²⁰But don't rejoice because evil spirits obey you; rejoice because your names are registered in heaven."

~ Luke 10:3, 5-9, 16-20

FORGIVING AGAIN AND AGAIN

One of the hardest things to do is to forgive someone who has trespassed against you more than once. God will give you the compassion, mercy and love to forgive someone who has trespassed against you repeatedly. God's grace is sufficient for you and me. His strength is made perfect in weakness.

¹One day Jesus said to his disciples, "There will always be temptations to sin, but what sorrow awaits the person who does the tempting! ²It would be better to be thrown into the sea with a millstone hung around your neck than to cause one of these little ones to fall into sin. ³So watch yourselves!

`If another believer sins, rebuke that person; then if there is repentance, forgive. ⁴Even if that person wrongs you seven times a day and each time turns again and asks forgiveness, you must forgive."

⁵The apostles said to the Lord, "Show us how to increase our faith."

⁶The Lord answered, "If you had faith even as small as a mustard seed, you could say to this mulberry tree, 'May you be uprooted and thrown into the sea,' and it would obey you!"

~ Luke 17:1-6

SEPTEMBER

THE WORD

Jesus is the Word. The more time we spend in the Word of God, the more we will become like the Master. This Bible is the only book that never ages. It is called the Living Word because it is alive. It states that the universe came into being with a word. That Word is God, Jesus Christ and the Holy Spirit.

[1]In the beginning the Word already existed.
  The Word was with God,
  and the Word was God.
[2]He existed in the beginning with God.
[3]God created everything through him,
and nothing was created except through him.
[4]The Word gave life to everything that was created,
  and his life brought light to everyone.
[5]The light shines in the darkness,
  and the darkness can never extinguish it.

[6]God sent a man, John the Baptist, [7]to tell about the light so that everyone might believe because of his testimony. [8]John himself was not the light; he was simply a witness to tell about the light. [9]The one who is the true light, who gives light to everyone, was coming into the world.

[10]He came into the very world he created, but the world didn't recognize him. [11]He came to his own people, and even they rejected him. [12]But to all who believed him and accepted him, he gave the right to become children of God. [13]They are reborn—not with a physical birth resulting from human passion or plan, but a birth that comes from God. [14]So the Word became human and made his home among us.

~ John 1:1-14

BREAD OF LIFE

Is there a hunger inside your soul for the Bread of Life today? Are you struggling to put bread on the table to feed your family? Then I have good news for you. Jesus says, "I am the bread of life." Believe in Him, and ask Him to provide you with your daily bread, physically and spiritually. Jesus promises that whoever comes to Him will never go hungry.

[35]Jesus replied, "I am the bread of life. Whoever comes to me will never be hungry again. Whoever believes in me will never be thirsty. [36]But you haven't believed in me even though you have seen me. [37]However, those the Father has given me will come to me, and I will never reject them. [38]For I have come down from heaven to do the will of God who sent me, not to do my own will. [39]And this is the will of God, that I should not lose even one of all those he has given me, but that I should raise them up at the last day. [40]For it is my Father's will that all who see his Son and believe in him should have eternal life. I will raise them up at the last day."

~ John 6:35-40

THROUGH EVERY BATTLE

Jesus Christ, the Son of the Living God, is our Lord and Savior. But He Is also God. He will be at our side through the toughest battles we will ever face, and in our darkest hour He will be there. He is before all things, and in Him all things hold together. We serve a great God!

²²It was now winter, and Jesus was in Jerusalem at the time of Hanukkah, the Festival of Dedication.

²³He was in the Temple, walking through the section known as Solomon's Colonnade. ²⁴The people surrounded him and asked, "How long are you going to keep us in suspense? If you are the Messiah, tell us plainly."

²⁵Jesus replied, "I have already told you, and you don't believe me. The proof is the work I do in my Father's name. ²⁶But you don't believe me because you are not my sheep. ²⁷My sheep listen to my voice; I know them, and they follow me. ²⁸I give them eternal life, and they will never perish. No one can snatch them away from me, ²⁹for my Father has given them to me, and he is more powerful than anyone else. No one can snatch them from the Father's hand. ³⁰The Father and I are one."

~ John 10:22-30

SEPTEMBER 4
NO GREATER LOVE

Jesus loves us so much that He laid down His life for us. He says, "I'm going to give you all the power you need. Get out there and do the job. Set the captives free. Heal the broken-hearted. Proclaim My gospel." That is what we should do today.

[9]"I have loved you even as the Father has loved me. Remain in my love. [10]When you obey my commandments, you remain in my love, just as I obey my Father's commandments and remain in his love. [11]I have told you these things so that you will be filled with my joy. Yes, your joy will overflow! [12]This is my commandment: Love each other in the same way I have loved you. [13]There is no greater love than to lay down one's life for one's friends. [14]You are my friends if you do what I command. [15]I no longer call you slaves, because a master doesn't confide in his slaves. Now you are my friends, since I have told you everything the Father told me. [16]You didn't choose me. I chose you. I appointed you to go and produce lasting fruit, so that the Father will give you whatever you ask for, using my name. [17]This is my command: Love each other."

~ John 15:9-17

GUIDANCE THROUGH PRAYER

Do you need to hear from God? Do you need to make an important decision and need guidance? Then pray to God. Ask Him to lead you through His Spirit in all truth so that you will know what you should do. Remember that the Bible says that if you seek the Lord with all your heart, you will find Him.

[5]"But now I am going away to the one who sent me, and not one of you is asking where I am going. [6]Instead, you grieve because of what I've told you. [7]But in fact, it is best for you that I go away, because if I don't, the Advocate won't come. If I do go away, then I will send him to you. [8]And when he comes, he will convict the world of its sin, and of God's righteousness, and of the coming judgment. [9]The world's sin is that it refuses to believe in me. [10]Righteousness is available because I go to the Father, and you will see me no more. [11]Judgment will come because the ruler of this world has already been judged. [12]There is so much more I want to tell you, but you can't bear it now. [13]When the Spirit of truth comes, he will guide you into all truth. He will not speak on his own but will tell you what he has heard. He will tell you about the future. [14]He will bring me glory by telling you whatever he receives from me. [15]All that belongs to the Father is mine; this is why I said, 'The Spirit will tell you whatever he receives from me.'

[16]"In a little while you won't see me anymore. But a little while after that, you will see me again."

~ John 16:5-16

CHRIST'S IDENTITY

Never forget the true identity of Jesus Christ. He is more than a conqueror, more than the King of kings and the Lord of lords, more even than your Savior and Redeemer. He is indeed the great I AM. If you are feeling discouraged and worthless today, remember that the great I AM is with you.

¹After saying these things, Jesus crossed the Kidron Valley with his disciples and entered a grove of olive trees. ²Judas, the betrayer, knew this place, because Jesus had often gone there with his disciples.

³The leading priests and Pharisees had given Judas a contingent of Roman soldiers and Temple guards to accompany him. Now with blazing torches, lanterns, and weapons, they arrived at the olive grove. ⁴Jesus fully realized all that was going to happen to him, so he stepped forward to meet them. "Who are you looking for?" he asked. ⁵"Jesus the Nazarene," they replied. "I AM he," Jesus said. (Judas, who betrayed him, was standing with them.)

⁶As Jesus said "I AM he," they all drew back and fell to the ground! ⁷Once more he asked them, "Who are you looking for?" And again they replied, "Jesus the Nazarene." ⁸"I told you that I AM he," Jesus said. "And since I am the one you want, let these others go." ⁹He did this to fulfill his own statement: "I did not lose a single one of those you have given me."

~ John 18:1-9

CLOSER THAN A BROTHER

The Lord tells us that we are not His servants, we are His friends. True friends are few and far between. But Jesus is a friend who sticks closer than a brother. The love that Jesus has for you and me is so deep that He gave His life for us, the ultimate price. You can't give someone any more than that. Remember, He chose us before we chose Him.

¹¹ Mary was standing outside the tomb crying, and as she wept, she stooped and looked in. ¹²She saw two white-robed angels, one sitting at the head and the other at the foot of the place where the body of Jesus had been lying. ¹³"Dear woman, why are you crying?" the angels asked her.

"Because they have taken away my Lord," she replied, "and I don't know where they have put him."

¹⁴She turned to leave and saw someone standing there. It was Jesus, but she didn't recognize him. ¹⁵"Dear woman, why are you crying?" Jesus asked her. "Who are you looking for?"

She thought he was the gardener. "Sir," she said, "if you have taken him away, tell me where you have put him, and I will go and get him."

¹⁶"Mary!" Jesus said. She turned to him and cried out, "Rabboni!" (which is Hebrew for "Teacher").

¹⁷"Don't cling to me," Jesus said, "for I haven't yet ascended to the Father. But go find my brothers and tell them, 'I am ascending to my Father and your Father, to my God and your God.'"

¹⁸Mary Magdalene found the disciples and told them, "I have seen the Lord!" Then she gave them his message.

~ John 20:11-18

Peter operated by the grace of God. And in his weakness, he was made strong. Peter, the man who ran away when they asked him if he knew Jesus, asked to be crucified upside down because he was not worthy to die in the same way as his Master. No matter what you did, choose today to live by the power of and grace of God.

¹⁵After breakfast Jesus asked Simon Peter, "Simon son of John, do you love me more than these?" "Yes, Lord," Peter replied, "you know I love you." "Then feed my lambs," Jesus told him. ¹⁶Jesus repeated the question: "Simon son of John, do you love me?" "Yes, Lord," Peter said, "you know I love you." "Then take care of my sheep," Jesus said.

¹⁷A third time he asked him, "Simon son of John, do you love me?" Peter was hurt that Jesus asked the question a third time. He said, "Lord, you know everything. You know that I love you."

Jesus said, "Then feed my sheep.

¹⁸"I tell you the truth, when you were young, you were able to do as you liked; you dressed yourself and went wherever you wanted to go. But when you are old, you will stretch out your hands, and others will dress you and take you where you don't want to go."

¹⁹Jesus said this to let him know by what kind of death he would glorify God. Then Jesus told him, "Follow me."

~ John 21:15-19

THE HOLY SPIRIT

The Holy Spirit was sent to comfort us and to help us spread the gospel. In fact, without the Holy Spirit we can do nothing. We need to allow Him to work through us and give Him more authority in our lives. Once we have received the power of the Holy Spirit, we will be able to witness to the world about Jesus.

¹In my first book I told you, Theophilus, about everything Jesus began to do and teach ²until the day he was taken up to heaven after giving his chosen apostles further instructions through the Holy Spirit. ³During the forty days after his crucifixion, he appeared to the apostles from time to time, and he proved to them in many ways that he was actually alive. And he talked to them about the Kingdom of God.

⁴Once when he was eating with them, he commanded them, "Do not leave Jerusalem until the Father sends you the gift he promised, as I told you before. ⁵John baptized with water, but in just a few days you will be baptized with the Holy Spirit."

⁶So when the apostles were with Jesus, they kept asking him, "Lord, has the time come for you to free Israel and restore our kingdom?"

⁷He replied, "The Father alone has the authority to set those dates and times, and they are not for you to know. ⁸But you will receive power when the Holy Spirit comes upon you. And you will be my witnesses, telling people about me everywhere—in Jerusalem, throughout Judea, in Samaria, and to the ends of the earth."

~ Acts 1:1-8

THE OUTPOURING

The upper room in Jerusalem was where the first church began after Jesus ascended to heaven. During that time the Holy Spirit was poured out. The disciples began speaking in tongues and the presence of God was tangible. The Holy Spirit still performs miracles through those who are prepared to trust in God.

¹On the day of Pentecost all the believers were meeting together in one place. ²Suddenly, there was a sound from heaven like the roaring of a mighty windstorm, and it filled the house where they were sitting. ³Then, what looked like flames or tongues of fire appeared and settled on each of them. ⁴And everyone present was filled with the Holy Spirit and began speaking in other languages, as the Holy Spirit gave them this ability.

⁵At that time there were devout Jews from every nation living in Jerusalem. ⁶When they heard the loud noise, everyone came running, and they were bewildered to hear their own languages being spoken by the believers.

⁷They were completely amazed. "How can this be?" they exclaimed. "These people are all from Galilee, ⁸and yet we hear them speaking in our own native languages! ⁹Here we are—Parthians, Medes, Elamites, people from Mesopotamia, Judea, Cappadocia, Pontus, the province of Asia, ¹⁰Phrygia, Pamphylia, Egypt, and the areas of Libya around Cyrene, visitors from Rome ¹¹(both Jews and converts to Judaism), Cretans, and Arabs. And we all hear these people speaking in our own languages about the wonderful things God has done!" ¹²They stood there amazed and perplexed. "What can this mean?" they asked each other.

~ Acts 2:1-12

PETER'S SERMON

Peter's sermon is a very clear demonstration of the power of the Holy Spirit. The same Peter who denied the Lord three times, now preached a sermon that led thousands of people to the Lord. With the help and guidance of the Holy Spirit, all things are possible.

[22]"People of Israel, listen! God publicly endorsed Jesus the Nazarene by doing powerful miracles, wonders, and signs through him, as you well know. [23]But God knew what would happen, and his prearranged plan was carried out when Jesus was betrayed. [24]But God released him from the horrors of death and raised him back to life, for death could not keep him in its grip.

[32]"God raised Jesus from the dead, and we are all witnesses of this. [33]Now he is exalted to the place of highest honor in heaven, at God's right hand. And the Father, as he had promised, gave him the Holy Spirit to pour out upon us, just as you see and hear today.

[36]"So let everyone in Israel know for certain that God has made this Jesus, whom you crucified, to be both Lord and Messiah!"

[37]Peter's words pierced their hearts, and they said to him and to the other apostles, "Brothers, what should we do?"

[38]Peter replied, "Each of you must repent of your sins and turn to God, and be baptized in the name of Jesus Christ for the forgiveness of your sins. Then you will receive the gift of the Holy Spirit."

[41]Those who believed what Peter said were baptized and added to the church that day—about 3,000 in all.

~ Acts 2:22-24, 32-33, 36-38, 41

TRUST IN GOD

A very powerful miracle took place at the gates of the temple where God used Peter and John to heal a lame man. Their faith in God and the gift of the Holy Spirit enabled them to do that which seemed impossible. Nothing is impossible for God. He can use anybody to perform miracles in His name.

[1]Peter and John went to the Temple one afternoon to take part in the three o'clock prayer service. [2]As they approached the Temple, a man lame from birth was being carried in. Each day he was put beside the Temple gate, the one called the Beautiful Gate, so he could beg from the people going into the Temple. [3]When he saw Peter and John about to enter, he asked them for some money.

[4]Peter and John looked at him intently, and Peter said, "Look at us!" [5]The lame man looked at them eagerly, expecting some money. [6]But Peter said, "I don't have any silver or gold for you. But I'll give you what I have. In the name of Jesus Christ the Nazarene, get up and walk!"

[7]Then Peter took the lame man by the right hand and helped him up. And as he did, the man's feet and ankles were instantly healed and strengthened. [8]He jumped up, stood on his feet, and began to walk! Then, walking, leaping, and praising God, he went into the Temple with them.

[9]All the people saw him walking and heard him praising God. [10]When they realized he was the lame beggar they had seen so often at the Beautiful Gate, they were absolutely astounded!

~ Acts 3:1-10

DON'T LIE

You can't deceive God. He is omnipotent and omniscient. When Ananias and Sapphira lied to the church by keeping a portion of the money they promised them, God knew about it and they paid the price with their lives. We cannot hide anything from the Holy Spirit, so let us honor God in all the things we say and do.

¹But there was a certain man named Ananias who, with his wife, Sapphira, sold some property. ²He brought part of the money to the apostles, claiming it was the full amount. With his wife's consent, he kept the rest.

³Then Peter said, "Ananias, why have you let Satan fill your heart? You lied to the Holy Spirit, and you kept some of the money for yourself. ⁴The property was yours to sell or not sell, as you wished. And after selling it, the money was also yours to give away. How could you do a thing like this? You weren't lying to us but to God!"

⁵As soon as Ananias heard these words, he fell to the floor and died. Everyone who heard about it was terrified.

⁷About three hours later his wife came in, not knowing what had happened. ⁸Peter asked her, "Was this the price you and your husband received for your land?"

"Yes," she replied, "that was the price." ⁹And Peter said, "How could the two of you even think of conspiring to test the Spirit of the Lord like this? The young men who buried your husband are just outside the door, and they will carry you out, too."

¹⁰Instantly, she fell to the floor and died. ¹¹Great fear gripped the entire church and everyone else who heard what had happened.

~ Acts 5:1-5, 7-11

THE WORK WILL CONTINUE

When God sets a plan in motion, nobody can stop it. Gamaliel knew this and told the Pharisees that they would only be able to stop the apostles if God did not send them. He used ordinary people to spread His Word. When God uses people to do His work, great things happen.

³³When they heard this, the high council was furious and decided to kill them. ³⁴But one member, a Pharisee named Gamaliel, who was an expert in religious law and respected by all the people, stood up and ordered that the men be sent outside the council chamber for a while. ³⁵Then he said to his colleagues, "Men of Israel, take care what you are planning to do to these men! ³⁶Some time ago there was that fellow Theudas, who pretended to be someone great. About 400 others joined him, but he was killed, and all his followers went their various ways. The whole movement came to nothing. ³⁷After him, at the time of the census, there was Judas of Galilee. He got people to follow him, but he was killed, too, and all his followers were scattered.

³⁸"So my advice is, leave these men alone. Let them go. If they are planning and doing these things merely on their own, it will soon be overthrown. ³⁹But if it is from God, you will not be able to overthrow them. You may even find yourselves fighting against God!"

⁴⁰The others accepted his advice. They called in the apostles and had them flogged. Then they ordered them never again to speak in the name of Jesus, and they let them go.

⁴¹The apostles left the high council rejoicing that God had counted them worthy to suffer disgrace for the name of Jesus.

~ Acts 5:33-41

THE FIRST MARTYR

Stephen so infuriated the Pharisees that they stoned him to death. While they were busy killing him, Stephen could see the heavens open and Jesus standing next to God. Stephen kept His eyes fixed on Jesus the whole time. Even when being persecuted, we must keep our eyes on Him.

51 "You stubborn people! You are heathen at heart and deaf to the truth. Must you forever resist the Holy Spirit? That's what your ancestors did, and so do you! 52Name one prophet your ancestors didn't persecute! They even killed the ones who predicted the coming of the Righteous One—the Messiah whom you betrayed and murdered. 53You deliberately disobeyed God's law, even though you received it from the hands of angels."

54The Jewish leaders were infuriated by Stephen's accusation, and they shook their fists at him in rage. 55But Stephen, full of the Holy Spirit, gazed steadily into heaven and saw the glory of God, and he saw Jesus standing in the place of honor at God's right hand. 56And he told them, "Look, I see the heavens opened and the Son of Man standing in the place of honor at God's right hand!"

57Then they put their hands over their ears and began shouting. They rushed at him 58and dragged him out of the city and began to stone him. His accusers took off their coats and laid them at the feet of a young man named Saul.

59As they stoned him, Stephen prayed, "Lord Jesus, receive my spirit." 60He fell to his knees, shouting, "Lord, don't charge them with this sin!" And with that, he died.

~ Acts 7:51-60

SAUL'S TURNING POINT

Few things are as powerful and can touch people's hearts as dramatically as a believer's testimony of conversion. Not all conversions are necessarily a Damascus Road experience like Saul's. Most important is that you meet your Savior personally.

¹Meanwhile, Saul was uttering threats with every breath and was eager to kill the Lord's followers. So he went to the high priest. ²He requested letters addressed to the synagogues in Damascus, asking for their cooperation in the arrest of any followers of the Way he found there. He wanted to bring them—both men and women—back to Jerusalem in chains.

³As he was approaching Damascus on this mission, a light from heaven suddenly shone down around him. ⁴He fell to the ground and heard a voice saying to him, "Saul! Saul! Why are you persecuting me?"

⁵"Who are you, lord?" Saul asked.

And the voice replied, "I am Jesus, the one you are persecuting! ⁶Now get up and go into the city, and you will be told what you must do."

⁷The men with Saul stood speechless, for they heard the sound of someone's voice but saw no one!

⁸Saul picked himself up off the ground, but when he opened his eyes he was blind. So his companions led him by the hand to Damascus. ⁹He remained there blind for three days and did not eat or drink.

~ Acts 9:1-9

PETER'S VISION

God showed Peter that He is no respecter of people or things and that He will not be dictated to by tradition. Basically what it means is that what God has cleansed, set free, and renewed is done. I thank God for the freedom this verse brings. We are not bound to any tradition, but only to Jesus.

⁹The next day as Cornelius's messengers were nearing the town, Peter went up on the flat roof to pray. It was about noon, ¹⁰and he was hungry. But while a meal was being prepared, he fell into a trance. ¹¹He saw the sky open, and something like a large sheet was let down by its four corners.

¹²In the sheet were all sorts of animals, reptiles, and birds.

¹³Then a voice said to him, "Get up, Peter; kill and eat them."

¹⁴"No, Lord," Peter declared. "I have never eaten anything that our Jewish laws have declared impure and unclean."

¹⁵But the voice spoke again: "Do not call something unclean if God has made it clean."

¹⁶The same vision was repeated three times. Then the sheet was suddenly pulled up to heaven.

¹⁷Peter was very perplexed. What could the vision mean?

~ Acts 10:9-17

SAVED

Silas and Paul's miraculous escape from prison saved not only them, but also the jailer and his family. The jailer witnessed how God cared for His own.

At Shalom we say, "one genuine miracle = 1,000 sermons." That jailer might have heard a thousand sermons, without being saved, but when he saw the miracle happen before his eyes, he believed.

[25]Around midnight Paul and Silas were praying and singing hymns to God, and the other prisoners were listening. [26]Suddenly, there was a massive earthquake, and the prison was shaken to its foundations. All the doors immediately flew open, and the chains of every prisoner fell off! [27]The jailer woke up to see the prison doors wide open. He assumed the prisoners had escaped, so he drew his sword to kill himself. [28]But Paul shouted to him, "Stop! Don't kill yourself! We are all here!"

[29]The jailer called for lights and ran to the dungeon and fell down trembling before Paul and Silas. [30]Then he brought them out and asked, "Sirs, what must I do to be saved?"

[31]They replied, "Believe in the Lord Jesus and you will be saved, along with everyone in your household." [32]And they shared the word of the Lord with him and with all who lived in his household. [33]Even at that hour of the night, the jailer cared for them and washed their wounds. Then he and everyone in his household were immediately baptized. [34]He brought them into his house and set a meal before them, and he and his entire household rejoiced because they all believed in God.

~ Acts 16:25-34

UPSIDE DOWN

In a time when Christians were severely persecuted, God's servants continued preaching the gospel. They turned the world upside down with their teachings and testimonies, even though it sometimes cost them their lives. We must keep our eyes on God and be fearless in spreading the gospel.

[2]As was Paul's custom, he went to the synagogue service, and for three Sabbaths in a row he used the Scriptures to reason with the people. [3]He explained the prophecies and proved that the Messiah must suffer and rise from the dead. He said, "This Jesus I'm telling you about is the Messiah." [4]Some of the Jews who listened were persuaded and joined Paul and Silas, along with many God-fearing Greek men and quite a few prominent women.

[5]But some of the Jews were jealous, so they gathered some troublemakers from the marketplace to form a mob and start a riot. They attacked the home of Jason, searching for Paul and Silas so they could drag them out to the crowd. [6]Not finding them there, they dragged out Jason and some of the other believers instead and took them before the city council. "Paul and Silas have caused trouble all over the world," they shouted, "and now they are here disturbing our city, too. [7]And Jason has welcomed them into his home. They are all guilty of treason against Caesar, for they profess allegiance to another king, named Jesus."

[8]The people of the city, as well as the city council, were thrown into turmoil by these reports. [9]So the officials forced Jason and the other believers to post bond, and then they released them.

~ Acts 17:2-9

PROMISES FOR TOUGH TIMES

God uses ordinary people to do His work. Aquila and Priscilla were tent makers, just like Paul. It is important if you are going into full-time ministry to have a specific calling from God, a specific event, so that through the tough times you can hold onto the promises of God.

¹Then Paul left Athens and went to Corinth. ²There he became acquainted with a Jew named Aquila, born in Pontus, who had recently arrived from Italy with his wife, Priscilla. ³Paul lived and worked with them, for they were tentmakers just as he was.

⁴Each Sabbath found Paul at the synagogue, trying to convince the Jews and Greeks alike. ⁵And after Silas and Timothy came down from Macedonia, Paul spent all his time preaching the word. He testified to the Jews that Jesus was the Messiah. ⁶But when they opposed and insulted him, Paul shook the dust from his clothes and said, "Your blood is upon your own heads—I am innocent. From now on I will go preach to the Gentiles."

⁷Then he left and went to the home of Titius Justus, a Gentile who worshiped God and lived next door to the synagogue. ⁸Crispus, the leader of the synagogue, and everyone in his household believed in the Lord. Many others in Corinth also heard Paul, became believers, and were baptized.

⁹One night the Lord spoke to Paul in a vision and told him, "Don't be afraid! Speak out! Don't be silent! ¹⁰For I am with you, and no one will attack and harm you, for many people in this city belong to me."

~ Acts 18:1-10

SPIRITUAL DISCERNMENT

The sons of Sceva meant well. They tried to cast out an evil spirit, but the evil spirit overpowered them. When we do the work of the Lord, we must be prepared spiritually, mentally and physically. We must pray for the ability to discern between true and false prophets and guard against being deceived.

[11]God gave Paul the power to perform unusual miracles. [12]When handkerchiefs or aprons that had merely touched his skin were placed on sick people, they were healed of their diseases, and evil spirits were expelled.

[13]A group of Jews was traveling from town to town casting out evil spirits. They tried to use the name of the Lord Jesus in their incantation, saying, "I command you in the name of Jesus, whom Paul preaches, to come out!" [14]Seven sons of Sceva, a leading priest, were doing this. [15]But one time when they tried it, the evil spirit replied, "I know Jesus, and I know Paul, but who are you?" [16]Then the man with the evil spirit leaped on them, overpowered them, and attacked them with such violence that they fled from the house, naked and battered.

[17]The story of what happened spread quickly all through Ephesus, to Jews and Greeks alike. A solemn fear descended on the city, and the name of the Lord Jesus was greatly honored. [18]Many who became believers confessed their sinful practices. [19]A number of them who had been practicing sorcery brought their incantation books and burned them at a public bonfire. The value of the books was several million dollars. [20]So the message about the Lord spread widely and had a powerful effect.

~ Acts 19:11-20

STEADFAST FAITH

We need to do what the Lord tells us to do and trust that He knows best. Paul never hesitated to fulfill his calling, even when it was prophesied that he would be killed. Paul wanted to honor the Lord and obey His instructions. He knew that there was much more beyond this life, therefore he didn't fear death.

⁸The next day we went on to Caesarea and stayed at the home of Philip the Evangelist, one of the seven men who had been chosen to distribute food. ⁹He had four unmarried daughters who had the gift of prophecy.

¹⁰Several days later a man named Agabus, who also had the gift of prophecy, arrived from Judea. ¹¹He came over, took Paul's belt, and bound his own feet and hands with it. Then he said, "The Holy Spirit declares, 'So shall the owner of this belt be bound by the Jewish leaders in Jerusalem and turned over to the Gentiles.'" ¹²When we heard this, we and the local believers all begged Paul not to go on to Jerusalem.

¹³But he said, "Why all this weeping? You are breaking my heart! I am ready not only to be jailed at Jerusalem but even to die for the sake of the Lord Jesus." ¹⁴When it was clear that we couldn't persuade him, we gave up and said, "The Lord's will be done."

¹⁵After this we packed our things and left for Jerusalem.

~ Acts 21:8-15

THE STORM

This is the account of the terrible storm that Paul endured. The people on the ship had no hope and thought they would die. But Paul encouraged them by saying that none of them would lose their lives. As servants of the Lord, we need to be confident in Him, especially when we are in the middle of a storm.

[16]We sailed along the sheltered side of a small island named Cauda, where with great difficulty we hoisted aboard the lifeboat being towed behind us. [17]Then the sailors bound ropes around the hull of the ship to strengthen it. They were afraid of being driven across to the sandbars of Syrtis off the African coast, so they lowered the sea anchor to slow the ship and were driven before the wind.

[18]The next day, as gale-force winds continued to batter the ship, the crew began throwing the cargo overboard. [19]The following day they even took some of the ship's gear and threw it overboard. [20]The terrible storm raged for many days, blotting out the sun and the stars, until at last all hope was gone.

[21]No one had eaten for a long time. Finally, Paul called the crew together and said, "Men, you should have listened to me in the first place and not left Crete. You would have avoided all this damage and loss. [22]But take courage! None of you will lose your lives, even though the ship will go down. [23]For last night an angel of the God to whom I belong and whom I serve stood beside me, [24]and he said, 'Don't be afraid, Paul, for you will surely stand trial before Caesar! What's more, God in his goodness has granted safety to everyone sailing with you.' [25]So take courage! For I believe God. It will be just as he said."

~ Acts 27:16-25

FINISHING WELL

Paul lived in Rome and preached for two years before he was killed. Even though he knew he was going to die, he continued preaching with confidence. We need to be like Paul. We must run the race with perseverance and finish well.

[17]Three days after Paul's arrival, he called together the local Jewish leaders. He said to them, "Brothers, I was arrested in Jerusalem and handed over to the Roman government, even though I had done nothing against our people or the customs of our ancestors. [20]I asked you to come here today so we could get acquainted and so I could explain to you that I am bound with this chain because I believe that the hope of Israel—the Messiah—has already come."

[21]They replied, "We have had no letters from Judea or reports against you from anyone who has come here. [22]But we want to hear what you believe, for the only thing we know about this movement is that it is denounced everywhere."

[23]So a time was set, and on that day a large number of people came to Paul's lodging. He explained and testified about the Kingdom of God and tried to persuade them about Jesus from the Scriptures. Using the law of Moses and the books of the prophets, he spoke to them from morning until evening. [24]Some were persuaded by the things he said, but others did not believe.

[30]For the next two years, Paul lived in Rome at his own expense. He welcomed all who visited him, [31]boldly proclaiming the Kingdom of God and teaching about the Lord Jesus Christ. And no one tried to stop him.

~ Acts 28:17, 20-24, 30-31

LIVING BY FAITH

When we are not ashamed to proclaim the gospel of Christ, then we have the power of God working in us. This Scripture verse touched and revolutionized the lives of Martin Luther and John Wesley. It made them realize that we will only reach heaven by grace through faith in Jesus Christ.

¹⁶For I am not ashamed of this Good News about Christ. It is the power of God at work, saving everyone who believes—the Jew first and also the Gentile. ¹⁷This Good News tells us how God makes us right in his sight. This is accomplished from start to finish by faith. As the Scriptures say, "It is through faith that a righteous person has life."

¹⁸But God shows his anger from heaven against all sinful, wicked people who suppress the truth by their wickedness. ¹⁹They know the truth about God because he has made it obvious to them. ²⁰For ever since the world was created, people have seen the earth and sky. Through everything God made, they can clearly see his invisible qualities—his eternal power and divine nature. So they have no excuse for not knowing God.

²¹Yes, they knew God, but they wouldn't worship him as God or even give him thanks. And they began to think up foolish ideas of what God was like. As a result, their minds became dark and confused. ²²Claiming to be wise, they instead became utter fools. ²³And instead of worshiping the glorious, ever-living God, they worshiped idols made to look like mere people and birds and animals and reptiles.

~ Romans 1:16-23

RIGHTEOUSNESS

Paul said clearly that there is only one path to righteousness: Jesus Christ. Our sinful nature stands in the way of righteousness, which is why Jesus Christ died for us. We can only be made righteous through the blood of Christ.

¹⁹Obviously, the law applies to those to whom it was given, for its purpose is to keep people from having excuses, and to show that the entire world is guilty before God. ²⁰For no one can ever be made right with God by doing what the law commands. The law simply shows us how sinful we are.

²¹But now God has shown us a way to be made right with him without keeping the requirements of the law, as was promised in the writings of Moses and the prophets long ago. ²²We are made right with God by placing our faith in Jesus Christ. And this is true for everyone who believes, no matter who we are.

²³For everyone has sinned; we all fall short of God's glorious standard. ²⁴Yet God, with undeserved kindness, declares that we are righteous. He did this through Christ Jesus when he freed us from the penalty for our sins. ²⁵For God presented Jesus as the sacrifice for sin. People are made right with God when they believe that Jesus sacrificed his life, shedding his blood. This sacrifice shows that God was being fair when he held back and did not punish those who sinned in times past, ²⁶for he was looking ahead and including them in what he would do in this present time. God did this to demonstrate his righteousness, for he himself is fair and just, and he declares sinners to be right in his sight when they believe in Jesus.

~ Romans 3:19-26

NOTHING TO BOAST ABOUT

A good example of a man justified by faith was Abraham. "Abraham believed God, and God counted him as righteous because of his faith" (Acts 4:3). Abraham was not a particularly good man, yet he was a man of great faith. He trusted God. We need to be men of great faith, then we can be made right with God.

¹Abraham was, humanly speaking, the founder of our Jewish nation. What did he discover about being made right with God? ²If his good deeds had made him acceptable to God, he would have had something to boast about. But that was not God's way. ³For the Scriptures tell us, "Abraham believed God, and God counted him as righteous because of his faith."

⁴When people work, their wages are not a gift, but something they have earned. ⁵But people are counted as righteous, not because of their work, but because of their faith in God who forgives sinners.

⁶David also spoke of this when he described the happiness of those who are declared righteous without working for it:

⁷"Oh, what joy for those
whose disobedience is forgiven,
whose sins are put out of sight.

⁸Yes, what joy for those
whose record the Lord has cleared of sin."

~ Romans 4:1-8

WHEN LIFE GETS TOUGH

Faith grows through hardship. Faith does not grow in a garden of prosperity, but in a desert of tribulation. Even though it is never pleasant to experience hardship, it teaches us to persevere and to cling to God. He will never desert us.

¹Therefore, since we have been made right in God's sight by faith, we have peace with God because of what Jesus Christ our Lord has done for us. ²Because of our faith, Christ has brought us into this place of undeserved privilege where we now stand, and we confidently and joyfully look forward to sharing God's glory.

³We can rejoice, too, when we run into problems and trials, for we know that they help us develop endurance. ⁴And endurance develops strength of character, and character strengthens our confident hope of salvation. ⁵And this hope will not lead to disappointment. For we know how dearly God loves us, because he has given us the Holy Spirit to fill our hearts with his love.

⁸But God showed his great love for us by sending Christ to die for us while we were still sinners. ⁹And since we have been made right in God's sight by the blood of Christ, he will certainly save us from God's condemnation. ¹⁰For since our friendship with God was restored by the death of his Son while we were still his enemies, we will certainly be saved through the life of his Son. ¹¹So now we can rejoice in our wonderful new relationship with God because our Lord Jesus Christ has made us friends of God.

~ Romans 5:1-5, 8-11

FREEDOM IN CHRIST

Never underestimate the destructive power of sin. If we give in to our sinful natures, we become prisoners of sin. Only Jesus can set us truly free. We walk by faith and not by sight. God raised Jesus from the dead and we can have life in our bodies, minds and souls. What a beautiful promise!

¹So now there is no condemnation for those who belong to Christ Jesus. ²And because you belong to him, the power of the life-giving Spirit has freed you from the power of sin that leads to death. ³The law of Moses was unable to save us because of the weakness of our sinful nature. So God did what the law could not do. He sent his own Son in a body like the bodies we sinners have. And in that body God declared an end to sin's control over us by giving his Son as a sacrifice for our sins. ⁴He did this so that the just requirement of the law would be fully satisfied for us, who no longer follow our sinful nature but instead follow the Spirit.

⁵Those who are dominated by the sinful nature think about sinful things, but those who are controlled by the Holy Spirit think about things that please the Spirit. ⁶So letting your sinful nature control your mind leads to death. But letting the Spirit control your mind leads to life and peace.

¹⁰And Christ lives within you, so even though your body will die because of sin, the Spirit gives you life because you have been made right with God. ¹¹The Spirit of God, who raised Jesus from the dead, lives in you. And just as God raised Christ Jesus from the dead, he will give life to your mortal bodies by this same Spirit living within you.

~ Romans 8:1-6, 10-11

EVERLASTING LOVE

If God is for us, nothing can stand against us. God's love for us is much greater than we can imagine. He loved us so much that He didn't even spare His own Son. Nothing will ever separate us from His love. Aren't we blessed?

³¹What shall we say about such wonderful things as these? If God is for us, who can ever be against us? ³²Since he did not spare even his own Son but gave him up for us all, won't he also give us everything else? ³³Who dares accuse us whom God has chosen for his own? No one—for God himself has given us right standing with himself. ³⁴Who then will condemn us? No one—for Christ Jesus died for us and was raised to life for us, and he is sitting in the place of honor at God's right hand, pleading for us.

³⁵Can anything ever separate us from Christ's love? Does it mean he no longer loves us if we have trouble or calamity, or are persecuted, or hungry, or destitute, or in danger, or threatened with death? ³⁶(As the Scriptures say, "For your sake we are killed every day; we are being slaughtered like sheep.") ³⁷No, despite all these things, overwhelming victory is ours through Christ, who loved us.

³⁸And I am convinced that nothing can ever separate us from God's love. Neither death nor life, neither angels nor demons, neither our fears for today nor our worries about tomorrow—not even the powers of hell can separate us from God's love. ³⁹No power in the sky above or in the earth below—indeed, nothing in all creation will ever be able to separate us from the love of God that is revealed in Christ Jesus our Lord.

~ Romans 8:31-39

OCTOBER

BELIEVE

What a beautiful passage from Scripture. God shows us again that He has a heart, first and foremost, for His people. He says clearly that if you call on His name, you will be saved. It is not about efforts or good works, but about confessing with your mouth and believing that Jesus Christ died and rose again.

¹Dear brothers and sisters, the longing of my heart and my prayer to God is for the people of Israel to be saved. ²I know what enthusiasm they have for God, but it is misdirected zeal. ³For they don't understand God's way of making people right with himself. Refusing to accept God's way, they cling to their own way of getting right with God by trying to keep the law. ⁴For Christ has already accomplished the purpose for which the law was given. As a result, all who believe in him are made right with God.

⁵For Moses writes that the law's way of making a person right with God requires obedience to all of its commands. ⁶But faith's way of getting right with God says, "Don't say in your heart, 'Who will go up to heaven?' (to bring Christ down to earth). ⁷And don't say, 'Who will go down to the place of the dead?' (to bring Christ back to life again)." ⁸In fact, it says, "The message is very close at hand; it is on your lips and in your heart."

And that message is the very message about faith that we preach: ⁹If you confess with your mouth that Jesus is Lord and believe in your heart that God raised him from the dead, you will be saved. ¹⁰For it is by believing in your heart that you are made right with God, and it is by confessing with your mouth that you are saved.

~ Romans 10:1-10

NO FANCY STORIES

We as Christians have an obligation to tell people about Jesus, not only with words, but also with our whole lives. It is not fancy stories that bring people to Christ, it is the undiluted Word of God. We must pay more attention to our words and deeds, because we can use them to lead people to God.

[14]But how can they call on him to save them unless they believe in him? And how can they believe in him if they have never heard about him? And how can they hear about him unless someone tells them? [15]And how will anyone go and tell them without being sent? That is why the Scriptures say, "How beautiful are the feet of messengers who bring good news!"

[16]But not everyone welcomes the Good News, for Isaiah the prophet said, "LORD, who has believed our message?" [17]So faith comes from hearing, that is, hearing the Good News about Christ. [18]But I ask, have the people of Israel actually heard the message? Yes, they have:

"The message has gone throughout the earth,
    and the words to all the world."

[19]But I ask, did the people of Israel really understand? Yes, they did, for even in the time of Moses, God said, "I will rouse your jealousy through people who are not even a nation.

    I will provoke your anger through the foolish Gentiles."

[20]And later Isaiah spoke boldly for God, saying,

"I was found by people who were not looking for me.
    I showed myself to those who were not asking for me."

~ Romans 10:14-20

ACT LIKE A CHRISTIAN

The Lord has called us to be separate and different from those in the world. In a world of so much uncertainty and fear, it is encouraging to see believers who are joyful. We need to refrain from acting like the world and stick to God's will for us. Leave justice and revenge to God.

¹And so, dear brothers and sisters, I plead with you to give your bodies to God because of all he has done for you. Let them be a living and holy sacrifice—the kind he will find acceptable. This is truly the way to worship him. ²Don't copy the behavior and customs of this world, but let God transform you into a new person by changing the way you think. Then you will learn to know God's will for you, which is good and pleasing and perfect.

⁶In his grace, God has given us different gifts for doing certain things well. So if God has given you the ability to prophesy, speak out with as much faith as God has given you. ⁷If your gift is serving others, serve them well. If you are a teacher, teach well. ⁸If your gift is to encourage others, be encouraging. If it is giving, give generously. If God has given you leadership ability, take the responsibility seriously. And if you have a gift for showing kindness to others, do it gladly.

⁹Don't just pretend to love others. Really love them. Hate what is wrong. Hold tightly to what is good. ¹⁰Love each other with genuine affection, and take delight in honoring each other. ¹¹Never be lazy, but work hard and serve the Lord enthusiastically. ¹²Rejoice in our confident hope. Be patient in trouble, and keep on praying. ¹³When God's people are in need, be ready to help them. Always be eager to practice hospitality.

~ Romans 12:1-2, 6-13

HONORING THE AUTHORITIES

The Lord is clear that we need to submit to those who are in authority over us, namely the government. If we owe tax, we need to pay it. We are to render unto Caesar what is Caesar's and what belongs to the Lord to the Lord.

¹Everyone must submit to governing authorities. For all authority comes from God, and those in positions of authority have been placed there by God.

²So anyone who rebels against authority is rebelling against what God has instituted, and they will be punished. ³For the authorities do not strike fear in people who are doing right, but in those who are doing wrong. Would you like to live without fear of the authorities? Do what is right, and they will honor you.

⁴The authorities are God's servants, sent for your good. But if you are doing wrong, of course you should be afraid, for they have the power to punish you. They are God's servants, sent for the very purpose of punishing those who do what is wrong. ⁵So you must submit to them, not only to avoid punishment, but also to keep a clear conscience.

⁶Pay your taxes, too, for these same reasons. For government workers need to be paid. They are serving God in what they do. ⁷Give to everyone what you owe them: Pay your taxes and government fees to those who collect them, and give respect and honor to those who are in authority.

~ Romans 13:1-7

STUMBLING BLOCKS

> The kingdom of God is not about eating and drinking, but about righteousness, love and peace. We must not be stumbling blocks to fellow believers, but a source of support and encouragement. Help other believers, because that's what God wants you to do.

[14]I know and am convinced on the authority of the Lord Jesus that no food, in and of itself, is wrong to eat. But if someone believes it is wrong, then for that person it is wrong. [15]And if another believer is distressed by what you eat, you are not acting in love if you eat it. Don't let your eating ruin someone for whom Christ died. [16]Then you will not be criticized for doing something you believe is good. [17]For the Kingdom of God is not a matter of what we eat or drink, but of living a life of goodness and peace and joy in the Holy Spirit. [18]If you serve Christ with this attitude, you will please God, and others will approve of you, too. [19]So then, let us aim for harmony in the church and try to build each other up.

[20]Don't tear apart the work of God over what you eat. Remember, all foods are acceptable, but it is wrong to eat something if it makes another person stumble. [21]It is better not to eat meat or drink wine or do anything else if it might cause another believer to stumble. [22]You may believe there's nothing wrong with what you are doing, but keep it between yourself and God. Blessed are those who don't feel guilty for doing something they have decided is right. [23]But if you have doubts about whether or not you should eat something, you are sinning if you go ahead and do it. For you are not following your convictions. If you do anything you believe is not right, you are sinning.

~ Romans 14:14-23

LIVE IN PEACE

As believers, we should live in peace and harmony with one another. Although this is sometimes difficult to do, we must remember that the church is at its strongest when the members work together. Not only does this strengthen us as believers, it also serves as an example to those who do not believe.

[5]May God, who gives this patience and encouragement, help you live in complete harmony with each other, as is fitting for followers of Christ Jesus. [6]Then all of you can join together with one voice, giving praise and glory to God, the Father of our Lord Jesus Christ.

[7]Therefore, accept each other just as Christ has accepted you so that God will be given glory. [8]Remember that Christ came as a servant to the Jews to show that God is true to the promises he made to their ancestors.

[9]He also came so that the Gentiles might give glory to God for his mercies to them.

[13]I pray that God, the source of hope, will fill you completely with joy and peace because you trust in him. Then you will overflow with confident hope through the power of the Holy Spirit.

~ Romans 15:5-9, 13

ONLY ONE CHRIST

Paul warns against divisions among believers. These divisions happen when believers do not look to the Lord anymore, but to people for guidance. While the Lord sends people to lead us in His ways, we should always remember that there is only one Christ and it is only He who can save us.

[10]I appeal to you, dear brothers and sisters, by the authority of our Lord Jesus Christ, to live in harmony with each other. Let there be no divisions in the church. Rather, be of one mind, united in thought and purpose. [11]For some members of Chloe's household have told me about your quarrels, my dear brothers and sisters. [12]Some of you are saying, "I am a follower of Paul." Others are saying, "I follow Apollos," or "I follow Peter," or "I follow only Christ."

[13]Has Christ been divided into factions? Was I, Paul, crucified for you? Were any of you baptized in the name of Paul? Of course not! [14]I thank God that I did not baptize any of you except Crispus and Gaius, [15]for now no one can say they were baptized in my name. [16](Oh yes, I also baptized the household of Stephanas, but I don't remember baptizing anyone else.) [17]For Christ didn't send me to baptize, but to preach the Good News—and not with clever speech, for fear that the cross of Christ would lose its power.

~ 1 Corinthians 1:10-17

GOD'S ECONOMY

When we try to work things out and calculate how God does things, it does not make sense in our eyes. In God's economy 2 + 2 = 7. If you place all your trust in God, He will perform miracles which man could never have done. All glory to God!

[26]Remember, dear brothers and sisters, that few of you were wise in the world's eyes or powerful or wealthy when God called you.

[27]Instead, God chose things the world considers foolish in order to shame those who think they are wise. And he chose things that are powerless to shame those who are powerful. [28]God chose things despised by the world, things counted as nothing at all, and used them to bring to nothing what the world considers important. [29]As a result, no one can ever boast in the presence of God.

[30]God has united you with Christ Jesus. For our benefit God made him to be wisdom itself. Christ made us right with God; he made us pure and holy, and he freed us from sin.

[31]Therefore, as the Scriptures say, "If you want to boast, boast only about the Lord."

~ 1 Corinthians 1:26-31

WAIT FOR THE LORD

No eye has seen and no ear has heard the things that God has in store for those who love Him. Let us wait expectantly to see what God wants to give us so abundantly. We should love the Lord and wait for what He has planned for our lives.

⁶Yet when I am among mature believers, I do speak with words of wisdom, but not the kind of wisdom that belongs to this world or to the rulers of this world, who are soon forgotten.

⁷No, the wisdom we speak of is the mystery of God—his plan that was previously hidden, even though he made it for our ultimate glory before the world began.

⁸But the rulers of this world have not understood it; if they had, they would not have crucified our glorious Lord. ⁹That is what the Scriptures mean when they say,

"No eye has seen, no ear has heard,
    and no mind has imagined
what God has prepared
    for those who love him."

¹⁰But it was to us that God revealed these things by his Spirit. For his Spirit searches out everything and shows us God's deep secrets.

~ 1 Corinthians 2:6-10

FATHERLY CARE

Men need to be fathered and mentored, and led by experience. We need to lead by example and from the front. We should be bold enough to say "Imitate me, as I imitate Jesus." We should set an example for our children.

¹⁴I am not writing these things to shame you, but to warn you as my beloved children. ¹⁵For even if you had ten thousand others to teach you about Christ, you have only one spiritual father. For I became your father in Christ Jesus when I preached the Good News to you. ¹⁶So I urge you to imitate me.

¹⁷That's why I have sent Timothy, my beloved and faithful child in the Lord. He will remind you of how I follow Christ Jesus, just as I teach in all the churches wherever I go.

¹⁸Some of you have become arrogant, thinking I will not visit you again. ¹⁹But I will come—and soon—if the Lord lets me, and then I'll find out whether these arrogant people just give pretentious speeches or whether they really have God's power.

²⁰For the Kingdom of God is not just a lot of talk; it is living by God's power. ²¹Which do you choose? Should I come with a rod to punish you, or should I come with love and a gentle spirit?

~ 1 Corinthians 4:14-21

DISCIPLINE

Paul is clear that although we are all running the race, only one receives the prize. This race is not just about getting to the finish line, but a case of winning the crown. Therefore, we need to discipline ourselves physically, mentally and spiritually so that God can use us.

[24]Don't you realize that in a race everyone runs, but only one person gets the prize? So run to win!

[25]All athletes are disciplined in their training. They do it to win a prize that will fade away, but we do it for an eternal prize.

[26]So I run with purpose in every step. I am not just shadow-boxing.

[27]I discipline my body like an athlete, training it to do what it should. Otherwise, I fear that after preaching to others I myself might be disqualified.

~ 1 Corinthians 9:24-27

TEMPTATION

Build yourself up in the things of God, discipline yourself and keep good company. This helps keep temptation at bay. Remember, God will never let you be tempted beyond what you can bear.

[1]I don't want you to forget, dear brothers and sisters, about our ancestors in the wilderness long ago. All of them were guided by a cloud that moved ahead of them, and all of them walked through the sea on dry ground. [2]In the cloud and in the sea, all of them were baptized as followers of Moses. [3]All of them ate the same spiritual food, [4]and all of them drank the same spiritual water. For they drank from the spiritual rock that traveled with them, and that rock was Christ. [5]Yet God was not pleased with most of them, and their bodies were scattered in the wilderness.

[6]These things happened as a warning to us, so that we would not crave evil things as they did, [7]or worship idols as some of them did. As the Scriptures say, "The people celebrated with feasting and drinking, and they indulged in pagan revelry." [8]And we must not engage in sexual immorality as some of them did, causing 23,000 of them to die in one day.

[9]Nor should we put Christ to the test, as some of them did and then died from snakebites. [10]And don't grumble as some of them did, and then were destroyed by the angel of death. [11]These things happened to them as examples for us. They were written down to warn us who live at the end of the age.

[12]If you think you are standing strong, be careful not to fall. [13]The temptations in your life are no different from what others experience. And God is faithful. He will not allow the temptation to be more than you can stand. When you are tempted, he will show you a way out so that you can endure.

~ 1 Corinthians 10:1-13

SPIRITUAL GIFTS

What I love about the Lord is that He has given us all different talents and spiritual gifts. When we unite our gifts and ministries together, things work so well. Let us rejoice in our diversity as we serve the Lord together.

¹Now, dear brothers and sisters, regarding your question about the special abilities the Spirit gives us. I don't want you to misunderstand this. ²You know that when you were still pagans, you were led astray and swept along in worshiping speechless idols. ³So I want you to know that no one speaking by the Spirit of God will curse Jesus, and no one can say Jesus is Lord, except by the Holy Spirit.

⁴There are different kinds of spiritual gifts, but the same Spirit is the source of them all. ⁵There are different kinds of service, but we serve the same Lord. ⁶God works in different ways, but it is the same God who does the work in all of us.

⁷A spiritual gift is given to each of us so we can help each other. ⁸To one person the Spirit gives the ability to give wise advice; to another the same Spirit gives a message of special knowledge. ⁹The same Spirit gives great faith to another, and to someone else the one Spirit gives the gift of healing. ¹⁰He gives one person the power to perform miracles, and another the ability to prophesy. He gives someone else the ability to discern whether a message is from the Spirit of God or from another spirit. Still another person is given the ability to speak in unknown languages, while another is given the ability to interpret what is being said. ¹¹It is the one and only Spirit who distributes all these gifts. He alone decides which gift each person should have.

~ 1 Corinthians 12:1-11

LOVE

Unless we have love, we have nothing. Love keeps no record of wrongs and never thinks of itself. The greatest virtue is love.

[4]Love is patient and kind. Love is not jealous or boastful or proud [5]or rude. It does not demand its own way. It is not irritable, and it keeps no record of being wronged. [6]It does not rejoice about injustice but rejoices whenever the truth wins out. [7]Love never gives up, never loses faith, is always hopeful, and endures through every circumstance.

[8]Prophecy and speaking in unknown languages and special knowledge will become useless. But love will last forever! [9]Now our knowledge is partial and incomplete, and even the gift of prophecy reveals only part of the whole picture! [10]But when the time of perfection comes, these partial things will become useless.

[11]When I was a child, I spoke and thought and reasoned as a child. But when I grew up, I put away childish things. [12]Now we see things imperfectly, like puzzling reflections in a mirror, but then we will see everything with perfect clarity. All that I know now is partial and incomplete, but then I will know everything completely, just as God now knows me completely.

[13]Three things will last forever—faith, hope, and love—and the greatest of these is love.

~ 1 Corinthians 13:4-13

HE IS ALIVE

We preach a risen Christ. We serve a God whose tomb is empty. Our God is alive and He is coming back for you and me. Let us not lose sight of the fact that the earth is but our temporary home.

[12]But tell me this—since we preach that Christ rose from the dead, why are some of you saying there will be no resurrection of the dead?

[13]For if there is no resurrection of the dead, then Christ has not been raised either. [14]And if Christ has not been raised, then all our preaching is useless, and your faith is useless. [15]And we apostles would all be lying about God—for we have said that God raised Christ from the grave. But that can't be true if there is no resurrection of the dead.

[16]And if there is no resurrection of the dead, then Christ has not been raised. [17]And if Christ has not been raised, then your faith is useless and you are still guilty of your sins. [18]In that case, all who have died believing in Christ are lost! [19]And if our hope in Christ is only for this life, we are more to be pitied than anyone in the world.

~ 1 Corinthians 15:12-19

OUR TRUE HOME

Paul says that we must continue steadfast, immoveable, always abounding in the work of the Lord. For we know it is not a waste of time. Look forward with longing to the day when you go to heaven. No more suffering, no more pain, no more fear, no more tears.

[50]What I am saying, dear brothers and sisters, is that our physical bodies cannot inherit the Kingdom of God. These dying bodies cannot inherit what will last forever.

[51]But let me reveal to you a wonderful secret. We will not all die, but we will all be transformed! [52]It will happen in a moment, in the blink of an eye, when the last trumpet is blown. For when the trumpet sounds, those who have died will be raised to live forever. And we who are living will also be transformed. [53]For our dying bodies must be transformed into bodies that will never die; our mortal bodies must be transformed into immortal bodies.

[54]Then, when our dying bodies have been transformed into bodies that will never die, this Scripture will be fulfilled:

"Death is swallowed up in victory.

[55]O death, where is your victory?

O death, where is your sting?"

[56]For sin is the sting that results in death, and the law gives sin its power. [57]But thank God! He gives us victory over sin and death through our Lord Jesus Christ.

[58]So, my dear brothers and sisters, be strong and immovable. Always work enthusiastically for the Lord, for you know that nothing you do for the Lord is ever useless.

~ 1 Corinthians 15:50-58

THE OPENED DOOR

Always remember that we are in a war that we have already won. But that is why Paul says there are many adversaries. Even though the Lord has opened the door for you to continue witnessing for Him, remember it always comes at a price, but it is always worthwhile.

⁵I am coming to visit you after I have been to Macedonia, for I am planning to travel through Macedonia. ⁶Perhaps I will stay awhile with you, possibly all winter, and then you can send me on my way to my next destination. ⁷This time I don't want to make just a short visit and then go right on. I want to come and stay awhile, if the Lord will let me. ⁸In the meantime, I will be staying here at Ephesus until the Festival of Pentecost. ⁹There is a wide-open door for a great work here, although many oppose me.

¹⁰When Timothy comes, don't intimidate him. He is doing the Lord's work, just as I am. ¹¹Don't let anyone treat him with contempt. Send him on his way with your blessing when he returns to me. I expect him to come with the other believers.

¹²Now about our brother Apollos—I urged him to visit you with the other believers, but he was not willing to go right now. He will see you later when he has the opportunity.

¹³Be on guard. Stand firm in the faith. Be courageous. Be strong.

~ 1 Corinthians 16:5-13

SUFFERING

Unless we are willing to go through the fire ourselves, we have no right to try and console others. We have to walk that road if we are going to identify with the hurting people of this world. We know that He understands what we are going through. He has walked the road of suffering.

¹This letter is from Paul, chosen by the will of God to be an apostle of Christ Jesus, and from our brother Timothy.

I am writing to God's church in Corinth and to all of his holy people throughout Greece.

²May God our Father and the Lord Jesus Christ give you grace and peace.

³All praise to God, the Father of our Lord Jesus Christ. God is our merciful Father and the source of all comfort. ⁴He comforts us in all our troubles so that we can comfort others. When they are troubled, we will be able to give them the same comfort God has given us.

⁵For the more we suffer for Christ, the more God will shower us with his comfort through Christ. ⁶Even when we are weighed down with troubles, it is for your comfort and salvation! For when we ourselves are comforted, we will certainly comfort you. Then you can patiently endure the same things we suffer. ⁷We are confident that as you share in our sufferings, you will also share in the comfort God gives us.

~ 2 Corinthians 1:1-7

THE FRAGRANCE

If we are demonstrating the fragrance of Jesus, to some we will be the aroma of death and to others the aroma of life. Let us pray that we will be the aroma of life to those who need it most.

¹²When I came to the city of Troas to preach the Good News of Christ, the Lord opened a door of opportunity for me. ¹³But I had no peace of mind because my dear brother Titus hadn't yet arrived with a report from you. So I said good-bye and went on to Macedonia to find him.

¹⁴But thank God! He has made us his captives and continues to lead us along in Christ's triumphal procession. Now he uses us to spread the knowledge of Christ everywhere, like a sweet perfume.

¹⁵Our lives are a Christ-like fragrance rising up to God. But this fragrance is perceived differently by those who are being saved and by those who are perishing. ¹⁶To those who are perishing, we are a dreadful smell of death and doom. But to those who are being saved, we are a life-giving perfume. And who is adequate for such a task as this?

¹⁷You see, we are not like the many hucksters who preach for personal profit. We preach the word of God with sincerity and with Christ's authority, knowing that God is watching us.

~ 2 Corinthians 2:12-17

NOT CRUSHED

Paul chose to die to self and live for others. As a result, the Lord used him very powerfully to touch the world. Paul had to endure many hardships. It is through hardship that we have a testimony that brings glory to God.

[7]We now have this light shining in our hearts, but we ourselves are like fragile clay jars containing this great treasure. This makes it clear that our great power is from God, not from ourselves.

[8]We are pressed on every side by troubles, but we are not crushed. We are perplexed, but not driven to despair. [9]We are hunted down, but never abandoned by God. We get knocked down, but we are not destroyed. [10]Through suffering, our bodies continue to share in the death of Jesus so that the life of Jesus may also be seen in our bodies.

[11]Yes, we live under constant danger of death because we serve Jesus, so that the life of Jesus will be evident in our dying bodies. [12]So we live in the face of death, but this has resulted in eternal life for you.

[13]But we continue to preach because we have the same kind of faith the psalmist had when he said, "I believed in God, so I spoke." [14]We know that God, who raised the Lord Jesus, will also raise us with Jesus and present us to himself together with you. [15]All of this is for your benefit. And as God's grace reaches more and more people, there will be great thanksgiving, and God will receive more and more glory.

~ 2 Corinthians 4:7-15

RECONCILIATION

You and I have been called to be ambassadors for Jesus Christ. The world is reaching out for reconciliation and peace. But there will be no reconciliation until a man is reconciled first and foremost to God. We have a message of hope: people can be reconciled by accepting Jesus Christ as Lord and Savior.

¹²Are we commending ourselves to you again? No, we are giving you a reason to be proud of us, so you can answer those who brag about having a spectacular ministry rather than having a sincere heart. ¹³If it seems we are crazy, it is to bring glory to God. And if we are in our right minds, it is for your benefit. ¹⁴Either way, Christ's love controls us. Since we believe that Christ died for all, we also believe that we have all died to our old life. ¹⁵He died for everyone so that those who receive his new life will no longer live for themselves. Instead, they will live for Christ, who died and was raised for them.

¹⁶So we have stopped evaluating others from a human point of view. At one time we thought of Christ merely from a human point of view. How differently we know him now! ¹⁷This means that anyone who belongs to Christ has become a new person. The old life is gone; a new life has begun!

¹⁸And all of this is a gift from God, who brought us back to himself through Christ. And God has given us this task of reconciling people to him. ¹⁹For God was in Christ, reconciling the world to himself, no longer counting people's sins against them. And he gave us this wonderful message of reconciliation. ²⁰So we are Christ's ambassadors; God is making his appeal through us. We speak for Christ when we plead, "Come back to God!"

~ 2 Corinthians 5:12-20

SPIRITUAL WAR

The Lord reminds us that the battle is not against flesh and blood but against principalities and powers of the air. We know that the weapons we have are more than capable of pulling down those strongholds. Do not fear, but put on the armor of God daily.

¹Now I, Paul, appeal to you with the gentleness and kindness of Christ—though I realize you think I am timid in person and bold only when I write from far away. ²Well, I am begging you now so that when I come I won't have to be bold with those who think we act from human motives.

³We are human, but we don't wage war as humans do. ⁴We use God's mighty weapons, not worldly weapons, to knock down the strongholds of human reasoning and to destroy false arguments.

⁵We destroy every proud obstacle that keeps people from knowing God. We capture their rebellious thoughts and teach them to obey Christ. ⁶And after you have become fully obedient, we will punish everyone who remains disobedient.

~ 2 Corinthians 10:1-6

AFFLICTION

We can ask God to remove the "thorn in the flesh" in our lives, but we mustn't be disheartened if a miracle doesn't happen. If your affliction has changed your character and made you into a person who is gentle, compassionate and patient – praise the Lord for that!

[6]If I wanted to boast, I would be no fool in doing so, because I would be telling the truth. But I won't do it, because I don't want anyone to give me credit beyond what they can see in my life or hear in my message, [7]even though I have received such wonderful revelations from God. So to keep me from becoming proud, I was given a thorn in my flesh, a messenger from Satan to torment me and keep me from becoming proud.

[8]Three different times I begged the Lord to take it away. [9]Each time he said, "My grace is all you need. My power works best in weakness." So now I am glad to boast about my weaknesses, so that the power of Christ can work through me.

[10]That's why I take pleasure in my weaknesses, and in the insults, hardships, persecutions, and troubles that I suffer for Christ. For when I am weak, then I am strong.

~ 2 Corinthians 12:6-10

OUR CHILDREN

Paul reminds the church that he does not want to be a burden to them. Like a father, he looks after his spiritual children. We need to look after the children and people entrusted into our care, whether spiritual or physical.

[14]Now I am coming to you for the third time, and I will not be a burden to you. I don't want what you have—I want you. After all, children don't provide for their parents. Rather, parents provide for their children. [15]I will gladly spend myself and all I have for you, even though it seems that the more I love you, the less you love me.

[16]Some of you admit I was not a burden to you. But others still think I was sneaky and took advantage of you by trickery. [17]But how? Did any of the men I sent to you take advantage of you? [18]When I urged Titus to visit you and sent our other brother with him, did Titus take advantage of you? No! For we have the same spirit and walk in each other's steps, doing things the same way.

[19]Perhaps you think we're saying these things just to defend ourselves. No, we tell you this as Christ's servants, and with God as our witness. Everything we do, dear friends, is to strengthen you. [20]For I am afraid that when I come I won't like what I find, and you won't like my response. I am afraid that I will find quarreling, jealousy, anger, selfishness, slander, gossip, arrogance, and disorderly behavior.

~2 Corinthians 12:14-20

ONLY ONE GOSPEL

Paul does not mix his words when he says there is only one gospel; anything else is not acceptable. What I love about Paul is that he is a straight speaker. There is no gospel plus or gospel minus, but one gospel as the Bible states.

¹This letter is from Paul, an apostle. I was not appointed by any group of people or any human authority, but by Jesus Christ himself and by God the Father, who raised Jesus from the dead.

²All the brothers and sisters here join me in sending this letter to the churches of Galatia.

³May God our Father and the Lord Jesus Christ give you grace and peace. ⁴Jesus gave his life for our sins, just as God our Father planned, in order to rescue us from this evil world in which we live. ⁵All glory to God forever and ever! Amen.

⁶I am shocked that you are turning away so soon from God, who called you to himself through the loving mercy of Christ. You are following a different way that pretends to be the Good News ⁷but is not the Good News at all. You are being fooled by those who deliberately twist the truth concerning Christ.

⁸Let God's curse fall on anyone, including us or even an angel from heaven, who preaches a different kind of Good News than the one we preached to you. ⁹I say again what we have said before: If anyone preaches any other Good News than the one you welcomed, let that person be cursed.

¹⁰Obviously, I'm not trying to win the approval of people, but of God. If pleasing people were my goal, I would not be Christ's servant.

~ Galatians 1:1-10

THE CALL

It is so important to get a clear call from God. Paul said he was called from the time when he was in his mother's womb. He also says no man taught him, but that his teaching came from the Holy Spirit through Jesus Christ. That is why he could withstand all types of onslaught from the evil one.

¹¹Dear brothers and sisters, I want you to understand that the gospel message I preach is not based on mere human reasoning. ¹²I received my message from no human source, and no one taught me. Instead, I received it by direct revelation from Jesus Christ.

¹³You know what I was like when I followed the Jewish religion—how I violently persecuted God's church. I did my best to destroy it. ¹⁴I was far ahead of my fellow Jews in my zeal for the traditions of my ancestors.

¹⁵But even before I was born, God chose me and called me by his marvelous grace. Then it pleased him ¹⁶to reveal his Son to me so that I would proclaim the Good News about Jesus to the Gentiles.

When this happened, I did not rush out to consult with any human being. ¹⁷Nor did I go up to Jerusalem to consult with those who were apostles before I was. Instead, I went away into Arabia, and later I returned to the city of Damascus.

~ Galatians 1:11-17

NOT BY LAW

This is such a beautiful passage, because it reminds us that we are not justified by works, but by the love and grace of Christ. God takes men who have fallen and He, by grace, makes them His representatives here on earth.

¹¹But when Peter came to Antioch, I had to oppose him to his face, for what he did was very wrong. ¹² When he first arrived, he ate with the Gentile Christians, who were not circumcised. But afterward, when some friends of James came, Peter wouldn't eat with the Gentiles anymore. He was afraid of criticism from these people who insisted on the necessity of circumcision.

¹⁴When I saw that they were not following the truth of the gospel message, I said to Peter in front of all the others, "Since you, a Jew by birth, have discarded the Jewish laws and are living like a Gentile, why are you now trying to make these Gentiles follow the Jewish traditions?

¹⁵"You and I are Jews by birth, not 'sinners' like the Gentiles."

¹⁹For when I tried to keep the law, it condemned me. So I died to the law—I stopped trying to meet all its requirements—so that I might live for God. ²⁰My old self has been crucified with Christ. It is no longer I who live, but Christ lives in me. So I live in this earthly body by trusting in the Son of God, who loved me and gave himself for me. ²¹I do not treat the grace of God as meaningless. For if keeping the law could make us right with God, then there was no need for Christ to die.

~ Galatians 2:11-12, 14-15, 19-21

FINISH BY FAITH

God is not interested in how you started the race, but rather how you finish. We have to get back to basics and we have to start with faith. Let us finish strong like we started, by faith!

¹Oh, foolish Galatians! Who has cast an evil spell on you? For the meaning of Jesus Christ's death was made as clear to you as if you had seen a picture of his death on the cross. ²Let me ask you this one question: Did you receive the Holy Spirit by obeying the law of Moses? Of course not! You received the Spirit because you believed the message you heard about Christ. ³How foolish can you be? After starting your Christian lives in the Spirit, why are you now trying to become perfect by your own human effort? ⁴Have you experienced so much for nothing? Surely it was not in vain, was it?

⁵I ask you again, does God give you the Holy Spirit and work miracles among you because you obey the law? Of course not! It is because you believe the message you heard about Christ.

⁶In the same way, "Abraham believed God, and God counted him as righteous because of his faith." ⁷The real children of Abraham, then, are those who put their faith in God.

⁸What's more, the Scriptures looked forward to this time when God would declare the Gentiles to be righteous because of their faith. God proclaimed this good news to Abraham long ago when he said, "All nations will be blessed through you." ⁹So all who put their faith in Christ share the same blessing Abraham received because of his faith.

~ Galatians 3:1-9

GOD'S PROMISES

God promises that He will do what He said He will do. So hang on to the promises of God. Even though It might take longer than we want, if we keep trusting, God will come through.

[15]Dear brothers and sisters, here's an example from everyday life. Just as no one can set aside or amend an irrevocable agreement, so it is in this case.

[16]God gave the promises to Abraham and his child. And notice that the Scripture doesn't say "to his children," as if it meant many descendants. Rather, it says "to his child"—and that, of course, means Christ.

[17]This is what I am trying to say: The agreement God made with Abraham could not be canceled 430 years later when God gave the law to Moses. God would be breaking his promise. [18]For if the inheritance could be received by keeping the law, then it would not be the result of accepting God's promise. But God graciously gave it to Abraham as a promise.

~ Galatians 3:15-18

NO LONGER A SLAVE

The Lord has told us that we are no longer slaves, but now sons and daughters in Christ. We can call out to our heavenly Father, because we are genuinely His sons and daughters because of the blood Jesus shed for us on the cross of Calvary.

[26]For you are all children of God through faith in Christ Jesus. [27]And all who have been united with Christ in baptism have put on Christ, like putting on new clothes. [28]There is no longer Jew or Gentile, slave or free, male and female. For you are all one in Christ Jesus. [29]And now that you belong to Christ, you are the true children of Abraham. You are his heirs, and God's promise to Abraham belongs to you.

[4]Think of it this way. If a father dies and leaves an inheritance for his young children, those children are not much better off than slaves until they grow up, even though they actually own everything their father had. [2]They have to obey their guardians until they reach whatever age their father set. [3]And that's the way it was with us before Christ came. We were like children; we were slaves to the basic spiritual principles of this world.

[4]But when the right time came, God sent his Son, born of a woman, subject to the law. [5]God sent him to buy freedom for us who were slaves to the law, so that he could adopt us as his very own children. [6]And because we are his children, God has sent the Spirit of his Son into our hearts, prompting us to call out, "Abba, Father." [7]Now you are no longer a slave but God's own child. And since you are his child, God has made you his heir.

~ Galatians 3:26-29; 4:1-7

TWO COVENANTS

This is such a profound insight by God to show us the difference of the world: the sons of the law and the sons of God. We are sons and daughters of God, children of liberty. Because we have believed in Jesus and are born again, we have the promise of eternal life.

²¹Tell me, you who want to live under the law, do you know what the law actually says? ²²The Scriptures say that Abraham had two sons, one from his slave wife and one from his freeborn wife. ²³The son of the slave wife was born in a human attempt to bring about the fulfillment of God's promise. But the son of the freeborn wife was born as God's own fulfillment of his promise.

²⁴These two women serve as an illustration of God's two covenants. The first woman, Hagar, represents Mount Sinai where people received the law that enslaved them. ²⁵And now Jerusalem is just like Mount Sinai in Arabia, because she and her children live in slavery to the law. ²⁶But the other woman, Sarah, represents the heavenly Jerusalem. She is the free woman, and she is our mother.

²⁸And you, dear brothers and sisters, are children of the promise, just like Isaac. ²⁹But you are now being persecuted by those who want you to keep the law, just as Ishmael, the child born by human effort, persecuted Isaac, the child born by the power of the Spirit.

³⁰But what do the Scriptures say about that? "Get rid of the slave and her son, for the son of the slave woman will not share the inheritance with the free woman's son." ³¹So, dear brothers and sisters, we are not children of the slave woman; we are children of the free woman.

~ Galatians 4:21-26, 28-31

NOVEMBER

DO GOOD

It is by our actions that we are recognized as children of God. We can fool people, but we can never fool God. He says that whatever we sow we will reap. If we do not grow weary in doing good deeds we will reap a harvest. Let us not lose heart.

¹Dear brothers and sisters, if another believer is overcome by some sin, you who are godly should gently and humbly help that person back onto the right path. And be careful not to fall into the same temptation yourself. ²Share each other's burdens, and in this way obey the law of Christ. ³If you think you are too important to help someone, you are only fooling yourself. You are not that important.

⁴Pay careful attention to your own work, for then you will get the satisfaction of a job well done, and you won't need to compare yourself to anyone else. ⁵For we are each responsible for our own conduct.

⁶Those who are taught the word of God should provide for their teachers, sharing all good things with them.

⁷Don't be misled—you cannot mock the justice of God. You will always harvest what you plant. ⁸Those who live only to satisfy their own sinful nature will harvest decay and death from that sinful nature. But those who live to please the Spirit will harvest everlasting life from the Spirit. ⁹So let's not get tired of doing what is good. At just the right time we will reap a harvest of blessing if we don't give up. ¹⁰Therefore, whenever we have the opportunity, we should do good to everyone—especially to those in the family of faith.

~ Galatians 6:1-10

SPIRITUAL WISDOM

We pray for many things for our children, but do we pray for spiritual wisdom and a discerning spirit? We need to pray for our children to have a spirit of wisdom, so that they can distinguish between what is of God and what is not.

[15]Ever since I first heard of your strong faith in the Lord Jesus and your love for God's people everywhere, [16]I have not stopped thanking God for you. I pray for you constantly, [17]asking God, the glorious Father of our Lord Jesus Christ, to give you spiritual wisdom and insight so that you might grow in your knowledge of God. [18]I pray that your hearts will be flooded with light so that you can understand the confident hope he has given to those he called—his holy people who are his rich and glorious inheritance.

[19]I also pray that you will understand the incredible greatness of God's power for us who believe him. This is the same mighty power [20]that raised Christ from the dead and seated him in the place of honor at God's right hand in the heavenly realms. [21]Now he is far above any ruler or authority or power or leader or anything else—not only in this world but also in the world to come.

[22]God has put all things under the authority of Christ and has made him head over all things for the benefit of the church. [23]And the church is his body; it is made full and complete by Christ, who fills all things everywhere with himself.

~ Ephesians 1:15-23

AMAZING GRACE

Grace means unmerited favor and undeserved loving kindness. This stops us from becoming proud and thinking we have something to do with our salvation. The workmanship in our lives is all from Jesus. Thank God today for His gift of grace.

¹Once you were dead because of your disobedience and your many sins. ²You used to live in sin, just like the rest of the world, obeying the devil—the commander of the powers in the unseen world. He is the spirit at work in the hearts of those who refuse to obey God. ³All of us used to live that way, following the passionate desires and inclinations of our sinful nature. By our very nature we were subject to God's anger, just like everyone else.

⁴But God is so rich in mercy, and he loved us so much, ⁵that even though we were dead because of our sins, he gave us life when he raised Christ from the dead. (It is only by God's grace that you have been saved!) ⁶For he raised us from the dead along with Christ and seated us with him in the heavenly realms because we are united with Christ Jesus. ⁷So God can point to us in all future ages as examples of the incredible wealth of his grace and kindness toward us, as shown in all he has done for us who are united with Christ Jesus.

⁸God saved you by his grace when you believed. And you can't take credit for this; it is a gift from God. ⁹Salvation is not a reward for the good things we have done, so none of us can boast about it.

~ Ephesians 2:1-9

GOD'S HOUSEHOLD

It is good to see families gathering around God's Word. They share their lives with one another and with God. That's what we are aiming for. That's what Jesus wants. We are fellow citizens and members of God's household. What a privilege!

[14]For Christ himself has brought peace to us. He united Jews and Gentiles into one people when, in his own body on the cross, he broke down the wall of hostility that separated us. [15]He did this by ending the system of law with its commandments and regulations. He made peace between Jews and Gentiles by creating in himself one new people from the two groups. [16]Together as one body, Christ reconciled both groups to God by means of his death on the cross, and our hostility toward each other was put to death.

[17]He brought this Good News of peace to you Gentiles who were far away from him, and peace to the Jews who were near. [18]Now all of us can come to the Father through the same Holy Spirit because of what Christ has done for us.

[19]So now you Gentiles are no longer strangers and foreigners. You are citizens along with all of God's holy people. You are members of God's family. [20]Together, we are his house, built on the foundation of the apostles and the prophets. And the cornerstone is Christ Jesus himself. [21]We are carefully joined together in him, becoming a holy temple for the Lord. [22]Through him you Gentiles are also being made part of this dwelling where God lives by his Spirit.

~ Ephesians 2:14-22

AN AMAZING GOD

God always does things bigger and better than we imagine. He is so generous, embracing and powerful. He longs for all people to be saved and to know His love. We will never be able to comprehend the incredible love He has for each of us.

[14]When I think of all this, I fall to my knees and pray to the Father, [15]the Creator of everything in heaven and on earth. [16]I pray that from his glorious, unlimited resources he will empower you with inner strength through his Spirit.

[17]Then Christ will make his home in your hearts as you trust in him. Your roots will grow down into God's love and keep you strong.

[18]And may you have the power to understand, as all God's people should, how wide, how long, how high, and how deep his love is. [19]May you experience the love of Christ, though it is too great to understand fully. Then you will be made complete with all the fullness of life and power that comes from God.

[20]Now all glory to God, who is able, through his mighty power at work within us, to accomplish infinitely more than we might ask or think.

~ Ephesians 3:14-20

DON'T LET THE SUN SET

When couples marry, they are often told that they mustn't let the sun go down on their wrath. The silent treatment is not of God. Settle any differences before the day is over, and by so doing you will not give the devil any place in your marriage.

[25]So stop telling lies. Let us tell our neighbors the truth, for we are all parts of the same body. [26]And "don't sin by letting anger control you." Don't let the sun go down while you are still angry, [27]for anger gives a foothold to the devil.

[28]If you are a thief, quit stealing. Instead, use your hands for good hard work, and then give generously to others in need. [29]Don't use foul or abusive language. Let everything you say be good and helpful, so that your words will be an encouragement to those who hear them.

[30]And do not bring sorrow to God's Holy Spirit by the way you live. Remember, he has identified you as his own, guaranteeing that you will be saved on the day of redemption.

[31]Get rid of all bitterness, rage, anger, harsh words, and slander, as well as all types of evil behavior. [32]Instead, be kind to each other, tenderhearted, forgiving one another, just as God through Christ has forgiven you.

~ Ephesians 4:25-32

SUBMIT AND LOVE

The Lord speaks clearly about the holy covenant of marriage. When we say on our wedding day, "Until death do us part," we need to really understand what that means. It means until the end. It is for as long as we live. Consider this carefully before entering into marriage.

²²For wives, this means submit to your husbands as to the Lord. ²³For a husband is the head of his wife as Christ is the head of the church. He is the Savior of his body, the church. ²⁴As the church submits to Christ, so you wives should submit to your husbands in everything.

²⁵For husbands, this means love your wives, just as Christ loved the church. He gave up his life for her ²⁶to make her holy and clean, washed by the cleansing of God's word. ²⁷He did this to present her to himself as a glorious church without a spot or wrinkle or any other blemish. Instead, she will be holy and without fault.

²⁸In the same way, husbands ought to love their wives as they love their own bodies. For a man who loves his wife actually shows love for himself. ²⁹No one hates his own body but feeds and cares for it, just as Christ cares for the church. ³⁰And we are members of his body.

³¹As the Scriptures say, "A man leaves his father and mother and is joined to his wife, and the two are united into one." ³²This is a great mystery, but it is an illustration of the way Christ and the church are one. ³³So again I say, each man must love his wife as he loves himself, and the wife must respect her husband.

~ Ephesians 5:22-33

HONOR YOUR PARENTS

"Honor your father and mother" is the first commandment in the Bible with a promise added to it. Often parents literally tease their children and break their confidence by the things they say. We need to encourage our children. They are our representatives. They need to know that we love them.

¹Children, obey your parents because you belong to the Lord, for this is the right thing to do.

²"Honor your father and mother." This is the first commandment with a promise:

³If you honor your father and mother, "things will go well for you, and you will have a long life on the earth."

⁴Fathers, do not provoke your children to anger by the way you treat them. Rather, bring them up with the discipline and instruction that comes from the Lord.

~ Ephesians 6:1-4

THE ARMOR OF GOD

From the day we are saved, we need to put God's armor on every day. Once that is done, we need to stand, because the battle is not ours, it is the Lord's. Put on the armor of God daily to enable you to fight the evil spirits in the heavenly realms.

[10]A final word: Be strong in the Lord and in his mighty power. [11]Put on all of God's armor so that you will be able to stand firm against all strategies of the devil. [12]For we are not fighting against flesh-and-blood enemies, but against evil rulers and authorities of the unseen world, against mighty powers in this dark world, and against evil spirits in the heavenly places.

[13]Therefore, put on every piece of God's armor so you will be able to resist the enemy in the time of evil. Then after the battle you will still be standing firm. [14]Stand your ground, putting on the belt of truth and the body armor of God's righteousness. [15]For shoes, put on the peace that comes from the Good News so that you will be fully prepared. [16]In addition to all of these, hold up the shield of faith to stop the fiery arrows of the devil. [17]Put on salvation as your helmet, and take the sword of the Spirit, which is the word of God.

[18]Pray in the Spirit at all times and on every occasion. Stay alert and be persistent in your prayers for all believers everywhere.

[19]And pray for me, too. Ask God to give me the right words so I can boldly explain God's mysterious plan that the Good News is for Jews and Gentiles alike. [20]I am in chains now, still preaching this message as God's ambassador. So pray that I will keep on speaking boldly for him, as I should.

~ Ephesians 6:10-20

NEVER GIVE UP

Our confidence in the work the Lord has given us is not up to us, but up to Him. We must do our best, work hard and listen to the direction of the Lord. Rejoice then and give Him all the praise when you achieve success.

[2]May God our Father and the Lord Jesus Christ give you grace and peace.

[3]Every time I think of you, I give thanks to my God. [4]Whenever I pray, I make my requests for all of you with joy, [5]for you have been my partners in spreading the Good News about Christ from the time you first heard it until now. [6]And I am certain that God, who began the good work within you, will continue his work until it is finally finished on the day when Christ Jesus returns.

[7]So it is right that I should feel as I do about all of you, for you have a special place in my heart. You share with me the special favor of God, both in my imprisonment and in defending and confirming the truth of the Good News. [8]God knows how much I love you and long for you with the tender compassion of Christ Jesus.

[9]I pray that your love will overflow more and more, and that you will keep on growing in knowledge and understanding. [10]For I want you to understand what really matters, so that you may live pure and blameless lives until the day of Christ's return. [11]May you always be filled with the fruit of your salvation—the righteous character produced in your life by Jesus Christ—for this will bring much glory and praise to God.

~ Philippians 1:2-11

DYING TO LIVE

With so many diseases and illnesses on the rampage, people seem so fearful of death. Yet, Paul said to live is Christ and to die is gain. You cannot frighten a Christian with death, because our reward is in heaven, where we will live with Jesus forever.

[19] For I know that as you pray for me and the Spirit of Jesus Christ helps me, this will lead to my deliverance.

[20] For I fully expect and hope that I will never be ashamed, but that I will continue to be bold for Christ, as I have been in the past. And I trust that my life will bring honor to Christ, whether I live or die.

[21] For to me, living means living for Christ, and dying is even better. [22] But if I live, I can do more fruitful work for Christ. So I really don't know which is better. [23] I'm torn between two desires: I long to go and be with Christ, which would be far better for me. [24] But for your sakes, it is better that I continue to live.

[25] Knowing this, I am convinced that I will remain alive so I can continue to help all of you grow and experience the joy of your faith. [26] And when I come to you again, you will have even more reason to take pride in Christ Jesus because of what he is doing through me.

~ Philippians 1:19-26

CHRIST IS OUR ALL

In today's Scripture passage, we see the dynamic love that Paul has for his Savior. We need to be of the same heart and mind. Everything outside of Christ is unimportant. Paul was prepared to go the distance for the Lord and we should be prepared to do the same.

[1]Whatever happens, my dear brothers and sisters, rejoice in the Lord. I never get tired of telling you these things, and I do it to safeguard your faith.

[2]Watch out for those dogs, those people who do evil, those mutilators who say you must be circumcised to be saved. [3]For we who worship by the Spirit of God are the ones who are truly circumcised. We rely on what Christ Jesus has done for us. We put no confidence in human effort, [4]though I could have confidence in my own effort if anyone could. Indeed, if others have reason for confidence in their own efforts, I have even more!

[7]I once thought these things were valuable, but now I consider them worthless because of what Christ has done. [8]Yes, everything else is worthless when compared with the infinite value of knowing Christ Jesus my Lord. For his sake I have discarded everything else, counting it all as garbage, so that I could gain Christ [9]and become one with him. I no longer count on my own righteousness through obeying the law; rather, I become righteous through faith in Christ. For God's way of making us right with himself depends on faith. [10]I want to know Christ and experience the mighty power that raised him from the dead. I want to suffer with him, sharing in his death, [11]so that one way or another I will experience the resurrection from the dead!

~ Philippians 3:1-4, 7-11

HOLD ON TO THAT

We need to press on and take hold of "that" which Jesus has prepared for us. We need to find out what it is that Christ has planned for us and requires of us in our lives. We need to hold on to that with everything we have got. Forget your past, and strive toward a bright future with Christ.

[12]I don't mean to say that I have already achieved these things or that I have already reached perfection. But I press on to possess that perfection for which Christ Jesus first possessed me.

[13]No, dear brothers and sisters, I have not achieved it, but I focus on this one thing: Forgetting the past and looking forward to what lies ahead, [14]I press on to reach the end of the race and receive the heavenly prize for which God, through Christ Jesus, is calling us.

[15]Let all who are spiritually mature agree on these things. If you disagree on some point, I believe God will make it plain to you. [16]But we must hold on to the progress we have already made.

~ Philippians 3:12-16

EVERYTHING THROUGH CHRIST

The Lord reminds us that we can do everything through Christ who strengthens us. At the end of the day it is all about the Lord, and He is the only one who can help us in our time of need. He is the only one who can empower us to do greater things than we could ever dream of – but only if we trust and believe Him.

⁸And now, dear brothers and sisters, one final thing. Fix your thoughts on what is true, and honorable, and right, and pure, and lovely, and admirable. Think about things that are excellent and worthy of praise. ⁹Keep putting into practice all you learned and received from me—everything you heard from me and saw me doing. Then the God of peace will be with you.

¹⁰How I praise the Lord that you are concerned about me again. I know you have always been concerned for me, but you didn't have the chance to help me. ¹¹Not that I was ever in need, for I have learned how to be content with whatever I have.

¹²I know how to live on almost nothing or with everything. I have learned the secret of living in every situation, whether it is with a full stomach or empty, with plenty or little. ¹³For I can do everything through Christ, who gives me strength.

~ Philippians 4:8-13

RECONCILED WITH HIM

Through Jesus' blood we are made friends with God. Through His death we have become holy and blameless in His sight. It is not us, but Christ in us that gives us the hope and ability to fulfill the godly calling on our lives.

¹⁹For God in all his fullness was pleased to live in Christ, ²⁰and through him God reconciled everything to himself. He made peace with everything in heaven and on earth by means of Christ's blood on the cross.

²¹This includes you who were once far away from God. You were his enemies, separated from him by your evil thoughts and actions. ²²Yet now he has reconciled you to himself through the death of Christ in his physical body. As a result, he has brought you into his own presence, and you are holy and blameless as you stand before him without a single fault.

²³But you must continue to believe this truth and stand firmly in it. Don't drift away from the assurance you received when you heard the Good News. The Good News has been preached all over the world, and I, Paul, have been appointed as God's servant to proclaim it.

²⁴I am glad when I suffer for you in my body, for I am participating in the sufferings of Christ that continue for his body, the church. ²⁵God has given me the responsibility of serving his church by proclaiming his entire message to you. ²⁶This message was kept secret for centuries and generations past, but now it has been revealed to God's people. ²⁷For God wanted them to know that the riches and glory of Christ are for you Gentiles, too. And this is the secret: Christ lives in you. This gives you assurance of sharing his glory.

~ Colossians 1:19-27

NOT MERE PHILOSOPHY

Our faith is based on the knowledge and relationship of Jesus Christ. When Sundar Singh was asked what made him change to the Christian religion, he said it was one man. Sundar preached all over the Himalayas and his bloody footprints could be seen in the snow. What a witness for Christ.

¹I want you to know how much I have agonized for you and for the church at Laodicea, and for many other believers who have never met me personally. ²I want them to be encouraged and knit together by strong ties of love. I want them to have complete confidence that they understand God's mysterious plan, which is Christ himself. ³In him lie hidden all the treasures of wisdom and knowledge.

⁴I am telling you this so no one will deceive you with well-crafted arguments. ⁵For though I am far away from you, my heart is with you. And I rejoice that you are living as you should and that your faith in Christ is strong.

⁶And now, just as you accepted Christ Jesus as your Lord, you must continue to follow him. ⁷Let your roots grow down into him, and let your lives be built on him. Then your faith will grow strong in the truth you were taught, and you will overflow with thankfulness.

⁸Don't let anyone capture you with empty philosophies and high-sounding nonsense that come from human thinking and from the spiritual powers of this world, rather than from Christ. ⁹For in Christ lives all the fullness of God in a human body. ¹⁰So you also are complete through your union with Christ, who is the head over every ruler and authority.

~ Colossians 2:1-10

LET PEACE RULE

When you belong to Christ, you should seek godly things. It shouldn't all be about what you wear and the car you drive. If you live a life committed to Christ, peace will rule in your heart, and others will want to be around you because you emulate Jesus.

¹Since you have been raised to new life with Christ, set your sights on the realities of heaven, where Christ sits in the place of honor at God's right hand. ²Think about the things of heaven, not the things of earth. ³For you died to this life, and your real life is hidden with Christ in God. ⁴And when Christ, who is your life, is revealed to the whole world, you will share in all his glory.

⁵So put to death the sinful, earthly things lurking within you. Have nothing to do with sexual immorality, impurity, lust, and evil desires. Don't be greedy, for a greedy person is an idolater, worshiping the things of this world.

⁸But now is the time to get rid of anger, rage, malicious behavior, slander, and dirty language.

¹²Since God chose you to be the holy people he loves, you must clothe yourselves with tenderhearted mercy, kindness, humility, gentleness, and patience. ¹³Make allowance for each other's faults, and forgive anyone who offends you. Remember, the Lord forgave you, so you must forgive others. ¹⁴Above all, clothe yourselves with love, which binds us all together in perfect harmony. ¹⁵And let the peace that comes from Christ rule in your hearts. For as members of one body you are called to live in peace. And always be thankful.

¹⁶Let the message about Christ, in all its richness, fill your lives. Teach and counsel each other with all the wisdom he gives.

~ Colossians 3:1-5, 8, 12-16

A GOOD WITNESS

Actions speak louder than words. The greatest example for any believer is the change in their lives from worshiping idols (money, health, possessions, fame) to worshiping the true and living God. That is what draws unbelievers to Jesus. It is not what you say that impresses them, but who you are.

³As we pray to our God and Father about you, we think of your faithful work, your loving deeds, and the enduring hope you have because of our Lord Jesus Christ.

⁴We know, dear brothers and sisters, that God loves you and has chosen you to be his own people. ⁵For when we brought you the Good News, it was not only with words but also with power, for the Holy Spirit gave you full assurance that what we said was true. And you know of our concern for you from the way we lived when we were with you. ⁶So you received the message with joy from the Holy Spirit in spite of the severe suffering it brought you. In this way, you imitated both us and the Lord. ⁷As a result, you have become an example to all the believers in Greece—throughout both Macedonia and Achaia.

⁸And now the word of the Lord is ringing out from you to people everywhere, even beyond Macedonia and Achaia, for wherever we go we find people telling us about your faith in God. We don't need to tell them about it, ⁹for they keep talking about the wonderful welcome you gave us and how you turned away from idols to serve the living and true God. ¹⁰And they speak of how you are looking forward to the coming of God's Son from heaven—Jesus, whom God raised from the dead. He is the one who has rescued us from the terrors of the coming judgment.

~ 1 Thessalonians 1:3-10

COMFORT EACH OTHER

The Lord tells us to comfort one another. We do that by praying without ceasing, and rejoicing always, especially when times are tough. Pray about your situation, whatever it may be, and leave your troubles at the foot of the cross. We must cast our cares upon Jesus.

[11]So encourage each other and build each other up, just as you are already doing.

[12]Dear brothers and sisters, honor those who are your leaders in the Lord's work. They work hard among you and give you spiritual guidance. [13]Show them great respect and wholehearted love because of their work. And live peacefully with each other.

[14]Brothers and sisters, we urge you to warn those who are lazy. Encourage those who are timid. Take tender care of those who are weak. Be patient with everyone.

[15]See that no one pays back evil for evil, but always try to do good to each other and to all people.

[16]Always be joyful. [17]Never stop praying. [18]Be thankful in all circumstances, for this is God's will for you who belong to Christ Jesus.

[19]Do not stifle the Holy Spirit. [20]Do not scoff at prophecies, [21]but test everything that is said. Hold on to what is good. [22]Stay away from every kind of evil.

~ 1 Thessalonians 5:11-22

THE LAZY MAN

The Bible says that those who are unwilling to work, don't deserve to eat. As an employer, you can never pay too much for a good worker. He will generate income that far exceeds his salary. There is nothing the Lord despises more than laziness.

⁶And now, dear brothers and sisters, we give you this command in the name of our Lord Jesus Christ: Stay away from all believers who live idle lives and don't follow the tradition they received from us.

⁷For you know that you ought to imitate us. We were not idle when we were with you. ⁸We never accepted food from anyone without paying for it. We worked hard day and night so we would not be a burden to any of you.

⁹We certainly had the right to ask you to feed us, but we wanted to give you an example to follow. ¹⁰Even while we were with you, we gave you this command: "Those unwilling to work will not get to eat."

¹¹Yet we hear that some of you are living idle lives, refusing to work and meddling in other people's business. ¹²We command such people and urge them in the name of the Lord Jesus Christ to settle down and work to earn their own living. ¹³As for the rest of you, dear brothers and sisters, never get tired of doing good.

¹⁴Take note of those who refuse to obey what we say in this letter. Stay away from them so they will be ashamed. ¹⁵Don't think of them as enemies, but warn them as you would a brother or sister.

~ 2 Thessalonians 3:6-15

QUALIFICATIONS

The Lord is clear about qualifications. To be a leader in His church, you don't necessarily need academic qualifications. Rather, you must lead by example. The way you live your life will make a way for you to be received by the leadership in your church and the world.

¹This is a trustworthy saying: "If someone aspires to be an elder, he desires an honorable position." ²So an elder must be a man whose life is above reproach. He must be faithful to his wife. He must exercise self-control, live wisely, and have a good reputation. He must enjoy having guests in his home, and he must be able to teach.

³He must not be a heavy drinker or be violent. He must be gentle, not quarrelsome, and not love money. ⁴He must manage his own family well, having children who respect and obey him. ⁵For if a man cannot manage his own household, how can he take care of God's church?

⁶An elder must not be a new believer, because he might become proud, and the devil would cause him to fall. ⁷Also, people outside the church must speak well of him so that he will not be disgraced and fall into the devil's trap.

~ 1 Timothy 3:1-7

LEAD BY EXAMPLE

We need to lead by example and not by so much as trying to condemn people and lead them into thinking what we want them to think, which is not necessarily God's way.

¹Now the Holy Spirit tells us clearly that in the last times some will turn away from the true faith; they will follow deceptive spirits and teachings that come from demons. ²These people are hypocrites and liars, and their consciences are dead.

³They will say it is wrong to be married and wrong to eat certain foods. But God created those foods to be eaten with thanks by faithful people who know the truth. ⁴Since everything God created is good, we should not reject any of it but receive it with thanks. ⁵For we know it is made acceptable by the word of God and prayer.

⁶If you explain these things to the brothers and sisters, Timothy, you will be a worthy servant of Christ Jesus, one who is nourished by the message of faith and the good teaching you have followed. ⁷Do not waste time arguing over godless ideas and old wives' tales. Instead, train yourself to be godly. ⁸"Physical training is good, but training for godliness is much better, promising benefits in this life and in the life to come." ⁹This is a trustworthy saying, and everyone should accept it. ¹⁰This is why we work hard and continue to struggle, for our hope is in the living God, who is the Savior of all people and particularly of all believers.

~ 1 Timothy 4:1-10

RESPECT

We need to show older men respect as fathers; we need to treat younger men as brothers, older women as mothers, and younger women as sisters. The biggest way the church should testify to the world is the way they treat widows and orphans.

[1]Never speak harshly to an older man, but appeal to him respectfully as you would to your own father. Talk to younger men as you would to your own brothers. [2]Treat older women as you would your mother, and treat younger women with all purity as you would your own sisters.

[3]Take care of any widow who has no one else to care for her. [4]But if she has children or grandchildren, their first responsibility is to show godliness at home and repay their parents by taking care of them. This is something that pleases God.

[5]Now a true widow, a woman who is truly alone in this world, has placed her hope in God. She prays night and day, asking God for his help. [6]But the widow who lives only for pleasure is spiritually dead even while she lives. [7]Give these instructions to the church so that no one will be open to criticism.

[8]But those who won't care for their relatives, especially those in their own household, have denied the true faith. Such people are worse than unbelievers.

[16]If a woman who is a believer has relatives who are widows, she must take care of them and not put the responsibility on the church. Then the church can care for the widows who are truly alone.

~ 1 Timothy 5:1-8, 16

DON'T BE GREEDY

We need to remember that we are sojourners and foreigners, passing through this world to reach our true home. The only way we can find contentment is to live a holy life. Let us not compromise our faith in order to satisfy a craving.

³Some people may contradict our teaching, but these are the wholesome teachings of the Lord Jesus Christ. These teachings promote a godly life.

⁴Anyone who teaches something different is arrogant and lacks understanding. Such a person has an unhealthy desire to quibble over the meaning of words. This stirs up arguments ending in jealousy, division, slander, and evil suspicions. ⁵These people always cause trouble. Their minds are corrupt, and they have turned their backs on the truth. To them, a show of godliness is just a way to become wealthy.

⁶Yet true godliness with contentment is itself great wealth. ⁷After all, we brought nothing with us when we came into the world, and we can't take anything with us when we leave it. ⁸So if we have enough food and clothing, let us be content.

⁹But people who long to be rich fall into temptation and are trapped by many foolish and harmful desires that plunge them into ruin and destruction. ¹⁰For the love of money is the root of all kinds of evil. And some people, craving money, have wandered from the true faith and pierced themselves with many sorrows.

~ 1 Timothy 6:3-10

THE GOOD FIGHT

We need to have a good testimony so that people will recognize us as children of God. Let us get away from things that don't give us a good name. When people go through tough times, they should be able to come to us for godly advice.

[11]But you, Timothy, are a man of God; so run from all these evil things. Pursue righteousness and a godly life, along with faith, love, perseverance, and gentleness.

[12]Fight the good fight for the true faith. Hold tightly to the eternal life to which God has called you, which you have confessed so well before many witnesses.

[13]And I charge you before God, who gives life to all, and before Christ Jesus, who gave a good testimony before Pontius Pilate, [14]that you obey this command without wavering. Then no one can find fault with you from now until our Lord Jesus Christ comes again.

[15]For at just the right time Christ will be revealed from heaven by the blessed and only almighty God, the King of all kings and Lord of all lords. [16]He alone can never die, and he lives in light so brilliant that no human can approach him. No human eye has ever seen him, nor ever will. All honor and power to him forever! Amen.

~ 1 Timothy 6:11-16

ENDURING HARDSHIP

Just like the athlete who competes for the medal and the hardworking farmer who waits for his crop to ripen, so we as believers must be prepared to endure all things for the sake of the gospel. God is looking for us to live Christian lifestyles and to be godly in our reactions when we face hardship.

³Endure suffering along with me, as a good soldier of Christ Jesus. ⁴Soldiers don't get tied up in the affairs of civilian life, for then they cannot please the officer who enlisted them. ⁵And athletes cannot win the prize unless they follow the rules. ⁶And hardworking farmers should be the first to enjoy the fruit of their labor. ⁷Think about what I am saying. The Lord will help you understand all these things.

⁸Always remember that Jesus Christ, a descendant of King David, was raised from the dead. This is the Good News I preach. ⁹And because I preach this Good News, I am suffering and have been chained like a criminal. But the word of God cannot be chained. ¹⁰So I am willing to endure anything if it will bring salvation and eternal glory in Christ Jesus to those God has chosen.

¹¹This is a trustworthy saying:

If we die with him,

we will also live with him.

¹²If we endure hardship,

we will reign with him.

~ 2 Timothy 2:3-12

THE EVANGELIST

It is preaching the Word that makes the difference. We can present the Word in any way, whether it is printed, spoken or sung – but we need to preach it all times, in our lifestyle, and by what we say. We need to be careful that our lives don't erase the message of Christ.

[1]I solemnly urge you in the presence of God and Christ Jesus, who will someday judge the living and the dead when he appears to set up his Kingdom: [2]Preach the word of God. Be prepared, whether the time is favorable or not. Patiently correct, rebuke, and encourage your people with good teaching.

[3]For a time is coming when people will no longer listen to sound and wholesome teaching. They will follow their own desires and will look for teachers who will tell them whatever their itching ears want to hear. [4]They will reject the truth and chase after myths.

[5]But you should keep a clear mind in every situation. Don't be afraid of suffering for the Lord. Work at telling others the Good News, and fully carry out the ministry God has given you.

[6]As for me, my life has already been poured out as an offering to God. The time of my death is near. [7]I have fought the good fight, I have finished the race, and I have remained faithful.

[8]And now the prize awaits me—the crown of righteousness, which the Lord, the righteous Judge, will give me on the day of his return. And the prize is not just for me but for all who eagerly look forward to his appearing.

~ 2 Timothy 4:1-8

THE LORD IS FAITHFUL

I can honestly say with Paul that the Lord has stood with me during all the tough times. When I address a crowd, I know that my Redeemer lives and that gives me the strength to preach with conviction and power. He is faithful and will never forsake you.

⁹Timothy, please come as soon as you can. ¹⁰Demas has deserted me because he loves the things of this life and has gone to Thessalonica. Crescens has gone to Galatia, and Titus has gone to Dalmatia. ¹¹Only Luke is with me. Bring Mark with you when you come, for he will be helpful to me in my ministry. ¹²I sent Tychicus to Ephesus. ¹³When you come, be sure to bring the coat I left with Carpus at Troas. Also bring my books, and especially my papers.

¹⁴Alexander the coppersmith did me much harm, but the Lord will judge him for what he has done. ¹⁵Be careful of him, for he fought against everything we said.

¹⁶The first time I was brought before the judge, no one came with me. Everyone abandoned me. May it not be counted against them. ¹⁷But the Lord stood with me and gave me strength so that I might preach the Good News in its entirety for all the Gentiles to hear. And he rescued me from certain death. ¹⁸Yes, and the Lord will deliver me from every evil attack and will bring me safely into his heavenly Kingdom. All glory to God forever and ever! Amen.

~ 2 Timothy 4:9-18

A GOOD AMBASSADOR

Remember today that you are an ambassador for Jesus Christ. It's not so much about what you say, but who you are that will persuade other people that you truly know and love the Lord.

¹Paul, a bondservant of God and an apostle of Jesus Christ, according to the faith of God's elect and the acknowledgment of the truth which accords with godliness, ²in hope of eternal life which God, who cannot lie, promised before time began, ³but has in due time manifested His word through preaching, which was committed to me according to the commandment of God our Savior;

⁴To Titus, a true son in our common faith:

Grace, mercy, and peace from God the Father and the Lord Jesus Christ our Savior.

¹⁰For there are many insubordinate, both idle talkers and deceivers, especially those of the circumcision, ¹¹whose mouths must be stopped, who subvert whole households, teaching things which they ought not, for the sake of dishonest gain. ¹²One of them, a prophet of their own, said, "Cretans are always liars, evil beasts, lazy gluttons." ¹³This testimony is true. Therefore rebuke them sharply, that they may be sound in the faith, ¹⁴not giving heed to Jewish fables and commandments of men who turn from the truth. ¹⁵To the pure all things are pure, but to those who are defiled and unbelieving nothing is pure; but even their mind and conscience are defiled.

~ Titus 1:1-4, 10-15

NO EXCUSES

The Word is wonderful! These few verses sum up the Christian lifestyle. It tells us how to run our homes, look after our families, respect our employers and trust our employees, and also cautions us to depart from evil and lust and live a sober life.

¹As for you, Titus, promote the kind of living that reflects wholesome teaching. ²Teach the older men to exercise self-control, to be worthy of respect, and to live wisely. They must have sound faith and be filled with love and patience.

³Similarly, teach the older women to live in a way that honors God. They must not slander others or be heavy drinkers. Instead, they should teach others what is good. ⁴These older women must train the younger women to love their husbands and their children, ⁵to live wisely and be pure, to work in their homes, to do good, and to be submissive to their husbands.

⁶In the same way, encourage the young men to live wisely. ⁷And you yourself must be an example to them by doing good works of every kind. Let everything you do reflect the integrity and seriousness of your teaching. ⁸Teach the truth so that your teaching can't be criticized. Then those who oppose us will be ashamed and have nothing bad to say about us.

¹²And we are instructed to turn from godless living and sinful pleasures. We should live in this evil world with wisdom, righteousness, and devotion to God, ¹³while we look forward with hope to that wonderful day when the glory of our great God and Savior, Jesus Christ, will be revealed. ¹⁴He gave his life to free us from every kind of sin, to cleanse us, and to make us his very own people, totally committed to doing good deeds.

~ Titus 2:1-8, 12-14

DECEMBER

SECOND CHANCES

Here Paul asks Philemon to take Onesimus, his run-away slave, back into his home and give him a second chance. Faith is a doing word – don't tell people you love them, show them you love them. It can be costly and come at a price, but we still need to do it.

⁴I always thank my God when I pray for you, Philemon, ⁵because I keep hearing about your faith in the Lord Jesus and your love for all of God's people. ⁸That is why I am boldly asking a favor of you. I could demand it in the name of Christ because it is the right thing for you to do. ⁹But because of our love, I prefer simply to ask you. Consider this as a request from me—Paul, an old man and now also a prisoner for the sake of Christ Jesus.

¹⁰I appeal to you to show kindness to my child, Onesimus. I became his father in the faith while here in prison. ¹¹Onesimus hasn't been of much use to you in the past, but now he is very useful to both of us. ¹²I am sending him back to you, and with him comes my own heart.

¹³I wanted to keep him here with me while I am in these chains for preaching the Good News, and he would have helped me on your behalf. ¹⁴But I didn't want to do anything without your consent. I wanted you to help because you were willing, not because you were forced. ¹⁵It seems you lost Onesimus for a little while so that you could have him back forever. ¹⁶He is no longer like a slave to you. He is more than a slave, for he is a beloved brother, especially to me. Now he will mean much more to you, both as a man and as a brother in the Lord.

¹⁷So if you consider me your partner, welcome him as you would welcome me.

~ Philemon 1:4-5, 8-17

DON'T DRIFT AWAY

The Lord warns us not to drift away and lose our first love. It would be better to never know God, than to know Him and turn away from Him. Avoid drifting from God by reading the Word of God, praying and spending time with fellow believers.

[1]So we must listen very carefully to the truth we have heard, or we may drift away from it. [2]For the message God delivered through angels has always stood firm, and every violation of the law and every act of disobedience was punished. [3]So what makes us think we can escape if we ignore this great salvation that was first announced by the Lord Jesus himself and then delivered to us by those who heard him speak?

[4]And God confirmed the message by giving signs and wonders and various miracles and gifts of the Holy Spirit whenever he chose. [5]And furthermore, it is not angels who will control the future world we are talking about. [6]For in one place the Scriptures say,

"What are mere mortals that you should think about them,
    or a son of man that you should care for him? [7]Yet you
made them only a little lower than the angels
    and crowned them with glory and honor.
[8]You gave them authority over all things."

Now when it says "all things," it means nothing is left out. But we have not yet seen all things put under their authority. [9]What we do see is Jesus, who was given a position "a little lower than the angels"; and because he suffered death for us, he is now "crowned with glory and honor." Yes, by God's grace, Jesus tasted death for everyone.

~ Hebrews 2:1-9

A NEW COVENANT

The new covenant sets us free from the law and that is why good people don't go to heaven – believers go to heaven. It is only by faith in Christ that we are saved. The gospel is so simple; it's about our love relationship with Jesus Christ.

⁶But now Jesus, our High Priest, has been given a ministry that is far superior to the old priesthood, for he is the one who mediates for us a far better covenant with God, based on better promises.

⁷If the first covenant had been faultless, there would have been no need for a second covenant to replace it. ⁸But when God found fault with the people, he said:

"The day is coming, says the LORD, when I will make a new covenant with the people of Israel and Judah.⁹This covenant will not be like the one I made with their ancestors when I took them by the hand and led them out of the land of Egypt. They did not remain faithful to my covenant, so I turned my back on them, says the LORD.

¹⁰But this is the new covenant I will make

with the people of Israel on that day, says the LORD:

I will put my laws in their minds, and I will write them on their hearts. I will be their God, and they will be my people.

¹¹And they will not need to teach their neighbors, nor will they need to teach their relatives, saying, 'You should know the LORD.'

For everyone, from the least to the greatest, will know me already.

¹²And I will forgive their wickedness, and I will never again remember their sins."

~ Hebrews 8:6-12

FAITH

St. Augustine said, "Faith is to believe what we cannot see and the reward of that is to see what we believe." Without faith we cannot please God, but he who believes will be rewarded by God. If you don't have faith, you cannot be a Christian. Grow in faith by obeying and studying the Word of God.

¹Faith is the confidence that what we hope for will actually happen; it gives us assurance about things we cannot see. ²Through their faith, the people in days of old earned a good reputation.

³By faith we understand that the entire universe was formed at God's command, that what we now see did not come from anything that can be seen.

⁴It was by faith that Abel brought a more acceptable offering to God than Cain did. Abel's offering gave evidence that he was a righteous man, and God showed his approval of his gifts. Although Abel is long dead, he still speaks to us by his example of faith.

⁵It was by faith that Enoch was taken up to heaven without dying—"he disappeared, because God took him." For before he was taken up, he was known as a person who pleased God.

⁷It was by faith that Noah built a large boat to save his family from the flood. He obeyed God, who warned him about things that had never happened before. By his faith Noah condemned the rest of the world, and he received the righteousness that comes by faith.

⁸It was by faith that Abraham obeyed when God called him to leave home and go to another land that God would give him as his inheritance.

~ Hebrews 11:1-5, 7-8,

A CLOUD OF WITNESSES

We are running in a race, but we are not on our own, there is a crowd of witnesses cheering us on. When an athlete runs a marathon, the support from the spectators keep them going. Can you imagine the Master Himself, at the finish line welcoming us home?

[1]Therefore, since we are surrounded by such a huge crowd of witnesses to the life of faith, let us strip off every weight that slows us down, especially the sin that so easily trips us up. And let us run with endurance the race God has set before us.

[2]We do this by keeping our eyes on Jesus, the champion who initiates and perfects our faith. Because of the joy awaiting him, he endured the cross, disregarding its shame. Now he is seated in the place of honor beside God's throne.

[3]Think of all the hostility he endured from sinful people; then you won't become weary and give up. [4]After all, you have not yet given your lives in your struggle against sin.

~ Hebrews 12:1-4

BE HOLY

What is holiness? It's the end product of obedience. We know our God is the God of grace, the God of love. Our God, however, is also the holy God. And without holiness no one will see God. Choose to consecrate yourself and be holy, because God, your Father, is holy.

¹⁴Work at living in peace with everyone, and work at living a holy life, for those who are not holy will not see the Lord. ¹⁵Look after each other so that none of you fails to receive the grace of God. Watch out that no poisonous root of bitterness grows up to trouble you, corrupting many. ¹⁶Make sure that no one is immoral or godless like Esau, who traded his birthright as the firstborn son for a single meal. ¹⁷You know that afterward, when he wanted his father's blessing, he was rejected. It was too late for repentance, even though he begged with bitter tears.

²⁵Be careful that you do not refuse to listen to the One who is speaking. For if the people of Israel did not escape when they refused to listen to Moses, the earthly messenger, we will certainly not escape if we reject the One who speaks to us from heaven! ²⁶When God spoke from Mount Sinai his voice shook the earth, but now he makes another promise: "Once again I will shake not only the earth but the heavens also." ²⁷This means that all of creation will be shaken and removed, so that only unshakable things will remain.

²⁸Since we are receiving a Kingdom that is unshakable, let us be thankful and please God by worshiping him with holy fear and awe. ²⁹For our God is a devouring fire.

~ Hebrews 12:14-17; 25-29

DECEMBER 7
GOD'S FAITHFULNESS

We have nothing to fear because the Lord is our help-er. If the Lord is on our side, we are in the majority. What can man do to us? Unlike man, the Lord never changes. The Lord is the same yesterday, today and forever. What wonderful news that is.

¹Keep on loving each other as brothers and sisters. ²Don't forget to show hospitality to strangers, for some who have done this have entertained angels without realizing it! ³Remember those in prison, as if you were there yourself. Remember also those being mistreated, as if you felt their pain in your own bodies. ⁴Give honor to marriage, and remain faithful to one another in marriage. God will surely judge people who are immoral and those who commit adultery.

⁵Don't love money; be satisfied with what you have. For God has said,

"I will never fail you.
    I will never abandon you."

⁶So we can say with confidence,

"The LORD is my helper,
    so I will have no fear.
        What can mere people do to me?"

⁷Remember your leaders who taught you the word of God. Think of all the good that has come from their lives, and follow the example of their faith.

⁸Jesus Christ is the same yesterday, today, and forever.

~ Hebrews 13:1-8

FAITH HAS FEET

James says that faith without action is no faith at all. He reminds us about Abraham, who had faith enough to sacrifice Isaac. God called Abraham His friend because he was faithful and obedient, and that touched God's heart deeply.

[14]What good is it, dear brothers and sisters, if you say you have faith but don't show it by your actions? Can that kind of faith save anyone? [15]Suppose you see a brother or sister who has no food or clothing, [16]and you say, "Good-bye and have a good day; stay warm and eat well"—but then you don't give that person any food or clothing. What good does that do?

[17]So you see, faith by itself isn't enough. Unless it produces good deeds, it is dead and useless. [18]Now someone may argue, "Some people have faith; others have good deeds." But I say, "How can you show me your faith if you don't have good deeds? I will show you my faith by my good deeds." [19]You say you have faith, for you believe that there is one God. Good for you! Even the demons believe this, and they tremble in terror. [20]How foolish! Can't you see that faith without good deeds is useless?

[21]Don't you remember that our ancestor Abraham was shown to be right with God by his actions when he offered his son Isaac on the altar? [22]You see, his faith and his actions worked together. His actions made his faith complete. [23]And so it happened just as the Scriptures say: "Abraham believed God, and God counted him as righteous because of his faith." He was even called the friend of God. [24]So you see, we are shown to be right with God by what we do, not by faith alone.

[26]Just as the body is dead without breath, so also faith is dead without good works.

~ James 2:14-24, 26

THE TONGUE

The Lord says we need to tame our tongues. The Bible says the tongue is like that tiny rudder on a huge ocean vessel which directs the ship through raging seas, or a bit in a horse's mouth that directs him. The tongue needs to be tamed; if it isn't, it can cause a lot of pain.

¹Dear brothers and sisters, not many of you should become teachers in the church, for we who teach will be judged more strictly. ²Indeed, we all make many mistakes. For if we could control our tongues, we would be perfect and could also control ourselves in every other way.

³We can make a large horse go wherever we want by means of a small bit in its mouth. ⁴And a small rudder makes a huge ship turn wherever the pilot chooses to go, even though the winds are strong. ⁵In the same way, the tongue is a small thing that makes grand speeches. But a tiny spark can set a great forest on fire. ⁶And the tongue is a flame of fire. It is a whole world of wickedness, corrupting your entire body. It can set your whole life on fire, for it is set on fire by hell itself.

⁷People can tame all kinds of animals, birds, reptiles, and fish, ⁸but no one can tame the tongue. It is restless and evil, full of deadly poison. ⁹Sometimes it praises our Lord and Father, and sometimes it curses those who have been made in the image of God. ¹⁰And so blessing and cursing come pouring out of the same mouth. Surely, my brothers and sisters, this is not right! ¹¹Does a spring of water bubble out with both fresh water and bitter water? ¹²Does a fig tree produce olives, or a grapevine produce figs? No, and you can't draw fresh water from a salty spring.

~ James 3:1-12

LORD-WILLING

When we say we are going to do something in the future, we must never forget to say, "God-willing". Because of God's grace toward us we can trust that we will be here tomorrow. Instead of making our own plans, rather say, "Lord, if You are willing, we will go here or there."

[13]Look here, you who say, "Today or tomorrow we are going to a certain town and will stay there a year. We will do business there and make a profit."

[14]How do you know what your life will be like tomorrow? Your life is like the morning fog—it's here a little while, then it's gone.

[15]What you ought to say is, "If the Lord wants us to, we will live and do this or that."

[16]Otherwise you are boasting about your own plans, and all such boasting is evil.

[17]Remember, it is sin to know what you ought to do and then not do it.

~ James 4:13-17

PILGRIMS

The Lord reminds us that earth is not our home – our home is in heaven. We are pilgrims in a foreign land and we must not become too comfortable in this world. We need to guard against the lusts and temptations of this world.

[11]Dear friends, I warn you as "temporary residents and foreigners" to keep away from worldly desires that wage war against your very souls.

[12]Be careful to live properly among your unbelieving neighbors. Then even if they accuse you of doing wrong, they will see your honorable behavior, and they will give honor to God when he judges the world.

[13]For the Lord's sake, respect all human authority—whether the king as head of state, [14]or the officials he has appointed. For the king has sent them to punish those who do wrong and to honor those who do right.

[15]It is God's will that your honorable lives should silence those ignorant people who make foolish accusations against you. [16]For you are free, yet you are God's slaves, so don't use your freedom as an excuse to do evil. [17]Respect everyone, and love your Christian brothers and sisters. Fear God, and respect the king.

~ 1 Peter 2:11-17

LOVE

We need to love one another as Christ loved us. Love covers a multitude of sins. If you have done something wrong and you really show love toward your fellow man, then that's half the battle won. Without love you could negotiate for days, but unless God and His love steps in, nothing will be resolved.

[7]The end of the world is coming soon. Therefore, be earnest and disciplined in your prayers.

[8]Most important of all, continue to show deep love for each other, for love covers a multitude of sins. [9]Cheerfully share your home with those who need a meal or a place to stay.

[10]God has given each of you a gift from his great variety of spiritual gifts. Use them well to serve one another.

[11]Do you have the gift of speaking? Then speak as though God himself were speaking through you. Do you have the gift of helping others? Do it with all the strength and energy that God supplies. Then everything you do will bring glory to God through Jesus Christ. All glory and power to him forever and ever! Amen.

~ 1 Peter 4:7-11

BE HUMBLE

We need to be humble. Jesus took the towel and basin and washed His disciples' feet. This is a wonderful example of humility. Remember, the Word says that He resists the proud but gives grace to the humble.

[5]In the same way, you younger men must accept the authority of the elders. And all of you, serve each other in humility, for

"God opposes the proud
   but favors the humble."

[6]So humble yourselves under the mighty power of God, and at the right time he will lift you up in honor. [7]Give all your worries and cares to God, for he cares about you.

[8]Stay alert! Watch out for your great enemy, the devil. He prowls around like a roaring lion, looking for someone to devour.

[9]Stand firm against him, and be strong in your faith. Remember that your Christian brothers and sisters all over the world are going through the same kind of suffering you are.

[10]In his kindness God called you to share in his eternal glory by means of Christ Jesus. So after you have suffered a little while, he will restore, support, and strengthen you, and he will place you on a firm foundation. [11]All power to him forever! Amen.

~1 Peter 5:5-11

PRODUCTIVE CHRISTIANS

This passage speaks of the virtues we need to demonstrate in our lives. Let's take heed and be productive and useful Christians. People need to know what we are, not by what we say, but by our actions.

⁵In view of all this, make every effort to respond to God's promises. Supplement your faith with a generous provision of moral excellence, and moral excellence with knowledge, ⁶and knowledge with self-control, and self-control with patient endurance, and patient endurance with godliness, ⁷and godliness with brotherly affection, and brotherly affection with love for everyone.

⁸The more you grow like this, the more productive and useful you will be in your knowledge of our Lord Jesus Christ. ⁹But those who fail to develop in this way are shortsighted or blind, forgetting that they have been cleansed from their old sins.

¹⁰So, dear brothers and sisters, work hard to prove that you really are among those God has called and chosen. Do these things, and you will never fall away. ¹¹Then God will give you a grand entrance into the eternal Kingdom of our Lord and Savior Jesus Christ.

~ 2 Peter 1:5-11

LIKE A THIEF

Peter reminds us that the Lord will come like a thief in the night. Martin Luther was once asked what he would do if he heard the Lord was coming tomorrow and he said he would plant an apple tree. In other words, he would carry on with life but always be ready for the coming of the King.

¹⁰But the day of the Lord will come as unexpectedly as a thief. Then the heavens will pass away with a terrible noise, and the very elements themselves will disappear in fire, and the earth and everything on it will be found to deserve judgment.

¹¹Since everything around us is going to be destroyed like this, what holy and godly lives you should live, ¹²looking forward to the day of God and hurrying it along. On that day, he will set the heavens on fire, and the elements will melt away in the flames. ¹³But we are looking forward to the new heavens and new earth he has promised, a world filled with God's righteousness. ¹⁴And so, dear friends, while you are waiting for these things to happen, make every effort to be found living peaceful lives that are pure and blameless in his sight.

¹⁵And remember, our Lord's patience gives people time to be saved. This is what our beloved brother Paul also wrote to you with the wisdom God gave him— ¹⁶speaking of these things in all of his letters. Some of his comments are hard to understand, and those who are ignorant and unstable have twisted his letters to mean something quite different, just as they do with other parts of Scripture. And this will result in their destruction.

~ 2 Peter 3:10-16

WE HAVE SEEN HIM

This is concrete proof that our Redeemer lives. John says that he has touched Him, his eyes have seen Him and his ears have heard Him. He is talking of the Word of life. If someone asks you to see Jesus, pick up a Bible and show it to them. Jesus is indeed the Word of God.

[1]We proclaim to you the one who existed from the beginning, whom we have heard and seen. We saw him with our own eyes and touched him with our own hands. He is the Word of life.

[2]This one who is life itself was revealed to us, and we have seen him. And now we testify and proclaim to you that he is the one who is eternal life. He was with the Father, and then he was revealed to us.

[3]We proclaim to you what we ourselves have actually seen and heard so that you may have fellowship with us. And our fellowship is with the Father and with his Son, Jesus Christ.

[4]We are writing these things so that you may fully share our joy.

~ 1 John 1:1-4

LOVE YOUR BROTHER

The Lord tells us categorically that if we say we love the Lord, but hate our brother, then we are liars and the truth is not in us. Again we are told that if we say that we love the Lord, we need to obey His commandments. We need to love our brother. There is nothing simpler than this commandment.

³And we can be sure that we know him if we obey his commandments. ⁴If someone claims, "I know God," but doesn't obey God's commandments, that person is a liar and is not living in the truth. ⁵But those who obey God's word truly show how completely they love him. That is how we know we are living in him. ⁶Those who say they live in God should live their lives as Jesus did.

⁷Dear friends, I am not writing a new commandment for you; rather it is an old one you have had from the very beginning. This old commandment—to love one another—is the same message you heard before. ⁸Yet it is also new. Jesus lived the truth of this commandment, and you also are living it. For the darkness is disappearing, and the true light is already shining.

⁹If anyone claims, "I am living in the light," but hates a Christian brother or sister, that person is still living in darkness. ¹⁰Anyone who loves another brother or sister is living in the light and does not cause others to stumble. ¹¹But anyone who hates another brother or sister is still living and walking in darkness. Such a person does not know the way to go, having been blinded by the darkness.

~ 1 John 2:3-11

THE CERTAINTY

Jesus is the Word of God. All who believe in Him have the certainty of salvation and eternal life. Look into your heart today and make sure that you believe.

[6]And Jesus Christ was revealed as God's Son by his baptism in water and by shedding his blood on the cross—not by water only, but by water and blood. And the Spirit, who is truth, confirms it with his testimony.

[7]So we have these three witnesses— [8]the Spirit, the water, and the blood—and all three agree. [9]Since we believe human testimony, surely we can believe the greater testimony that comes from God. And God has testified about his Son.

[10]All who believe in the Son of God know in their hearts that this testimony is true. Those who don't believe this are actually calling God a liar because they don't believe what God has testified about his Son.

[11]And this is what God has testified: He has given us eternal life, and this life is in his Son. [12]Whoever has the Son has life; whoever does not have God's Son does not have life.

[13]I have written this to you who believe in the name of the Son of God, so that you may know you have eternal life.

~ 1 John 5:6-13

ANTICHRIST

This is a severe warning from God to us to be careful of deceivers. If anyone comes to you and wants to add something to the Word of God, do not accept it because the Word of God is complete. Do not even let that person into your home.

[7]I say this because many deceivers have gone out into the world. They deny that Jesus Christ came in a real body. Such a person is a deceiver and an antichrist.

[8]Watch out that you do not lose what we have worked so hard to achieve. Be diligent so that you receive your full reward.

[9]Anyone who wanders away from this teaching has no relationship with God. But anyone who remains in the teaching of Christ has a relationship with both the Father and the Son.

[10]If anyone comes to your meeting and does not teach the truth about Christ, don't invite that person into your home or give any kind of encouragement. [11]Anyone who encourages such people becomes a partner in their evil work.

~ 2 John 1:7-11

The Lord challenges us on being truthful: telling the truth and walking in the truth. As you and I conduct our businesses, our families and our social lives according to God's Word, we will become known as truthful people. Others will be drawn to us because people need to hear the truth in love.

¹This letter is from John, the elder.

I am writing to Gaius, my dear friend, whom I love in the truth.

²Dear friend, I hope all is well with you and that you are as healthy in body as you are strong in spirit. ³Some of the traveling teachers recently returned and made me very happy by telling me about your faithfulness and that you are living according to the truth.

⁴I could have no greater joy than to hear that my children are following the truth. ⁵Dear friend, you are being faithful to God when you care for the traveling teachers who pass through, even though they are strangers to you.

⁶They have told the church here of your loving friendship. Please continue providing for such teachers in a manner that pleases God. ⁷For they are traveling for the Lord, and they accept nothing from people who are not believers. ⁸So we ourselves should support them so that we can be their partners as they teach the truth.

~ 3 John 1:1-8

LIFE WITH GOD

We need to keep ourselves holy and have compassion on those who are struggling in the faith. We also need a sense of urgency in telling the unsaved about the Truth which will keep them from going to hell. It needs to be spoken in love with no compromise.

[20]But you, dear friends, must build each other up in your most holy faith, pray in the power of the Holy Spirit, [21]and await the mercy of our Lord Jesus Christ, who will bring you eternal life. In this way, you will keep yourselves safe in God's love.

[22]And you must show mercy to those whose faith is wavering. [23]Rescue others by snatching them from the flames of judgment. Show mercy to still others, but do so with great caution, hating the sins that contaminate their lives.

[24]Now all glory to God, who is able to keep you from falling away and will bring you with great joy into his glorious presence without a single fault. [25]All glory to him who alone is God, our Savior through Jesus Christ our Lord. All glory, majesty, power, and authority are his before all time, and in the present, and beyond all time! Amen.

~ Jude 1:20-25

CLOUD WATCHERS

Some people are cloud watchers. The Lord says that He is coming back in the clouds. He also says He is the Alpha and Omega. If you have Jesus in your life you don't need anything else. Let us wake up every morning and ask the Lord if today is the day He is coming to fetch us to take us home.

⁴This letter is from John to the seven churches in the province of Asia.

Grace and peace to you from the one who is, who always was, and who is still to come; from the sevenfold Spirit before his throne; ⁵and from Jesus Christ. He is the faithful witness to these things, the first to rise from the dead, and the ruler of all the kings of the world.

All glory to him who loves us and has freed us from our sins by shedding his blood for us. ⁶He has made us a Kingdom of priests for God his Father. All glory and power to him forever and ever! Amen.

⁷Look! He comes with the clouds of heaven.

And everyone will see him—

even those who pierced him.

And all the nations of the world

will mourn for him.

Yes! Amen!

⁸"I am the Alpha and the Omega—the beginning and the end," says the Lord God. "I am the one who is, who always was, and who is still to come—the Almighty One."

~ Revelation 1:4-8

FIRST LOVE

This passage was part of a turning point in my life. The Lord said to me that I had forsaken my first love. He told me to put my plans on hold, go home and spend time with Him. He told me He needed me to mentor men and that was the beginning of the Mighty Men phenomenon.

[1]"Write this letter to the angel of the church in Ephesus. This is the message from the one who holds the seven stars in his right hand, the one who walks among the seven gold lampstands:

[2]"I know all the things you do. I have seen your hard work and your patient endurance. I know you don't tolerate evil people. You have examined the claims of those who say they are apostles but are not. You have discovered they are liars. [3]You have patiently suffered for me without quitting.

[4]"But I have this complaint against you. You don't love me or each other as you did at first! [5]Look how far you have fallen! Turn back to me and do the works you did at first. If you don't repent, I will come and remove your lampstand from its place among the churches. [6]But this is in your favor: You hate the evil deeds of the Nicolaitans, just as I do.

[7]"Anyone with ears to hear must listen to the Spirit and understand what he is saying to the churches. To everyone who is victorious I will give fruit from the tree of life in the paradise of God."

~ Revelation 2:1-7

CONFIRMATION

Seek God's confirmation through His Word. We need to obey His commands. If we do that to the end, He will give us the nations. Whenever we need confirmation from God, we can run backwards and forwards between people, pastors and leaders, but if we turn to the Word we get God's best.

²⁴"But I also have a message for the rest of you in Thyatira who have not followed this false teaching ('deeper truths,' as they call them—depths of Satan, actually). I will ask nothing more of you ²⁵except that you hold tightly to what you have until I come. ²⁶To all who are victorious, who obey me to the very end,
    To them I will give authority over all the nations.
        ²⁷They will rule the nations with an iron rod
        and smash them like clay pots.
²⁸They will have the same authority I received from my Father, and I will also give them the morning star!
    ²⁹"Anyone with ears to hear must listen to the Spirit and understand what he is saying to the churches."

~ Revelation 2:24-29

OPEN DOORS

If we walk in God's ways, He will open a door for us that no one can break down. When God closes a door, don't go through it, when God opens a door, don't hesitate to go through it. He will give us what we need. Hold fast to what He has given us until His return.

[7]"Write this letter to the angel of the church in Philadelphia.

This is the message from the one who is holy and true,
the one who has the key of David.

What he opens, no one can close;
and what he closes, no one can open:

[8]"I know all the things you do, and I have opened a door for you that no one can close. You have little strength, yet you obeyed my word and did not deny me. [9]Look, I will force those who belong to Satan's synagogue—those liars who say they are Jews but are not—to come and bow down at your feet. They will acknowledge that you are the ones I love.

[10]"Because you have obeyed my command to persevere, I will protect you from the great time of testing that will come upon the whole world to test those who belong to this world. [11]I am coming soon. Hold on to what you have, so that no one will take away your crown. [12]All who are victorious will become pillars in the Temple of my God, and they will never have to leave it. And I will write on them the name of my God, and they will be citizens in the city of my God—the new Jerusalem that comes down from heaven from my God. And I will also write on them my new name.

[13]"Anyone with ears to hear must listen to the Spirit and understand what he is saying to the churches."

~ Revelation 3:7-13

WELCOME HIM IN

Jesus appeals to the unbeliever to open the door and welcome Him in. The Lord wants to clothe us, feed us, and give us a second chance, but we need to open the door to our heart. The Lord waits for us. Let us not waste any more time.

[17]"You say, 'I am rich. I have everything I want. I don't need a thing!' And you don't realize that you are wretched and miserable and poor and blind and naked. [18]So I advise you to buy gold from me—gold that has been purified by fire. Then you will be rich. Also buy white garments from me so you will not be shamed by your nakedness, and ointment for your eyes so you will be able to see. [19]I correct and discipline everyone I love. So be diligent and turn from your indifference.

[20]"Look! I stand at the door and knock. If you hear my voice and open the door, I will come in, and we will share a meal together as friends. [21]Those who are victorious will sit with me on my throne, just as I was victorious and sat with my Father on his throne.

[22]"Anyone with ears to hear must listen to the Spirit and understand what he is saying to the churches."

~ Revelation 3:17-22

OVERCOMING THE DEVIL

The Lord says if we lift Him up, He will draw all men unto Himself. However, how do we overcome the devil? We overcome the devil by the blood of the Lamb and by the word of our testimony. When you speak out about what Jesus has done in your life, the devil runs a mile.

[7]Then there was war in heaven. Michael and his angels fought against the dragon and his angels. [8]And the dragon lost the battle, and he and his angels were forced out of heaven. [9]This great dragon—the ancient serpent called the devil, or Satan, the one deceiving the whole world—was thrown down to the earth with all his angels.

[10]Then I heard a loud voice shouting across the heavens, "It has come at last—
    salvation and power
and the Kingdom of our God,
    and the authority of his Christ.
For the accuser of our brothers and sisters
    has been thrown down to earth—
the one who accuses them before our God day and night.
[11]And they have defeated him by the blood of the Lamb
    and by their testimony.
And they did not love their lives so much
    that they were afraid to die.
[12]Therefore, rejoice, O heavens!
    And you who live in the heavens, rejoice!
But terror will come on the earth and the sea,
    for the devil has come down to you in great anger,
knowing that he has little time."

~ Revelation 12:7-12

REAPING THE HARVEST

Blessed are those who die in the Lord. It is a time for rejoicing, because a believer automatically enters heaven. It is a tragedy when an unbeliever dies, because there is no hope for him. Everywhere we look there is pain and suffering. We need to work hard, because the coming of the Lord is at hand.

[13]And I heard a voice from heaven saying, "Write this down: Blessed are those who die in the Lord from now on. Yes, says the Spirit, they are blessed indeed, for they will rest from their hard work; for their good deeds follow them!"

[14]Then I saw a white cloud, and seated on the cloud was someone like the Son of Man. He had a gold crown on his head and a sharp sickle in his hand.

[15]Then another angel came from the Temple and shouted to the one sitting on the cloud, "Swing the sickle, for the time of harvest has come; the crop on earth is ripe."

[16]So the one sitting on the cloud swung his sickle over the earth, and the whole earth was harvested.

~ Revelation 14:13-16

COMING BACK

What a day it will be when we see the Lord riding that white horse! That will be a great day for believers, but a fearful day for those who have turned their back on God. Let us at all costs preach the gospel so that the lost may be saved.

¹¹Then I saw heaven opened, and a white horse was standing there. Its rider was named Faithful and True, for he judges fairly and wages a righteous war. ¹²His eyes were like flames of fire, and on his head were many crowns. A name was written on him that no one understood except himself. ¹³He wore a robe dipped in blood, and his title was the Word of God. ¹⁴The armies of heaven, dressed in the finest of pure white linen, followed him on white horses. ¹⁵From his mouth came a sharp sword to strike down the nations. He will rule them with an iron rod. He will release the fierce wrath of God, the Almighty, like juice flowing from a winepress. ¹⁶On his robe at his thigh was written this title: King of all kings and Lord of all lords.

~ Revelation 19:11-16

Our one objective is to see that the names of as many people as possible are written in the Book of Life. It is not good people that go to heaven, but believers – people who believe that Jesus Christ is the Son of God. We need God in our last days.

¹¹And I saw a great white throne and the one sitting on it. The earth and sky fled from his presence, but they found no place to hide.

¹²I saw the dead, both great and small, standing before God's throne. And the books were opened, including the Book of Life. And the dead were judged according to what they had done, as recorded in the books.

¹³The sea gave up its dead, and death and the grave gave up their dead. And all were judged according to their deeds.

¹⁴Then death and the grave were thrown into the lake of fire. This lake of fire is the second death.

¹⁵And anyone whose name was not found recorded in the Book of Life was thrown into the lake of fire.

~ Revelation 20:11-15

I AM COMING QUICKLY

What we see happening in the last days is that the unjust are becoming more unjust, but the righteous are becoming more righteous. John says "Amen, come Lord Jesus." Keep short accounts with God and with men. The time is now very short.

[6]Then the angel said to me, "Everything you have heard and seen is trustworthy and true. The Lord God, who inspires his prophets, has sent his angel to tell his servants what will happen soon."

[7]"Look, I am coming soon! Blessed are those who obey the words of prophecy written in this book."

[8]I, John, am the one who heard and saw all these things. And when I heard and saw them, I fell down to worship at the feet of the angel who showed them to me. [9]But he said, "No, don't worship me. I am a servant of God, just like you and your brothers the prophets, as well as all who obey what is written in this book. Worship only God!"

[10]Then he instructed me, "Do not seal up the prophetic words in this book, for the time is near. [11]Let the one who is doing harm continue to do harm; let the one who is vile continue to be vile; let the one who is righteous continue to live righteously; let the one who is holy continue to be holy."

[20]He who is the faithful witness to all these things says, "Yes, I am coming soon!"

Amen! Come, Lord Jesus!

[21]May the grace of the Lord Jesus be with God's holy people.

~ Revelation 22:6-11, 20-21

Scripture Index